DATE DUE

HOW
TO
BUY
FOREIGN
SECURITIES

HOW
TO
BUY
FOREIGN
SECURITIES

THE COMPLETE BOOK OF
INTERNATIONAL INVESTING

by Rainer Esslen

With a Preface by Willard F. Rockwell, Jr.

Columbia Publishing Company, Inc.
Frenchtown, New Jersey

Columbia Publishing Company, Inc.
Frenchtown, New Jersey 08825

Publisher's Note: Special thanks are due to
Walter E. Dunsby, Jr., Partner, *Printon, Kane & Co.,*
Summit, New Jersey, for his painstaking reading
of this manuscript in all of its stages
and for offering so much insight and understanding.
His expert assistance is acknowledged with gratitude.
Many thanks are also due to *Pine Tree Composition Service*
in Lewiston, Maine, for their invaluable
cooperation beyond the call of duty.

ACKNOWLEDGMENTS

More than 100 investment professionals in Europe and the United States were interviewed during the research for this book, and I would like to thank all of them for their time, patience, and cooperation. My particular thanks are due to a number of people who went out of their way to help me maintain the greatest possible factual accuracy by reviewing parts of the manuscript. They include: Jose Anguiano and Robert D. Lamont, *Allen W. Lloyd y Asociados, S.A.*, Guadalajara; C. Austin Barker, *Hornblower & Weeks-Hemphill Noyes, Inc.*, New York; Gonzalo Corral, *Banco de Santander*, New York; Richard J. DeAgazio, *ABD Securities Corporation*, Boston; David J. Cremin, *James Capel & Co.*, London; Dr. Harald Eichler, *Vienna Stock Exchange*, Vienna; David A. Friedrich, *EuroPartners Securities Corporation*, New York; L. Genoud, *Swiss Reinsurance Company*, Zurich; Joseph Gordon, *Loeb, Rhoades & Co.*, New York; Dr. C. Grüebler, *Union Bank of Switzerland*, Zurich; Takashi Kawasaki, *The Nikko Securities Co. International, Inc.*, New York; G. D. Renardel de Lavalette, *Amro Bank*, Rotterdam; Jeanpierre Molin, *Suez American Corporation*, New York; Patrique Segal, *French American Capital Corporation*, New York; Hugh Seymour, *Hoare & Co. Govett Ltd.*, London; Naomichi Shimao, *Nomura Securities International, Inc.*, New York; Cedric J. Olivestone, *Leumi Securities Corporation*, New York; Gilbert Thulliez and J. Van Tuyckom, *Société Générale de Banque*, Brussels; N. W. Veer, *Robeco*, Rotterdam; Jean-Max Villars, *Lombard Odier & Cie*, Geneva; Leif Vindevåg, *Skandinaviska Enskilda*

Banken, Stockholm; Valentine A. Weber, Jr., *James Capel,* Chicago; and Partners of *J. B. Were & Son,* Melbourne.

John Fountain of *White, Weld & Co., Inc.,* one of the richest fountains of international investment intelligence, was the most exacting checker of facts and prolific provider of information.

Many members of the new internationally thundering herd of *Merrill Lynch, Pierce, Fenner & Smith, Inc.,* too numerous to mention individually, were most helpful in many countries to shepherd me to the right sources.

A very special citation belongs to Euan Malcolmson of *Shearson, Hammill & Co., Inc.,* who acted as a catalyst in generating the idea for this book.

Last but not least, my sincere thanks to Carolyn Lee, Kathy McMahon, and Dolores Petruzzi of *Ketchum, MacLeod & Grove, Inc.,* who worked beyond the call of duty to assemble the manuscript, and to Edward T. Parrack, Chairman of the Board of *Ketchum, MacLeod & Grove, Inc.,* and Richard H. Conner, Executive Vice President, for the opportunity to research this book in conjunction with my regular work for the clients of the firm.

— Rainer Esslen
November 1973

CONTENTS

NOTE

This book was on the presses when the United States government announced that, effective January 30, 1974, the Interest Equalization Tax on the purchase price of foreign stocks and bonds was reduced to zero. Thus, the reader should ignore any references to the tax in the book.

The reader is also cautioned that the Arab oil embargo may radically change the economic prospects of many of the countries reviewed in this book.

PREFACE

It will no doubt be a long time before the average American small investor feels at ease buying and selling shares of foreign-based companies, but Rainer Esslen's *How to Buy Foreign Securities* may be all that some investors will need to make that first purchase.

For Mr. Esslen's book on international investing reveals investment opportunities, including the most actively traded stocks, in more than 20 countries. The novice investor in overseas businesses will benefit from the author's comprehensive listing of stocks by industry, and the names and addresses of banks, including United States offices, providing investment information. The more experienced trader in foreign stocks will find the up-to-date reports on stock market activity around the world informative and useful.

Mr. Esslen's suggestion that American investors can no longer ignore the outside world may be viewed as un-American in some quarters, considering the state of our own economy and the exodus of the small investor from Wall Street.

But I believe the thoughtful reader will regard the author's view as logical and, in the long run, in the best interest of both the United States and the global world economy which is evolving. A good investment policy, as Mr. Esslen notes, is one that takes the global view. It is true for individuals, just as it is true for corporations.

Thousands of Americans owe their jobs directly or indirectly to foreign-based companies, and doubtless there will be many thousands more whose employment will be made possible by the multinational thrust of overseas firms. Three out of every ten workers employed by Swedish-owned firms are now outside Sweden. Japanese companies are only beginning to go multinational, but they are moving rapidly. And European firms, one American company reported, are now investing as much, if not more, of their countries' gross national product outside their home countries as American firms are.

The people of the United States now depend on other countries for many products once exclusively American enterprises. An Associated Press writer reported recently nine out of ten home radios sold in the United States come from overseas, as do half of the shoes, 52% of all black and white television sets, 95% of all motorcycles, 90% of all baseball gloves, 76% of all tennis rackets, 65% of all sewing machines, and 16% of all automobiles.

The United States still leads the world in the development of new technologies, but the flow of technology is no longer all one way from this country to other countries. Other nations have given us the radial tire, the diesel engine, doubleknit clothing, cassette tape recorders, and the Wankel engine, to name just a few developments which have had an impact on our way of life. These developments are providing thousands of jobs here and overseas.

I personally feel somewhat responsible for this book, for *How to Invest in Foreign Stocks,* like Mr. Esslen's earlier book on marketing securities in Europe, grew out of a 1966 report he wrote for what is now the Rockwell-Standard Division of *Rockwell International.*

I have a high regard for Rainer Esslen and his professional approach to a problem. It is my hope that in the months and years ahead you will be able to make similar statements about the investment advice you are about to receive.

—Willard F. Rockwell, Jr.
Chairman and Chief Executive Officer
Rockwell International

December 1973

INTRODUCTION
OWN A SHARE OF THE WORLD

Hindsight in investing is about as useful as a bag of sawdust in a bar—good only for sweeping up spilled beer.

After the second dollar devaluation in February 1973, there were an increasing number of Monday morning quarterbacks who, in the 1969 to 1973 bear market, discovered that their substantial losses could have been substantial gains had they put their money into foreign markets during that time.

One of my investing friends had calculated that he could have tripled his money on the Tokyo Stock Exchange between 1967 and 1972 if he had done only as well as the averages; and that he could have done far better had he picked some winners like *Sony* or *Calpis Food Industry Co. Ltd.* which had gained more than 1000%. Besides, on the two yen revaluations alone he would have had a gain of about 35% in terms of dollars.

He had also reasoned that by switching from a national stock market that had run its course to one that was about to take off, he could have become a millionaire in 10 years on an initial investment of $1,000. I pointed out to him that by putting his chips on yesterday's roulette results he could have become a theoretical millionaire in a day.

My friend was in good company, however. According to American brokers handling foreign business, an increasing number of American professional portfolio managers became interested in foreign securities

11

in 1973 when the news had seeped through even to them that their counterparts in other countries had done considerably better than they.

A New Ball Game

Usually such missed-opportunity discoveries are made too late—at a time when the pendulum begins to swing in the other direction. When my friend lamented "the one that got away abroad," foreign investors were coming back into the American stock market and some foreign industrial countries seemed more threatened by the energy crisis than the United States. Nevertheless, after the disastrous years on Wall Street from 1969 to 1973, things will never be quite the same again on the international investment scene. While Wall Street obviously still remains the largest stock market in the world, many fledglings abroad in those distress years cut themselves loose from their American apron strings and greatly strengthened their own stock markets. The Japanese market staged the most spectacular "hit" performance, but other formerly quiet and narrow markets also came to life between 1969 and 1973, among them Paris, Brussels, Amsterdam, Frankfurt, Tel Aviv, Madrid, and Melbourne. London, once ahead of New York, made a strong comeback with international financing and stock trading, even if its own domestic issues were not always as attractive as those of many other countries. What is most important, professional investors abroad, on their own behalf and for their nonprofessional customers, perfected truly international investment strategies and expertise. Many portfolios throughout the world are now international rather than domestic in composition, and funds are switched from one country to another on the basis of the changing economic cycles and other factors affecting the investment climates.

Wall Street Parish

Compared to the international investment expertise in other countries, New York has become increasingly parochial in the ten years since 1963—and for two main reasons: one, the apparent successes with growth, glamor, and "concept" stocks in the 1960s had hypnotized American investment professionals so that they had no eyes for what went on elsewhere in the world; and two, the Federal government, in 1963, introduced a tax on the purchase price of foreign securities which effectively discouraged most Americans from buying foreign stocks and bonds. This made it uneconomical for most American brokerage houses to maintain an information service on foreign markets. Thus, an information vacuum developed that was largely responsible for the fact that most Americans missed the great opportunities that foreign investment markets offered from 1963 to 1973 in spite of the tax.

This tax, called Interest Equalization Tax, and amounting to 11.25% of the purchase price of a foreign common stock, may soon be allowed to expire, possibly by the end of 1974. If so, it would mean a new surge of interest in foreign securities. Even if the tax is extended once more, American investors can no longer ignore the outside world. Many of them know by now that a good investment policy is one that takes a global view; that there are many foreign stocks for which it would have been worthwhile to pay the tax; and that there are many foreign securities that are either exempt from the tax or for which the tax has already been paid by someone else and need not be paid again if purchased by another American investor. The tax is explained in detail in Chapter 1.

There were at least three other important developments between 1969 and 1973 that radically changed the investment picture, apart from affecting practically everybody's life throughout the world: (1) the collapse of the dollar as an international monetary standard; (2) rampant world-wide inflation; and (3) the first shortages in a number of vital natural resources.

Collapse of the Dollar

After rotting inside like a sick tree, the dollar came tumbling down in August 1971 as a result of the alarming rise of the United States debt to foreigners during the late 1960s. The dollar was devalued a second time in February 1973, when the debt of the United States to foreigners had reached the staggering amount of $100 billion. At that point, the dollar had probably found its true value in relation to most other currencies and it was possibly even undervalued; and in 1973 no more major changes in the value of the dollar were expected. Nevertheless, the $100 billion debt remained, and at some time soon foreign creditors will obviously want to receive some tangible value for their money. If they can't use that much money for buying American products, they may buy entire companies, as they started doing in 1973; but it takes only about $7.5 billion to buy a controlling interest in *General Motors,* and the United States has only one *G.M.* No doubt, this "overhang" of dollars will continue to be a major factor on the international investment scene.

Floating Relations

The devaluation of the dollar resulted in so-called "floating" exchange rates. This means that exchange rates between many of the currencies of the world change almost daily in relation to demand and supply. Unfortunately, demand and supply are not only controlled by the purchase and sale of goods and services; they may also be affected by emotions and speculation. This introduces an element of instability into all international financial and trading transactions. Nevertheless, in 1973, it was difficult to see how these floating rates or frequent currency readjustments were to be avoided for quite a while since various economies were moving at completely different speeds. The economic fact is that somebody who has more to sell than others gets more money. Money flows primarily to these countries that work harder than others or have valuable raw materials that are much in demand. It was no coincidence that the Japanese, German, Dutch, Swiss, and Australian currencies were among those that turned in the strongest performances in the days of currency readjustments. The Japanese, Germans, Dutch, and Swiss have the habit, disturbing to more leisure-loving people, of working exceptionally hard and productively. Australians have an abundance of natural resources. Currency variations are a major factor in international investment strategy, and an investor must always keep them in mind.

A Contagious Disease

The huge debt of $100 billion that the United States owes foreign creditors was also the major cause of a world-wide inflation. This money, outside the control of any fiscal authority or central bank, added greatly to the local money supply. Whenever the money supply rises faster than the amount of goods and services produced, inflation occurs. Money is simply becoming worth less in relation to something of tangible value, such as a parcel of land or a piece of gold. (This is discussed in greater detail in Chapter 2.)

Inflation was further fanned in many countries by the fiction that "easy" money—i.e. generous money supply—stimulates the economic growth and keeps unemployment away. This theory, which originated with the British economist John Maynard Keynes in the 1930s, has never been conclusively substantiated—in fact, there are examples throughout history of sound money having created very healthy economic growths, most recently in post-World War II West Germany, Holland, and Switzerland—but like other unproven modern old wives' tales, such as "Vitamin C keeps colds away," this theory doesn't seem to die. It is particularly popular with politicians because "easy" money makes generous election promises possible without having to ask the electorate for higher taxes to pay for them.

"But then," in the words of economist John Kenneth Galbraith, "there is the remarkable non-accountability of economists—something of which, as an economist, I am very reluctant to complain. A surgeon, in a general way, is held accountable for results. If, delving for a brain tumor he gets a prostate, he is open to criticism. Even lawyers are held to certain standards of performance; . . . but not economists. No matter how great the disaster, we are still revered."

And so, indeed, is Lord Keynes, in spite of the world-wide disaster of inflation.

In the long run, inflation has a serious corroding effect on the economy and the social fabric of a country. It creates distortions in production and injustices in compensation for work performed. It usually hits the poorest hardest—those with hard-earned savings and small pensions. If it gets out of hand, a cry for "price controls" leads to shortages and stagnating or declining production.

Inflation is an important consideration for the investor. The theory that common stocks are a hedge against inflation is unfortunately not true in most cases. The physical assets of manufacturing companies often become obsolete quickly, and the main value of their common stock lies in their earnings potential, which may be seriously impaired by inflation and price controls.

The chief type of common stock that may offer protection against inflation is that of a company sitting on almost inexhaustible natural resources that are in demand, or one that can reproduce natural resources, such as forests. If the natural resources can be depleted quickly, there is, of course, no protection either.

Bonds are no hedge against inflation unless interest rates are higher than the rate of inflation. A 15-year bond, at an interest rate of 6%, during an average annual inflation rate of 8%, at redemption time is only worth about one-third the original value in terms of purchasing power.

In 1973, many countries tried to combat inflation by raising money rates—rather than using the more effective, but more unpopular, method of raising taxes and cutting budget deficits. At the time this book went to press, it was impossible to say whether these efforts were effective. An investor, however, should be aware that rising money rates usually depress common stock prices as well as the prices of older bonds sold at lower interest rates, and vice versa.

Limits to Growth

The third new element that suddenly appeared in 1972 like a threatening thundercloud on the international economic skies was the first sign of shortages in a number of natural resources, accompanied by energy crises and pollution alarms. Only a year or two earlier, people were laughed off the national discussion stage if they predicted the possibility of the rationing of natural gas, gasoline, fuel oil, newsprint, electricity, and other resources. And who would have believed at that time that the United States would deplete in a single year its huge food surplus? Yet, this had all become reality in 1973. Unfortunately, these first signs of rationing did not seem to make Americans rational about the situation. It was much easier to blame the "wicked" oil companies for having artificially created the gasoline shortage than to blame oneself for driving oversized cars. A rational solution to preserving oil reserves and keeping the Arabs in their place would have been to slam a higher tax on gasoline. Not only would this have encouraged Americans to drive less and buy smaller cars, but it could have eliminated the national budget deficit and reduced inflation. Besides, even 40 extra cents on the American gasoline price would still have left it well below the price prevailing in most other countries. Yet, such a tax was not considered a political possibility and instead the government kept gasoline prices artificially low through price controls. Such expediency, as it usually does, led to a far more serious crisis and drastic action later.

The United States, with only 6% of the world's population, accounts for about 30% of the world's consumption of resources. Most other countries in the world have ambitions to increase their material consumption to at least the same level. Yet, if we are already experiencing shortages at our present rate of consumption, where are the limits to growing world consumption? What will the limits of consumption mean in terms of growth economies and growth stocks—a concept that has governed investment thinking for the last 25 years? And what will it mean for the prices of shrinking natural resources, and the stocks of the companies sitting on them? And will governments allow private companies to continue sitting on them?

Yields Back in Style?

With the possibility of a decreasing supply of growth companies, it is perhaps worth remembering that there was a time when most investors invested for yield—in fact, in many countries many investors still do so. They still regard a company's divided rate a more important gauge of the value of a stock than reported (and often inaccurately reported) earnings. In 1973, yield on fixed-income securities in the United States and other countries of the world reached 10%, and went even higher in some. High interest rates (which mean high yield for those lending money to borrowers) may be the result of scarce money or of government policy intended to "cool" the economy. Or it simply is the price a borrower must pay to get money during inflation. When the annual inflation rate is 8%, a wise investor wants more than that to lend money to a bond issuer. And if he is convinced there are no reliable growth stocks left, what kind of yield would he be looking for in a common stock where the investment risk is greater than with a bond? If he expects more yield from a common stock than from a bond, what would this do to the price/earnings ratios of most common stocks?

This book provides no answers to these questions—only information and thoughts that might help an investor find his own answers and to encourage him to look upon the investment scene with a global point of view. It is becoming more and more obvious that individual investment markets are increasingly affected by world-wide trends, rather than strictly national ones, because of the increasing interdependence of the main producing countries upon each other for natural resources, production capacity, labor supply, and finance. Thus, the interested investor, whether he buys foreign securities or not, can only benefit from knowing what goes on in other parts of the world.

Leading You to Water

This book tries to fill part of the information gap that has arisen because of the long neglect of foreign securities in the United States. It tries to tell what has happened in the main investment markets in recent years. It is not an investment guide, but merely presents many of the sources where investment information on specific foreign securities can be obtained. Whenever a company is mentioned in the text, this is done to illustrate past history or give examples of current thinking—not as a recommendation to buy the stock. A seasoned investor need not be reminded that past history for investment decisions is about as useful as a bird in a bush is for an evening meal.

This book tries to tell where and how to buy foreign securities, *but not why to buy them or what to buy.* That is the province of the professional investment advisor.

Nor does this book want to make a case for securities as the best investment vehicle at this time—it may be real estate, or precious metals, or commodities, or a combination of all four. Each of the other three would require a book by itself; this is a book about foreign securities. Since it is trying to chart neglected waters, with very few up-to-date maps available in the United States, the book is offered with the E. & O. E. that British merchants used to put under the end sum of their invoices—Errors and Omissions Excepted. The errors, omissions, and opinions are, of course, the author's.

Obviously, when considering other countries outside the United States in his investment policy, an investor will find that his task of decision-making has become a good deal more complex. In general, investment information is more limited in most countries of the world than in the United States. Most foreign companies disclose far less information to their stockholders than do American companies. The United States Securities and Exchange Commission is far ahead of comparable organizations in most other countries in establishing and policing fair trading and information practices. In spite of the difficulties of the years 1969 to 1973, and the disappearance of the small investor, the American stock markets are still a good deal more active and liquid than most other stock markets in the world—and liquidity means that it is easier to buy and sell stock within a narrow price range of easily accessible quotations.

But other countries are fast catching up in trading practices and information services. Some are well ahead in investment sophistication and knowledge of the international scene. And some countries offer exceptional investment opportunities of a kind no longer easily found in the United States.

Fringe Benefits

This book relates some of these developments as they appeared in 1973, but events often move fast on the investment scene, and it is hoped that the reader will be encouraged by the book to keep abreast of events after having read it. This, in itself, may offer him an important fringe benefit—that of opening new horizons and vistas. When in the 1960s investment clubs sprang up in the United States, many of the members found that what they learned about American business, economics, politics, and various industries and regions of the country was at least as valuable as what they accomplished with their investments. There would be nothing more gratifying to the author if a reader finds this book rewarding because it has widened his interests. I found such an unexpected reward as a boy when I collected stamps. My voluminous stamp album provided blank spaces for most of the main issues of all of the countries of the world (that was in the 1920s, when Liechtenstein was about the only country that printed "special issues" strictly for collectors). The album also had some brief facts about each country's history, population, and economy. The tantalizing brevity of these descriptions often aroused my curiosity to read more about a country in the encyclopedia and look it up in my atlas. As a result, I had nothing but straight A's in history and geography throughout my school career.

I continued collecting stamps for about ten years without thinking about their potential monetary value. When about to leave Europe for the other side of the world, I gave the collection as a present to a musician friend who built his own portable pipe organs. He soon discovered the monetary value of the collection by selling it to a dealer. Then he used the money to buy scarce copper and tin to make more pipes. Now, 35 years later, those pipes are still part of an organ that produces lovely sounds in a house in the Avenue district of San Francisco, where my friend makes a living as a restorer of antique instruments, such as calliopes and pianolas.

Currency Conversion Rates: National Currencies in U.S. cents (¢)

	1968*	1969*	1970*	1971*	1972**	1973**
Australia (A$1 =)	111.04¢	111.79¢	111.42¢	119.40¢	119.10¢	149.0¢
Austria (1 Schilling =)	3.87¢	3.87¢	3.87¢	4.23¢	4.33¢	5.65¢
Belgium (1 BFranc =)	1.99¢	2.01¢	2.01¢	2.23¢	2.26¢	2.71¢
Brazil (1 Cruzeiro =)	26.11¢	22.99¢	20.20¢	17.74¢	16.80¢	16.60¢
Canada (C$1 =)	93.21¢	93.18¢	98.98¢	99.78¢	101.71¢	99.30¢
Denmark (1 DKrone =)	13.33¢	13.34¢	13.35¢	14.16¢	14.51¢	17.58¢
Finland (1 FMark =)	23.81¢	23.81¢	23.81¢	24.39¢	24.76¢	27.3¢†
France (1FFranc =)	20.21¢	17.99¢	18.21¢	19.14¢	19.96¢	23.65¢
Germany (1 DMark =)	25.00¢	27.10¢	27.41¢	30.60¢	31.23¢	41.39¢
Israel (1 I£ =)	28.57¢	28.57¢	28.57¢	23.81¢	23.81¢†	23.81¢†
Italy (1 Lira =)	0.160¢	0.160¢	0.160¢	0.168¢	0.172¢	0.177¢
Japan (1 Yen =)	0.279¢	0.279¢	0.279¢	0.317¢	0.332¢	0.376¢
Luxembourg (1 LFranc =)	1.99¢	2.01¢	2.01¢	2.23¢	2.26¢	2.71¢
Mexico (1 Peso =)	8.01¢	8.01¢	8.01¢	8.01¢	8.01¢	8.01¢
The Netherlands (1 guilder =)	27.73¢	27.59¢	27.80¢	30.73¢	30.90¢	39.83¢
Norway (1 NKrone =)	14.01¢	14.01¢	14.01¢	14.90¢	15.13¢	18.19¢
Portugal (1 Escudo =)	3.48¢	3.49¢	3.48¢	3.63¢	3.73¢	4.32¢
Singapore (1 S$ =)	32.47¢	32.36¢	32.36¢	34.48¢	36.20¢†	42.90¢†
South Africa (1 Rand =)	138.97¢	139.88¢	139.43¢	130.67¢	124.40¢	149.50¢
Spain (1 Peseta =)	1.43¢	1.43¢	1.43¢	1.51¢	1.59¢	1.80¢
Sweden (1 SKrone =)	19.30¢	19.34¢	19.34¢	20.55¢	21.14¢	23.82¢
Switzerland (1 SFranc =)	23.24¢	23.16¢	23.17¢	25.54¢	26.56¢	33.53¢
United Kingdom (1 £ =)	238.44¢	240.04¢	239.35¢	255.23¢	242.45¢	241.60¢

* Tabulated from information supplied by the International Monetary Fund as published in *United Nations 1972–1973 Statistical Yearbook* (New York, 1973), pp. 630–634.

** From the *New York Times*, October 3, 1973.

† From the *Wall Street Journal*, October 3, 1972 and October 3, 1973.

NOTES TO THE READER

The information presented in this book was collected from the best available sources during May to October 1973. Every effort was made to have the facts in each chapter checked by investment professionals in the country described. Nevertheless, not all sources are reliable, the author is not infallible, and regulations and other factors affecting the investment scene change frequently in almost all countries. Thus the reader is cautioned to check any facts that might influence his investment decisions.

Wherever dollar equivalents to local currency figures are given, these were converted at exchange rates prevailing in October 1973, even if some of the figures refer to an earlier time. This was done in order to allow comparisons at a constant value. A table at the beginning of this section presents historical conversion rates between the U.S. dollar and the currencies of the countries covered in the book, for the period 1969 to 1973.

All stock exchanges publish indices to reflect the average price action of the stocks traded on the exchange. However, all these indices are composed of different elements and therefore they are not truly comparable with each other. *Capital International Perspective,* a quarterly international stock chart guide, has devised a formula to bring all major stock exchange indices on to a common denominator and it publishes quarterly charts to reflect the price action of each exchange. The charts up to and including the third quarter of 1973 are reproduced at the end of this book by permission of the publisher, *Capital International S.A.,* Geneva.

Most of the technical investment terms used in this book, as well as some other commonly used investment terms, are explained in the glossary of this book. More complete investment glossaries can be found in a publication of the New York Stock Exchange and in various stock market and investment handbooks.

1

LOCAL SHOPPING
HOW TO INVEST ABROAD FROM HOME

When the subject of foreign stocks comes up, an old-timer on Wall Street never fails to mention that he buys foreign securities in much the same way that he used to date girls in his courting days—very close to his own backyard. "It saves a lot of time," he says, "and it is easier to keep an eye on the situation."

There is a sizable backyard for foreign stocks in the United States. Many foreign securities are actively traded here. It is faster and easier to buy these than to buy shares traded only abroad, and it is also much easier to keep an eye on them. Trading volume and prices for the most active stocks are reported in the financial press; and for all others, they can easily be obtained from an American broker. Investment information on at least a good number of them is readily available in the United States. Besides, in most cases, the Interest Equalization Tax that an American investor must pay when he buys a foreign security has already been paid (this tax is paid only by the first American buyer of the shares); and there are a good number of foreign stocks exempt from this Interest Equalization Tax.

What is the Interest Equalization Tax?

In the words of a conservative economist, the Interest Equalization Tax (IET) is one of those lead weights that the government, whenever it has made an economic blunder, puts in our backpack of tax burdens and other impediments to free enterprise.

When in the early 1960s, not entirely without some fault of its own, the United States government saw the dollar drain out of the country, it imposed the Interest Equalization Tax to discourage American investors from buying foreign bonds and stocks and reduce the outflow of dollars. It was named "Interest Equalization Tax" because its official purpose was to "equalize" the difference between the higher interest rates paid on bonds sold abroad and the lower rates paid on bonds sold at home.

The tax is a graduated percentage of the actual value of the foreign bonds when acquired. It ranges from 0.79% on bonds or other debt obligations that have at least one year but less than 1¼ years to run before they are redeemed, to 11.25% on those that have 28½ years or more left before redemption.*

On common stocks, there is no interest rate to equalize, but the government levies the tax anyway without bothering to change its name. In 1973, it was a flat rate of 11.25% of the purchase price of foreign stock. The tax officially expires on June 30, 1974, and at the time of publication of this book, it was expected to be phased out by the end of 1974. Removal would not only revive the international investment business in the United States, but actually benefit our economy.

Like so many government interferences in economics, the Interest Equalization Tax did not have the desired effect—the reduction of the dollar drain. It had the opposite effect. It lost valuable foreign currency income. A foreign organization, for instance, that would have borrowed $100 million at 5% in 1962 for ten years would have paid back $150 million by 1972—the $100 million capital plus $50 million in interest. In other words, the United States lost $50 million of foreign exchange income. The dollar drain after 1962 continued at an accelerated rate and by 1973 was more than double what it was in 1962, or about $100 billion.

In addition, American investment bankers and brokers lost a considerable amount of foreign business that would have brought in foreign currency. At a time when investment management became truly international in all major countries of the world, Wall Street became more and more parochial because most American brokers, as a result of the tax, could not maintain and develop the staff and expertise necessary to be knowledgeable about foreign stocks and

* Detailed information on the Interest Equalization Tax is found in publication 565(10-72) available from the Internal Revenue Service.

execute orders. At a time when internationally-oriented foreign brokers and banks handling investments were thriving, many American brokerage houses were in deep financial trouble.

In addition to its financial nuisance value, the Interest Equalization Tax represents a practical nuisance that acts as a deterrent to anyone who does not like to cope with bureaucratic procedures. A United States resident who has bought a foreign security on which the tax is due must file an Interest Equalization Quarterly Tax Return and enclose payment not later than 30 days after the end of the quarter during which he made the purchase—or sooner if he sells the stock again before the end of the quarter. The tax return must be accompanied by the original (not a photocopy) purchase confirmation from his broker and proof of his United States citizenship. A United States resident who is not a citizen must provide evidence of his resident status, such as his alien registration card, plus the original or photocopy of the first pages of his last two Federal income tax returns. There are so many exceptions, deviations, and "angles" to these tax rules that an investor going through the formalities for the first time is best advised to consult his nearest Internal Revenue Service office.

The most practical way, however, is to deal in foreign shares subject to the tax through a "participating" broker—that is, a broker who maintains records of foreign stock transactions for the inspection of the Internal Revenue Service and who pays the tax where applicable, billing the customer a so-called "net" price which includes the tax. In this case, the investor must buy and sell the security through the same participating broker and keep the stock certificate in the custody of the broker. If the investor wants to sell the foreign security through another broker, he must go through the formality of having the certificates validated by the Internal Revenue Service as "American-owned."

Once a foreign stock is owned by a United States resident, and the tax has been paid, it can be sold to another United States resident without the tax becoming due again.The price of the stock on which the tax has been paid often reflects the tax. In 1973 it was usually about 11 to 12% higher than the price of the foreign stock on which no tax had been paid. Demand for American-owned certificates of a foreign stock may sometimes drive the premium higher than 12% when ownership of the stock is limited by the foreign company or its government to a certain percentage of outstanding shares or there are other restrictions.

If an American-owned foreign stock is sold back to a foreigner, the

United States seller cannot recover the Interest Equalization Tax from the Internal Revenue Service. And if that foreigner should sell the same stock to an American the tax again becomes due.

Many foreign securities are exempt from the Interest Equalization Tax. (A recent list of exempt foreign stocks is found at the end of this chapter.) Exemption rules are quite complicated, and details can be obtained from the Internal Revenue Service. There are two categories of exempt foreign securities: (1) those that are treated as domestic issues (many Canadian securities fall in this category because of predominant stock ownership by United States citizens), and (2) those that are issued in countries that have been classified as less-developed. The IRS has published a list of countries that will never be designated as less-developed, either because of their recognized economic stability or because of political considerations. The latter applies primarily to countries of the Sino-Soviet block. Israel is rated by the IRS as a less-developed country and practically all of its securities are exempt from the Interest Equalization Tax.

Many foreign common stocks are exempt from the Interest Equalization Tax only when bought by a United States investor within a certain specified time (as indicated by the dates in the list at the end of this chapter). They remain exempt if validated as "American-owned." If not validated, or bought outside the specified time, such stocks are subject to the Interest Equalization Tax. Many of the corporations involved apply for extensions of the exempt period.

American Depositary Receipts (ADRs)

Anyone venturing into foreign stocks for the first time would be wise to limit himself to those that are American-owned and actively traded in the United States. Enough of them are available from various parts of the world to build up a diversified international portfolio.

Most foreign shares available in the United States are traded in the form of American Depositary Receipts (ADRs). An ADR is comparable to a stand-in at a wedding ceremony when one of the spouses is in a distant land and cannot attend personally. When buying an ADR, the investor, by proxy, becomes the owner of a foreign stock held on deposit with a custodian bank in a foreign country. One ADR may represent either one foreign share or several, depending on the price of the original share. When introducing a new ADR in the United States, the American bank tries to establish a price that lies within the range of popular United States common stocks.

ADRs are traded like any American stock, and the same brokerage commissions apply. Some foreign companies have their original common shares or other types of certificates such as American Depositary Shares, listed on the New York or American Stock Exchanges, or traded over-the-counter, but for most practical purposes these are like ADRs to the American investor.

The investor can take physical possession of the ADRs or other foreign certificates, or he can leave them with his broker. He will automatically receive dividends due from the custodian bank if he has the ADRs registered in his own name, or he gets a credit for them from his broker if he has left them in "street name" (that is, in the name and custody of the broker). The ADR bank sells the foreign currency in which it receives dividends and pays it in dollars. The bank also takes care of any rights offering, stock splits, and stock dividends that arise with the underlying shares. If a foreign rights issue is not registered in the United States with the Securities and Exchange Commission (and it rarely is), the subscription cannot be legally offered to United States shareholders by American brokers or banks. In such a case, the ADR bank sells the rights and transfers the proceeds to the holders of the ADRs. However, an American investor who does not want to lose the rights can give instructions to the ADR bank to deliver the rights to a foreign bank or broker and deal there with them directly.

When buying an ADR, an investor should not assume that the Interest Equalization Tax has been paid. ADRs can be traded either with certificates of American ownership or without (foreign-owned). A United States investor should specify American-owned ADRs to his broker.

The New York and the American Stock Exchanges publish lists of all ADRs and other foreign stock certificates traded on the exchanges and they indicate in their ticker symbols when an ADR is traded on the exchanges, both American- and foreign-owned. The National Association of Securities Dealers in Washington publishes lists of ADRs and foreign shares traded over-the-counter in the United States and quoted on the NASDAQ (National Association of Securities Dealers Automatic Quotation) system that reaches practically all brokerage offices in the United States. The NASDAQ prices are for American-owned stock.

A complete list of ADRs, including those not regularly quoted on any exchange or the NASDAQ system, is published from time to time by *Model, Roland & Co., Inc.*, New York. The list includes the American banks that hold the underlying foreign shares abroad and issue the ADRs here in the United States. The leading banks are

Morgan Guaranty Trust Company of New York; First National City Bank, New York; *Irving Trust Company*, New York; *Chemical Bank*, New York; and *Chase Manhattan Bank*, New York. The banks make available lists of the ADRs which they have issued.

The number of ADRs is increasing every year. When a foreign stock finds a substantial investment interest, the broker or brokers making a market in the stock may approach one of the ADR banks with a request that ADRs be issued for the stock, or a bank may decide to do so on its own.

The New York and American Stock Exchanges are making efforts to encourage foreign companies to list on their exchanges to compete with the increasing international investment business that is being developed on many of the foreign stock exchanges. At the end of 1972 there were 34 foreign stocks listed on the New York Stock Exchange, plus about 80 foreign bonds. Among the better known common shares are *Sony Corporation* (which multiplied 50 times in price in 10 years), *KLM, Royal Dutch Petroleum, Unilever Ltd.*, and *Unilever N.V.* (the one British, the other Dutch).

On the American Stock Exchange, in 1973, there were 50 Canadian issues listed, plus 23 other foreign issues.

The NASDAQ quotation system carries prices and trading volume for about 50 ADRs and about 50 foreign shares traded over-the-counter; most of the latter being Canadian.

The most actively traded foreign stocks are the Canadian, Israeli, and Japanese stocks and South African gold mining issues. These are discussed in separate chapters.

Sources of Information in the United States

ADRs and other foreign stocks quoted on the New York and American Stock Exchanges are included in the daily stock tables published in all major American newspapers. Both the *New York Times* and the *Wall Street Journal* have daily trading volume and prices for a number of ADRs traded over-the-counter; and in *Barron's* they can be found on a weekly basis.

All foreign issues traded on the New York Stock Exchange, most of those traded on the American Stock Exchange, and a few traded over-the-counter are covered by the regular stock report service of *Standard & Poor's* and *Moodies*. In addition, *Standard & Poor's* has an *International Stock Report Service* that covers about 75 foreign issues at regular intervals.

Capital International S.A., Geneva, a subsidiary of *The Capital Group, Inc.* and *Chase Manhattan Bank*, publishes *Capital International Perspective*, in monthly and quarterly editions, giving charts and statistics on about 1100 foreign stocks of 16 countries.

Some American brokerage houses publish, from time to time, individual stock reports for actively traded foreign stocks.

Practically all American brokerage houses have ceased publishing regular market letters on foreign security markets. Among the few exceptions which still make such information available to customers on a regular basis are *Drexel Burnham & Co., Inc., Smith Barney & Co., Inc.*, and *Arnhold and S. Bleichroeder, Inc.*

Investment Funds in the United States with Foreign Portfolios

The two funds that headed the 1972 and 1973 best performers lists for funds of $10 million or more in assets of the *Institutional Investor* magazine were *International Investors* and *Scudder International Investments*. Except for about 5% of general foreign industrial and financial stocks, the entire portfolio of *International Investors* in 1973 consisted of gold mining shares. The fund tries to buy only American-owned foreign securities for its portfolio, avoiding thereby the payment of the Interest Equalization Tax. Thus, an investor in the fund does not pay the tax, but he is charged a "front-end load" commission of 8¾%, which is reduced on a sliding scale for larger orders.

Scudder International Investments is legally a Canadian fund, but shares are sold in the United States through *Scudder Fund Distributors Inc.*, Boston. It is a "no-load closed-end" fund (which means that buyers pay no sales commission) but fund shares are subject to the Interest Equalization Tax unless already American-owned. Except for about 3% in United States securities, the portfolio at the end of March 1973, consisted entirely of foreign securities, with Canada leading with 28%, followed by Japan (17%), France (14%), and Holland (10%). The balance was spread in smaller percentages among a number of different countries.

Throughout the late 1960s and until 1972, when the Japanese stock market began to level off, one of the best performing funds was the *Japan Fund,* a closed-end fund traded on the New York Stock Exchange. The portfolio consists entirely of Japanese securities. Shares can be acquired either United States- or foreign-owned.

ASA Ltd., also listed on the New York Stock Exchange, both United States- and foreign-owned, is a closed-end investment fund with about 75% of its assets in South African gold mining shares, about 12% in diamond shares, and the balance in cash or other securities.

Capital Research and Management, in 1973, launched the $130 million *New Perspective Fund,* with the objective of investing up to 30% of its assets in foreign securities.

Investment companies with substantial Israeli holdings include *Israel Investors Corporation* and *Israel Development Corporation.*

A United States-based fund with primarily Canadian stock is the *Canadian Fund Inc.* No Interest Equalization Tax is payable on the purchase of these shares.

How to Buy Foreign Earnings in the United States

A relatively unknown New York Stock Exchange-listed company with a sales volume of about $200 million, making a relatively obscure and completely unglamorous product—frit—has run up record earnings every year since 1967. Headquartered in Cleveland, the company is *Ferro Corporation,* and its main product, frit, is the raw material for porcelain enameling used on appliances, plumbing fixtures, and comparable products. In 1972, 77% of Ferro's income came from abroad. While good management obviously has something to do with its good performance, the international diversification helped to counterbalance the ups and downs of the United States economy, and the company benefitted from currency gains in relation to the dollar.

Whenever pork and beans and ketchup are discussed in England, *H.J. Heinz* comes up as *the* household word, and many a Britisher who is confronted with the irrefutable evidence that *H.J. Heinz* is an American company headquartered in Pittsburgh seems to feel like a child who discovers for the first time that Santa Claus is really the handyman in disguise. The company has been operating in England since before World War I, and during the early 1960s, when its United States operations were less profitable, the British earnings accounted for more than 75% of the total and helped buoy the company's stock. Today, foreign earnings from England and other countries still account for almost 50% of the total, and the *Heinz* stock price held up strongly in the poor markets of 1969 to 1973.

In other words, an investor does not necessarily have to buy foreign stocks to invest in foreign earnings. He can get international portfolio diversification by buying United States stocks of companies with substantial foreign earnings.

A word of caution, however: it is earnings that count, not foreign sales. Many United States companies who ventured abroad in the 1960s did worse than those who stayed at home. The learning curve for starting foreign operations can be a deep and long one in the red, as many corporations discovered when they rushed into foreign countries expecting to do business there as it is done in the United States. Untold multimillions were lost by such seasoned giants as *General Electric, Raytheon,* and *Deere & Company.* Many of the foreign companies that were snapped up by American companies were the ones that were in trouble. And there are still quite a number of American corporations with foreign lemons on their hands.

Nevertheless, on balance in the early 1970s, many United States multinational companies had their foreign learning expenses behind them. A number of very profitable companies derive a major part of their earnings from abroad and came more or less unscratched through the bear markets of 1969 to 1973. Foremost among them are three New York Stock Exchange-listed banking giants that operate worldwide—*First National City Corporation,* holding company for *First National City Bank*; *BankAmerica Corp.*, holding company for *Bank of America,* the largest bank in the world; and *J.P. Morgan & Co., Inc.*, holding company for *Morgan Guaranty Trust,* the veteran among United States international banks. *First National City,* in 1972, derived 54% of its net income from abroad; the other two, 28% and 35% respectively.

Coca-Cola, another steady stock market performer, in 1972 derived 55% of its soft drink earnings from abroad. *Pepsi-Cola* earned 23% of its income abroad. More than half of *Colgate-Palmolive*'s business is done abroad. Other companies with a large percentage of foreign earnings, but not necessarily a good stock market record, include *CPC International* (61%), the world's largest corn refiner; *Engelhard Minerals & Chemical* (76%), a world-wide mineral trader and fabricator of precious metals, partly foreign owned; *Grolier Inc.* (89%), publisher of the *Encyclopedia Americana* and other reference books; and *Mobil Oil Corporation* (60%). Many of the international oil companies derive a good portion of their income from abroad although not all of them give a precise breakdown of the sources of their earnings.

For most companies, the percentage of income derived from abroad varies from year to year. The best way to select a representative number of companies with substantial foreign earnings is to leaf through the *Standard & Poor's* stock reports available at practically every brokerage house. Whenever a company has broken down its earnings by geographic origin, this is mentioned in the *Standard & Poor's* report.

How to Buy Foreign Stocks Not Traded in the United States

An investor wanting to venture beyond the foreign securities traded in the United States is entering deep waters. Only a handful of American brokerage houses will accept orders from retail customers for securities traded abroad. In answer to a questionnaire sent to leading brokerage houses and checked out through personal interviews, only two stated unequivocally that they will accept any size of account, even small ones, for foreign investments and that they are fully equipped to execute orders abroad. They are *Drexel Burnham & Co., Inc.*, New York, and *Loeb, Rhoades & Co.*, New York. Others with great expertise in trading foreign securities will deal only with institutional investors or large private customers, notably *Carl Marks & Co. Inc.*, and *Arnhold and S. Bleichroeder, Inc.*, New York. Some foreign brokers or affiliates of foreign banks established in New York as brokerage houses will accept orders for stocks of specific countries (these are listed in the chapters on the countries involved).

A number of United States brokerage houses will accept orders for foreign securities from customers but will leave the execution to other brokerage houses specializing in the business or to foreign brokers and banks. This may increase the commission cost.

Most of the trading of foreign securities in the United States is so-called arbitrage business. This means that a broker buys a stock on one market and sells it at the same time on another to make money on the difference of price that exists in the two markets. There is a great deal of arbitrage business with ADRs traded in the United States and the underlying shares traded on the foreign stock markets. If an ADR, for instance, is in strong demand in the United States and sells at a premium over the underlying stock abroad, an arbitrage dealer will buy the shares abroad and convert them into ADRs for sale in the United States. Vice versa, if the price is higher abroad, he will buy ADRs in the United States, "undo" them, and sell the underlying shares abroad.

Arbitragers are the market lubricants who make the wheels go round. Their trading assures that a stock, other things being equal, sells at pretty much the same price all over the world wherever it is traded and that there is a liquid market for the stock. Liquidity of a market means that a stock can be easily bought and sold whenever desired. An illiquid market in a stock represents a risk for the investor. When he wants to sell, he may find there are no buyers, or there are buyers only at a much lower price than the one nominally quoted. Many foreign stocks are illiquid even in their home markets. An investor should avoid these and make sure he or his broker is buying only actively traded stocks.

Information

Information about foreign stocks not traded in the United States is difficult to come by and most of it must be obtained from sources abroad (many of these are listed at the end of the various chapters). No broker or bank wants to disseminate information in the United States about a foreign security in a way that could be interpreted as soliciting business, unless the security is in the clear under the so-called blue-sky laws in all the states where the firm operates. The blue-sky laws antedate the Federal Securities Act of 1933 and the Securities Exchange Act of 1934 and they vary from state to state. New issues of foreign stocks cannot be offered in the United States at all unless they are registered with the SEC.

A stockholder of ADRs for foreign shares will get little or no information about the company of which he is a part owner unless he asks the ADR bank to put him on its mailing list. Many foreign securities are traded in the form of bearer certificates with coupons attached, like many American bonds. These are not registered in the name of the owner, and unless he asks to be put on the company's mailing list he will not receive reports. Bearer shares are like cash and may be sold by anyone who presents them to a broker or bank. Even with registered shares, it is a long way from a foreign company's headquarters to the American owner, and the stockholder cannot rely on receiving stockholder information promptly. Besides, most foreign companies disclose far less information than United States companies and less frequently. In general, it can be said that many foreign companies tend to understate earnings rather than overstate them, perhaps because foreign investors still look to dividends as a guide for the value of a security.

In summary: an investor who wants to make his own decisions about foreign stocks not traded in the United States must make it his business to keep himself informed by subscribing to foreign investment information services and by writing directly to the companies or other foreign sources.

The best solution, however, for an investor who wants to have a fairly substantial international portfolio of securities is to open an account with one of the few American brokers who handle such business or with a foreign broker or bank seasoned in international investment. Many British brokers and Dutch and Swiss banks have a long-standing tradition of managing international portfolios; and these are discussed in the chapters devoted to these countries.

The *U.S. Trust Company,* a New York trust bank, offers management of large private portfolios that include a substantial percentage of foreign securities or are entirely composed of foreign securities.

An investor who is not a resident of the United States may find it advantageous from a tax point of view to open an account with one of the banks or brokers established in Luxembourg, Holland, or Switzerland. A United States citizen or resident opening an account with a foreign broker or bank must report this on his Federal income tax return, and he must pay Interest Equalization Tax on all foreign securities bought abroad even if they are not held in the United States.

The only practical way of holding foreign securities not traded in the United States is to leave them in the custodial hands of the investor's broker and bank. Bearer shares, for instance, do not receive dividends automatically. A coupon must be detached and cashed through a bank. The owner will not be informed when the dividend is due. Nor will he be informed of any rights offering or other benefits due to him. A custodian bank will take care of these matters. Even with registered shares it is advisable to leave them in the hands of a custodian. To physically send the shares back and forth can be a drawn-out process; and communications may be delayed or get lost completely.

A broker or bank will in most cases charge a custodial fee in addition to the commission for each transaction. Portfolio management usually involves payment of a management fee. Commissions vary greatly from country to country and with the size of the transactions involved, but most foreign commissions are comparable to or even lower than commissions charged in the United States. Nevertheless, when negotiating a foreign stock transaction or the management of a foreign portfolio with a broker or bank, the investor should reach a clear understanding about all fees and commissions involved before he starts doing business.

Taxes

Most foreign governments withhold a tax on dividends and interest from securities held by non-residents of their countries. Withholding taxes vary from country to country and are generally discussed in the respective chapters of this book. If he files IRS Form 1116 with his Form 1140, a United States citizen or resident can offset the taxes withheld abroad against his taxable income, subject to certain limitations.

An increasing number of countries levy a capital gains tax on security transactions, but this applies normally only to residents of the country and is not withheld. In a few rare instances, such as investment trusts subject to a capital gains tax, a foreign owner of the shares of the trust may indirectly pay a capital gains tax. It appears that such indirect payment of a foreign capital gains tax cannot be recovered or deducted from Federal income taxes. A United States citizen or resident filing a Federal income tax return must, of course, pay tax on capital gains made from foreign stock transactions at the same rate he pays for domestic transactions.

A Partial List of United States Brokerage Houses Accepting Retail and Institutional Orders for Foreign Stocks Not Traded in the United States

Drexel Burnham & Co., Inc. / 60 Broad Street / New York, New York 10004
Fahnestock & Co. / 110 Wall Street / New York, New York 10005
Loeb, Rhoades & Co. / 42 Wall Street / New York, New York 10005
Merrill Lynch, Pierce, Fenner & Smith, Inc. / 1 Liberty Plaza / New York, New York 10006

A Partial List of United States Brokerage Houses Accepting Only Institutional Business or Large Private Portfolios

Arnhold and S. Bleichroeder, Inc. / 30 Broad Street / New York, New York 10004
Carl Marks & Co., Inc. / 77 Water Street / New York, New York 10005
Model, Roland & Co., Inc. / 120 Broadway / New York, New York 10005
Oppenheimer & Co. / 1 New York Plaza / New York, New York 10004
Smith, Barney & Co., Inc. / 1345 Avenue of the Americas / New York, New York 10019
White, Weld & Co., Inc. / 1 Liberty Plaza and 91 Liberty Street / New York, New York 10016

Investment Funds Available in the United States with Substantial Foreign Securities Portfolios

ASA Ltd. / 54 Marshall Street / Johannesburg, South Africa
[closed end; gold mining shares; traded on the New York Stock Exchange; American or foreign-owned shares]
Canadian Fund, Inc. / 1 Wall Street / New York, New York 10005
[open end; primarily Canadian securities; no Interest Equalization Tax]
International Investors Inc. / 420 Lexington Avenue / New York, New York 10017
[open end; primarily gold mining shares; no Interest Equalization Tax]
Israel Development Corp. / 30 East 42nd Street / New York, New York 10017
[closed end; Israeli securities; no Interest Equalization Tax]
Israel Investors Corp. / 850 Third Avenue / New York, New York 10022
[closed end; Israeli securities; no Interest Equalization Tax]
Japan Fund / 25 Broad Street / New York, New York 10004
[closed end; Japanese securities; traded on the New York Stock Exchange; American- or foreign-owned shares]
New Perspective Fund (Capital Research Co.) / 1 Chase Manhattan Plaza / New York, New York 10005
[open end; about 30% foreign securities; diversified]
Scudder International Investments Ltd. (Scudder Fund Distributors Inc.) / 10 Post Office Square / Boston, Massachusetts 02109
[closed end; diversified Canadian and international portfolio; Interest Equalization tax must be paid]

Fund shares not listed on an exchange can be bought either directly from the fund management or through a broker.

Independent Information Services on Foreign Stocks

International Stock Reports (Standard and Poor's Reports) / 345 Hudson Street / New York, New York 10014
Capital International Perspective (Capital International S.A.) / 15 rue du Cendrier / 1201 Geneva, Switzerland
For information on stocks of specific countries, see the listings following each chapter. *Capital International Perspective* offers monthly and quarterly information and charts on more than 1,000 foreign stocks.

Selected United States Multinational Companies with an Estimated 25% or More in Foreign Earnings

AMF Inc.
AMP Inc.
Addressograph-Multigraph Corp.
BankAmerica Corp.
Black & Decker Mfg. Co.
Burroughs Corp.
CPC International
Caterpillar Tractor Co.
Cheesebrough-Pond's Inc.
Coca-Cola Co.
Colgate-Palmolive Co.
Dow Chemical Co.
E.I. duPont de Nemours & Co.
Eastman Kodak Co.
Engelhard Minerals & Chemicals Corp.
Ferro Corp.
Firestone Tire & Rubber Co.
First National City Corp.
Gillette Co.
Goodyear Tire & Rubber Co.
W.R. Grace & Co.
Grolier Inc.
Halliburton Co.
H.J. Heinz Co.
Honeywell, Inc.
Hoover Co.
Huyck Corp.

IBM Corp.
International Flavors & Fragrances Inc.
International Harvester Co.
International Telephone & Telegraph Corp.
Eli Lilly & Co.
Merck & Co., Inc.
Minnesota Mining & Manufacturing Co.
Mobil Oil Corp.
J.P. Morgan & Co., Inc.
National Cash Register Co.
Pfizer, Inc.
Procter & Gamble Co.
Richardson-Merrell Inc.
Schering-Plough Corp.
Schlumberger Ltd.
Squibb Corp.
Sterling Drug Inc.
Sunbeam Corp.
Tektronix, Inc.
Union Carbide Corp.
Uniroyal, Inc.
Warner-Lambert Co.
F.W. Woolworth Co.
Xerox Corp.

Foreign Stocks Traded on the New York Stock Exchange *

* Products and country listed if not specified in corporate name.

Alcan Aluminium Limited (Canada)
ASA Ltd. (financial [South Africa])

Benguet Consolidated, Inc. (mining [Philippines])
British Petroleum Company Ltd.
Campbell Red Lake Mines, Ltd. (Canada)
Canadian Southern Railway Co.
Canadian Breweries, Ltd.
Canadian Pacific Limited (railroad)
Deltec International Limited (foods, commodities [Canada])
Distillers Corp. -Seagrams Ltd. (Canada)
Dome Mines, Limited (Canada)
EMI Limited (electronics, records, entertainment [United Kingdom])
Genstar Limited (building [Canada])
Granby Mining Co., Ltd. (Canada)
Hudson's Bay Mining and Smelting Co. (Canada)
International Nickel Co. of Canada Ltd.
KLM Royal Dutch Airlines
Massey-Ferguson, Ltd. (agricultural machinery, diesel engines [Canada])
Matsushita Electric Industrial Co., Ltd. (Japan)
McIntyre Porcupine Mines, Ltd. (Canada)
Norlin Corporation (holding company [Panama])
Northern & Central Gas Corp. Ltd. (utility [Canada])
Northgate Exploration Limited (mining [Canada])
Pacific Petroleums Ltd. (Canada)
Plessey Company Ltd. (electronic equipment, systems [United Kingdom])
Roan Selection Trust Ltd. (mining [Zambia])
Royal Dutch Petroleum Co.
Schlumberger, N.V. (petroleum [the Netherlands])
"Shell" Transport and Trading Co., Ltd. (petroleum [United Kingdom])
Sony Corporation (radios, recorders, televisions [Japan])
Unilever Ltd. (foods, commodities [United Kingdom])
Unilever, N.V. (foods commodities [the Netherlands])
Walker (Hiram) -Gooderham & Worts, Ltd. (distilleries [Canada])
West Coast Transmission Co., Ltd. (natural gas distributor [Canada])

Canadian Stocks Traded on the American Stock Exchange

Asterisk (*) indicates securities "admitted to unlisted trading privileges"

Aquitaine Company of Canada Ltd. (oil exploration)
Asamera Oil Corporation Ltd. (oil)
Ashland Oil Canada Ltd. (oil)
Bow Valley Industries, Ltd. (oil and gas exploration)
*Brascan Ltd.** (holding company with Canadian and Brazilian properties)
Campbell Chibougamau Mines Ltd. (mining)
Canadian Export Gas & Oil Ltd. (oil)
Canadian Homestead Oils Ltd. (oil)
Canadian Hydrocarbons Limited (petrochemicals)
Canadian International Power Co. Ltd. (utility)
Canadian Javelin Limited (mineral exploration)
*Canadian Marconi Company** (telecommunications)
Canadian Merrill Ltd. (minerals, oil, gas)
Canadian Occidental Petroleum, Ltd. (oil)

Canadian Superior Oil Co. Ltd. (oil)
Cominco Ltd.* (zinc, lead, fertilizers)
Dome Petroleum Ltd. (oil)
Domtar Limited* (forest products)
Ford Motor Co. of Canada Ltd.* (automotive)
Giant Yellowknife Mines Ltd. (mining)
Gulf Oil Canada, Limited* (oil)
Hollinger Mines Ltd.* (mining)
Home Oil Co. Ltd. (oil)
Hudson's Bay Oil & Gas Co. Ltd. (oil and gas)
Husky Oil Ltd. (oil)
Imperial Oil Ltd.* (oil)
Kilembe Copper Cobalt Ltd. (mining)
Lake Shore Mines Ltd.* (mining)
Neonex International Ltd. (various consumer businesses)
North Canadian Oils Ltd. (oil)
Numac Oil & Gas Ltd. (oil)
Pato Consolidated Gold Dredging Ltd. (mining)
Peel-Elder Limited (real estate)
Placer Development Company Limited (mining)
Prairie Oil Royalties Co. Ltd. (oil)
Preston Mines Ltd. (mining)
Quebecor Inc. (oil)
Ranger Oil (Canada) Limited (oil)
Revenue Properties Co. Ltd. (real estate)
Rio Algom Mines Ltd. (mining)
Scurry-Rainbow Oil Ltd. (oil)
Supercrete Ltd. (building products)
Total Petroleum (North America) Ltd. (oil)
Union Gas Co. of Canada, Ltd.* (gas)
United Asbestos Corp. Ltd. (asbestos)
Wainoco Oil Ltd. (oil)
Western Decalta Petroleum Ltd. (oil)
Wright-Hargreaves Mines, Ltd.* (mining)

Foreign Stocks Other than Canadian Traded on the American Stock Exchange

Asterisk (*) indicates securities "admitted to unlisted trading privileges"

Alliance Tire and Rubber Company Limited (Israel)
American Israel Paper Mills Limited (Israel)
Anglo Company Limited (holding company [Bahama Islands])
Atlas Consolidated Mining and Development Corp. (Philippines)
Brewer & Co. Ltd. (agriculture, real estate [Hawaii])
British-American Tobacco Company Ltd.* (United Kingdom)
Courtaulds Ltd.* (synthetic fibers [United Kingdom])
Dunlop Holdings Ltd.* (tires and rubber [United Kingdom])
Etz Lavud Limited (wood products [Israel])
Imperial Chemical Industries, Ltd.* (United Kingdom)

*Imperial Tobacco Group Ltd.** (United Kingdom)
Kesko Oy (retail buying and distribution service [Finland])
Marinduque Mining & Industrial Corp. (Philippines)
Mortgage Bank and Financial Agency of the Kingdom of Denmark
O'okiep Copper Co. Ltd. (South Africa)
Philippine Long Distance Telephone Co.
San Carlos Milling Co., Inc. (sugar [Philippines])
Sumitomo Chemical Company Ltd. (Japan)
Syntex Corporation (pharmaceuticals [Panama])
Tubos de Acero de Mexico, S.A. (steel)
Woolworth (F.W.) & Company Ltd. (retail [United Kingdom])

Foreign Stocks Traded on the Pacific Stock Exchange

Alcan Aluminium Limited (Canada)
ASA, Ltd. (financial [South Africa])
Asamera Oil Corporation Ltd. (Canada)
Benguet Consolidated, Inc. (mining [Philippines])
Campbell Red Lake Mines, Ltd. (Canada)
Canada Southern Petroleum, Ltd.
Canadian Breweries, Ltd.
Canadian Pacific, Ltd. (railroad)
Canadian Superior Oil Co. Ltd.
Dome Mines, Limited (Canada)
EMI Limited (electronics, records, entertainment [United Kingdom])
Granby Mining Co., Ltd. (Canada)
Home Oil Co. Ltd. (Canada)
International Nickel Co. of Canada, Ltd.
KLM Royal Dutch Airlines
Massey-Ferguson, Ltd. (agricultural machinery, diesel engines [Canada])
Matsushita Electric Industrial Co., Ltd. (Japan)
McIntyre Porcupine Mines, Ltd. (Canada)
Pacific Petroleums Ltd. (Canada)
Peel-Elder Ltd. (real estate [Canada])
Philippine Long Distance Telephone Co.
Plessey Company Ltd. (electronic equipment, systems [United Kingdom])
Roan Selection Trust Ltd. (mining [Zambia])
Royal Dutch Petroleum Co.
Schlumberger, Ltd. (petroleum [France])
"Shell" Transport & Trading Co., Ltd. (petroleum [United Kingdom])
Sony Corporation (radios, recorders, televisions [Japan])
Supercrete Ltd. (building products [Canada])
Syntex Corporation (pharmaceuticals [Panama])
Tubos de Acero de Mexico, S.A. (steel)
Ulster Petroleum, Ltd. (oil)
Unilever, Ltd. (foods, commodities [United Kingdom])
Unilever, N.V. (foods, commodities [The Netherlands])
United Canso Oil & Gas, Ltd. (Canada)
West Coast Transmission Company, Ltd. (natural gas distributor [Canada])
Western Decalta Petroleum, Ltd. (Canada)

Foreign Stocks Traded on the Midwest Stock Exchange

Alcan Aluminium Limited (Canada)
Asamera Oil Company, Limited (Canada)
Benguet Consolidated, Inc. (mining [Philippines])
British Petroleum Co., Ltd.
Canadian Export Gas & Oil Ltd.
Canadian Pacific Ltd. (railroad)
Dome Mines, Limited (Canada)
EMI Limited (electronics, records, entertainment [United Kingdom])
International Nickel Company of Canada, Ltd.
Massey-Ferguson, Ltd. (agricultural machinery, diesel engines [Canada])
Matsushita Electric Industries Co., Ltd. (Japan)
Northgate Exploration Limited (mining [Canada])
Pacific Petroleums Ltd. (Canada)
Plessey Company Ltd. (electronic equipment, systems [United Kingdom])
Roan Selection Trust Ltd. (mining [Zambia])
Royal Dutch Petroleum Company
Schlumberger, Ltd. (petroleum [France])

Foreign Stocks Traded on the Boston Stock Exchange

ASA Ltd. (financial [South Africa])
British Petroleum Company Ltd.
KLM Royal Dutch Airlines
Matsushita Electric Industrial Co., Ltd. (Japan)
Pacific Petroleums Ltd. (Canada)
Royal Dutch Petroleum Co.
"Shell" Transport and Trading Co., Ltd. (petroleum [United Kingdom])
Slater Walker Canada (bank and financial holding company)
Sony Corporation (radios, recorders, televisions [Japan])
Unilever Ltd. (foods, commodities [United Kingdom])
Unilever N.V. (foods, commodities [the Netherlands])

Foreign Stocks Traded on the PBW (Philadelphia-Baltimore-Washington) Stock Exchange

Matsushita Electric Industrial Co., Ltd. (Japan)
Plessey Company, Ltd. (electronic equipment, systems [United Kingdom])
Sony Corporation (radios, recorders, televisions [Japan])

Foreign Stocks Traded Over-the-Counter in Spokane

Reeves MacDonald Mines, Ltd. (Canada)
Silver Ridge Mining Co. (Canada)

Foreign Stocks Traded on the Honolulu Stock Exchange

Bogo-Medellin Milling Co., Inc. (sugar [Philippines])
Hawaiian-Philippine Company (sugar [Philippines])
San Carlos Milling Co., Inc. (sugar [Philippines])

ADR Securites Traded Over-the-Counter and Quoted on the NASDAQ System

Anglo American Corp. of South Africa Ltd. (holding company of natural resources)

Anglo American Gold Investment Co., Ltd. (gold investment fund [South Africa])

Bank Leumi le-Israel B.M.

Bayer A.G. (chemicals [Germany])

Beecham Group Ltd. (pharmaceuticals [United Kingdom])

Blyvooruitzicht Gold Mining Co. (South Africa)

Botswana RST, Ltd. (mining [Botswana])

Bowater Corp., Ltd. (paper [United Kingdom])

British Petroleum Co., Ltd.

Broken Hill Proprietary Co., Ltd. (steel, heavy manufacturing, oil [Australia])

Buffelsfontein Gold Mining Co., Ltd. (South Africa)

Burmah Oil Co., Ltd. (United Kingdom)

Canon, Inc. (photographic equipment [Japan])

DeBeers Consolidated Mines, Ltd. (diamond mining [South Africa])

Dresdner Bank A.G. (Germany)

Fiat S.p.A. (automotive [Italy])

Free State Geduld Mines, Ltd. (South Africa)

Fuji Photo Film (Japan)

Glaxo Holdings, Ltd. (drugs, foods [United Kingdom])

Gold Fields of South Africa, Ltd. (mining)

Hitachi, Ltd (industrial machinery [Japan])

Honda Motor Co., Ltd. (Japan)

IDB Bankholding Corp., Ltd. (Israel)

Industria Electrica de Mexico, S.A.

Japan Air Lines

Kansai Electric Power Co., Inc. (Japan)

Kirin Brewery, Ltd. (Japan)

Kloff Gold Mining, Ltd. (South Africa)

Matsushita Electric Works, Ltd. (lighting equipment and wiring devices [Japan])

Mitsui & Co., Ltd. (trading company [Japan])

Nippon Electric Co., Ltd. (Japan)

Nissan Motors Co., Ltd. (Japan)

Palabora Mining Co., Ltd. (South Africa)

Philips Gloeilampenfabrieken, N.V. (lamps and electrical equipment [the Netherlands])

Potgeitersrust Platinums, Ltd. (South Africa)

President Brand Gold Mining Co., Ltd. (South Africa)

President Steyn Gold Mining, Ltd. (South Africa)

Rank Organisation Ltd. (leisure time industry [United Kingdom])

Royal Dutch Petroleum

St. Helena Gold Mines (South Africa)

Telefonos de Mexico S.A.

Tokio Marine & Fire Insurance Co.

Tokyo Shibaura Electric Co., Ltd. (equipment)

Toyota Motor Co., Ltd. (Japan)
Union Corp., Ltd. (gold mining [South Africa])
Welkom Gold Mining Co., Ltd. (South Africa)
West Driefontein Gold Mining Co., Ltd. (South Africa)
Western Deep Levels, Ltd. (gold mining [South Africa])
Western Holdings Ltd. (Gold mining [South Africa])
Zambian Anglo American Ltd. (mining [Bermuda])

Foreign Securities Quoted on the NASDAQ System

Abitibi Paper Co., Ltd. (Canada)
Agnico-Eagle Mines, Ltd. (Canada)
Alcan Aluminium, Ltd. (Canada)
American International Reinsurance Co., Inc. (Bermuda)
Bankeno Mines, Ltd. (Canada)
Bell Telephone Co. of Canada
Brilund Mines, Ltd. (Canada)
Brinco, Ltd. (utility [Canada])
Can Del Oil Co., Ltd. (Canada)
Captain International Industries, Ltd. (refrigeration service [Canada])
Charter Oil Co., Ltd (Canada)
Chieftan Development Co., Ltd. (oil and gas [Canada])
Consumers Distributing Co., Ltd. (distribution catalogue [Canada])
Crown Life Insurance Company (Canada)
Denison Mines, Ltd. (Canada)
Dupont of Canada, Ltd.
Elscint, Ltd. (medical equipment [Israel])
L.M. Ericsson Telephone Co. (Sweden)
Falconbridge Nickel Mines, Ltd. (Canada)
GCL Graphic Communications, Inc. (printing [Canada])
Granisle Copper Ltd. (Canada)
Great Plains Development Co. of Canada Ltd. (oil and ga)
Great-West Life Assurance Co. (Canada)
Imasco, Ltd. (tobacco and food [Canada]
Interpool, Ltd. (Canada)
International Nickel Co. of Canada, Ltd.
Investors Group, Ltd. (investment fund [Canada]
Keen Industries, Ltd. (railway contractor [Canada])
Kerr Addison Mines, Ltd. (Canada)
Liberian Iron Ore, Ltd. (Sweden)
MIM Holdings, Ltd. (mining [Australia])
MacMillan Bloedel Ltd. (paper [Canada])
Maritime Fruit Carriers Co., Ltd. (Israel)
Moore Corp., Ltd. (business forms [Canada])
Noranda Mines Ltd. (Canada)
Overseas Inns, S.A. (Luxembourg)
Patino N.V. (mining [Canada])
Power Corp. of Canada Ltd.
Shell Canada Ltd. (oil)
Sherritt Gordon Mines, Ltd. (Canada)
Steel Co. of Canada. Ltd.

Trans-Canada Pipe Lines, Ltd.
United Canso Oil & Gas, Ltd. (Canada)
United Keno Hill Mines, Ltd. (Canada)
Universal Gas & Oil Co., Inc. (Panama)
Van Der Hout Associates, Ltd. (Canada)
Velcro Industries N.V. (fasteners [Canada])
Westcoast Petroleum Ltd. (Canada)

Foreign Stock Exempt from IET under
Code Section 4916 or 4920(b)

This notification advises you of foreign corporations which have received favorable rulings under the provisions of section 4916(c) or 4920(b) of the Internal Revenue Code.

Section 4916 relates to less-developed-country corporations. Section 4920(b) applies to certain classes of foreign stock which are treated as domestic issues.

Asterisk * designates a "shipping company" less-developed-country corporation as that term is defined in Section 955(c)(2) of the code. With certain limited exceptions, acquisitions of stock or debt obligations of such corporations, issued after January 29, 1973, will be subject to Interest Equalization Tax.

The following is a complete updated listing as of September 21, 1973.

Corporations Which Qualify as Less-Developed-Country
Corporations for the Stated Periods

*Aaron Maritime Co., Ltd.—10-27-66 to 1-29-67 and 6-30-70 to 6-30-73
*Acacia Navigation Ltd.—9-4-70 to 9-28-73
*Academy Trading, Ltd.—11-25-72 to 9-28-73
Adela Investment Company, S.A.—9-24-64 to 9-28-73
*Adonis Navigation Co., Ltd.—1-17-69 to 9-28-73
*Aegean Marine Corporation—4-23-69 to 5-29-70
Agronorte Ltd., S.A.—8-7-68 to 6-29-71
*Air Caribbean Transport Limited—12-4-67 to 3-31-70
*Alliance Tankers, Inc.—6-10-70 to 6-29-73
American-Asiatic Oil Corporation—7-30-68 to 1-31-73
American Israel Paper Mills, Ltd.—7-19-63 to 7-30-73
American Marine Singapore—6-24-71 to 9-27-73
*Amoco Carrier Company—7-1-71 to 4-2-73
*Amoco Tankers Company—7-29-71 to 4-2-73
*Amoco Transport Company (formerly Interhemisphere Transport Co.)
    —6-29-66 to 4-1-74
Andacollo Mining Company, Ltd.—9-16-66 to 7-29-71
*Angelicoussis Shipholding Group, Ltd.—3-17-73 to 4-1-74
Anglo-Lautaro Nitrate Company, Ltd.—7-19-63 to 12-29-71
Anglo-Philippine Oil & Mining Corporation—1-22-70 to 9-28-73
Antilles International Salt Company, N.V.—10-26-65 to 4-1-74
Antilles Steamship Company, Ltd.—8-31-67 to 3-31-69 and 5-29-70 to
    4-2-74

*Arger Navigation Ltd.—10-27-66 to 7-29-67
*Argon Maritime Ltd.—1-31-73 to 9-28-73
*Aris Steamship Company, Ltd.—3-27-67 to 1-29-68
*Artic LNG Transportation Company—4-19-68 to 3-31-69
Associates of Fiji, Limited—8-26-72 to 9-28-73
Atlas Consolidated Mining and Development Corporation—7-16-70 to 4-1-74
*Atlastor Navigation, Ltd.—12-30-72 to 9-28-73
*Attica Maritime Ltd.—12-26-68 to 9-28-73
Banco Centroamericano de Integracion Economica—9-1-70 to 9-28-73
Banco de Investimento and Desenvoluimento Industrial, S.A.—3-29-67 to 4-1-68
Banco Granai & Townson, S.A.—12-4-69 to 3-30-72
Banco Inmobiliario, S.A.—12-4-69 to 3-30-72
Bank Leumi le-Israel B.M.—5-3-65 to 4-1-74
Banque Internationale pour L'Afrique Occidentale—4-1-65 to 4-1-68
*Bantry Transportation Co.—9-6-66 to 4-1-74
*Barracuda Tanker Corp.—2-8-65 to 9-28-73
Basic Resources International, Ltd.—6-29-72 to 4-1-74
Basic Resources International (Bahamas) Limited—7-1-70 to 4-1-74
Benquet Consolidated, Inc.—7-19-63 to 8-15-68
Bogo-Medellin Milling Co., Inc.—7-20-65 to 12-31-73
Botswana RST Limited—3-20-68 to 4-2-73 and 9-13-73 to 4-1-74
Boundsgreen Company, Limited—3-25-72 to 4-1-74
Brascan, Limited—2-18-65 to 4-1-74 (formerly Brazilian Light & Power Co., Inc.)
*British West Indian Airways Limited—8-29-68 to 4-2-73
Brown Brothers de Mexico, S.A.—4-11-66 to 3-31-70
Brunei LNG Limited—7-1-72 to 4-1-74
Caja Central de Ahorros y Prestamos para la Vivienda—11-25-69 to 4-1-74
Calabrian (Thailand) Co., Ltd.—6-30-67 to 6-30-69
Calbiochem Africa Limited—4-30-69 to 3-31-70
Canadian International Power Co., Ltd.—7-19-63 to 4-1-74
Caribbean Cement Company, Ltd.—6-2-67 to 4-1-74
Caribbean Empire Company, Ltd.—7-2-68 to 3-31-69
Caribbean Leisurewear Inc.—8-24-71 to 6-29-72
*Caribbean Sulphur Shipping Company of Liberia—6-22-67 to 3-30-72
Casasus, Trigueros y Cia, S.A.—9-15-72 to 11-29-73
Caxinas, S. de R.L.—5-20-66 to 3-31-69
*Cayman Island Shipping Company, Ltd. (formerly Island Shipping Company, Ltd.)—7-6-67 to 3-31-69
Central American Allied Investors, S.A.—1-12-66 to 3-31-70
CE-rrey, S.A.—6-24-66 to 3-30-72
Coastal Caribbean Oil & Minerals, Ltd.—4-4-65 to 4-1-74
Coco Palms Resort, Ltd.—4-19-73 to 9-28-73
Comercial Flor Amarillo C.A.—5-16-70 to 2-28-74
Commercial Investment Properties, Ltd.—4-19-73 to 9-28-73
Communicaciones, S.A.—7-29-66 to 1-29-68
Companhia-Minera do Lobito, S.A.R.L.—4-5-67 to 4-1-74
Compania de Luz y Fuerza del Centro, S.A.—11-25-64 to 3-31-69

Compania de Celulose do Ultramar Portuges, S.A.R.L.—2-4-66 to 3-31-67
Compania Desarroladora Panamena, S.A.—6-27-67 to 3-31-69
Compania Hotelera EL Presidente, S.A. de C.V. (formerly Inmobiliario Rocasola, S.A.)—9-9-69 to 4-1-74
Compania Shell de Venezuela, Ltd.—5-25-65 to 4-1-74
Consolidated Mines, Inc.—10-13-65 to 3-31-66
Construcciones Gilbane de Colombia, S.A.—4-28-67 to 3-31-71
Construcciones Populares, S.A. de C.V.—7-8-65 to 3-31-66 and 12-29-71 to 4-1-74
Constructora de Vivendas de Bogota, Ltda.—11-28-66 to 6-30-67
Constructora y Urbanizadora Escambia, S.A. de C.V.—8-15-68 to 3-31-70
Continental Development, Ltd.—5-25-73 to 4-1-74
Continental Homes, Ethiopia, Private Limited—10-22-71 to 4-2-73
Credit and Development Corporation—5-17-65 to 4-1-73 (See Filinvest Credit Corporation)
Deltec Panamerican, S.A.—3-13-66 to 12-29-69
ECL Industries, Ltd.—7-19-63 to 3-31-70
EHMO S.A.—3-7-68 to 12-30-68
Elscint Limited—8-31-72 to 4-1-74
Ensome City Limited—4-23-65 to 3-31-66
*Enterprise Shipping Corporation S.A.—7-29-71 to 4-1-74
Equadorian Corporation, Limited—7-19-63 to 3-31-66
Etz Lavud Limited—7-22-69 to 6-29-73
*Evergreen Tankers, Inc.—10-27-71 to 6-29-72
*Evie Navigation Co., Ltd.—10-24-67 to 11-29-68 and 6-30-70 to 9-28-73
Executive Investment Co., Ltd.—10-16-70 to 3-31-71
Falconbridge Dominicana, C. por A.—1-1-70 to 4-1-74
Federacion Hondurena de Cooperatives de Vivienda, Ltd.—5-23-72 to 4-1-74
*Fieldston Navigation Co., Inc.—8-7-68 to 9-28-73
Filinvest Credit Corporation (formerly Credit and Development Corp.) —5-17-65 to 4-1-74
Financiera Bancomer, S.A.—3-18-69 to 4-1-74
Financiera Metrolitana, S.A.—12-10-68 to 4-1-74
Ford Brasil, S.A.—3-28-73 to 4-1-74
Fundacion Institute de Vivienda Cooperativa de Venezuela—7-26-73 to 4-1-74.
*Golarfruit, Inc.—4-11-66 to 3-31-67
*Grand Bassa Tankers, Inc.—1-25-65 to 4-1-74
Guana Island Club (The)—3-24-70 to 1-29-74
Guyana Securities Limited—10-28-72 to 5-1-73
Hawaiian-Philippine Company—8-3-65 to 12-29-73
Heinz Alimentos S.A. de C.V.—12-31-66 to 7-29-67
Hotel Condesa del Mar, S.A. (formerly Hotel Ritz Acapulco, S.A.)— 7-24-68 to 4-1-74
H. M. B. Holdings, Ltd.—10-27-71 to 4-1-74
IDB Bankholding Corporation Limited—12-30-69 to 4-1-74
Inagua Spray, Inc.—7-25-67 to 3-31-69
Inagua Spray, Inc. 7-25-67 to 3-31-69
Industria Electrica de Mexico, S.A.—7-19-63 to 4-1-74
Industrial Development Bank of Israel, Ltd.—12-30-71 to 4-1-74

Inmobiliaria Urbana, S.A.—8-26-71 to 4-1-74
*Intercontinental Maritime Ltd.—9-27-67 to 9-30-68 and 6-30-70 to 9-28-73
Interhemisphere Transport Co. (See Amoco Transport Co.)
Intermediaria de Viviendas Cia, Ltds.—12-3-69 to 4-2-73
International Halliwell Mines, Ltd. (formerly Consolidated Halliwell, Ltd.)—7-19-63 to 2-22-72
International Investment Corporation for Yugoslavia, S.A.—11-25-69 to 3-30-72
International Scientific, Ltd.—6-28-68 to 3-31-69 and 11-29-69 to 3-31-70
IPC Finance Ltd.—3-7-66 to 5-29-74
*Iran Shell, N.V.—7-27-66 to 3-31-67
Island Gem Enterprise Ltd. N.V.—10-27-72 to 2-28-74
Israel Bank of Agriculture Ltd.—3-1-72 to 6-29-73
Israel Corporation Ltd. (The)—6-30-69 to 6-28-73
Israel Discount Bank, Ltd. —1-1-64 to 4-1-74
Israel Land Development Company, Ltd. —5-1-70 to 9-28-70
Jamaica Financing Association, Ltd.—6-27-73 to 4-1-74
Jamaica Public Service Company, Ltd. —1-11-65 to 4-1-74
Jamaica Telephone Company, Ltd. (The)—7-16-69 to 4-1-74
Jardines de Guadelupe, S.A.—5-25-67 to 11-29-68
Kilembe Copper Cobalt Ltd.—11-4-65 to 4-1-74
Korea Explosives Co., Ltd.—9-22-69 to 3-30-72
Korea Polyester, Inc.—4-27-73 to 4-1-74
Kupat-Am Bank Ltd.—8-3-65 to 3-31-69
Kyung In Energy Co., Ltd.—1-10-70 to 4-1-74
La Gloria Palacios, S.A. de C.V.—9-30-65 to 3-31-67
La Luz Mines Limited—11-23-65 to 12-31-73
Lapanto Consolidated Mining Co.—6-9-66 to 4-1-74
La Tabacalero Mexicana, S.A.—7-19-63 to 11-2-64 and 5-7-65 to 3-31-66
Latin American Agribusiness Development Corp.—11-26-69 to 1-29-74
Liberian Iron Ore Limited—7-19-63 to 4-1-74
*Luzon Stevedoring Corp.—9-30-65 to 3-31-67
Marcopper Mining Corp.—10-5-67 to 3-30-72
Marinduque Mining and Industrial Corporation—5-16-67 to 4-1-74
Marpac, Inc.—9-25-71 to 3-30-72
Mexican Light and Power Co., Ltd.—7-19-63 to 3-31-69 and 1-31-70 to 3-31-71
Micron, Inc.—7-30-70 to 3-31-71
Midepsa Industries Limited—11-24-65 to 10-30-72
Montego Freeport Limited—8-1-72 to 11-29-73
*Moran International Towing Corp.—3-31-66 to 3-31-71
*Motorship Tankers, Inc.—11-30-64 to 3-31-66
Mufulira Copper Mines, Limited (See Roan Consolidated Mines Ltd.)
Nadi Beach Hotel, Ltd.—6-24-72 to 9-28-73
*National Iranian Tanker Company (Monrovia), Ltd.—7-19-63 to 11-2-64 and 11-30-64 to 3-31-66
Naviera Panamerica, S.A.—4-11-66 to 3-31-67
Nchanga Consolidated Copper Mines Limited—7-25-67 to 9-28-70
Nchanga Consolidated Copper Mines, Ltd. (formerly Bancroft Mines, Ltd.—9-1-70 to 7-1-74

Nicaraguan Hotel Company, Ltd. (The)—11-30-67 to 3-31-71
Norlin Corporation (formerly ECL Industries, Inc.)—5-26-69 to 4-1-74
Norsul Oil and Mining Ltd.—3-9-65 to 7-30-73
*Ocean Charters Corporation—10-1-69 to 3-31-71
*Ocean Oil Shipping Corp.—2-13-73 to 4-1-74
*Ocean Oil Traders, Inc.—4-11-66 to 3-31-67
*Ocean Oil Transport, Inc.—4-11-66 to 3-31-67
*Ocean Ore Shipping Corp.—4-11-66 to 3-31-67
Oriental Petroleum & Minerals Corp.—3-26-71 to 12-29-73
*Oriole Shipping Corp.—4-11-66 to 3-31-67
*Oswego Chemical Carriers Corp.—7-24-65 to 4-1-74
*Oswego Latex Carrier Corp.—12-1-71 to 4-1-74
*Oswego Marine Corp.—8-27-65 to 4-1-74
*Oswego Merchant Corp.—7-1-71 to 4-1-74
*Oswego Navigation Corp.—10-21-65 to 4-1-74
*Oswego Tanker Corp.—2-25-65 to 4-1-74
*Oswego Unity Corp.—11-10-65 to 4-1-74
Otsar La "Taasiya" Limited—10-28-72 to 4-1-74
Pago Mining Limited—5-20-68 to 3-31-69
Paper Industries Corporation of the Philippines—5-28-70 to 4-1-74
Parimentos Mexicanos—8-2-67 to 3-31-68
Pasco International Limited—6-16-67 to 3-30-72
Pato Consolidated Gold Dredging Limited—7-19-63 to 4-1-74
Petroleum Exploration and Development Company Limited—3-30-73 to
    4-1-74
Peruvian Investment & Finance, Ltd.—6-16-68 to 9-28-67
Philex Mining Corp.—10-28-68 to 4-1-74
Philippine Long Distance Telephone Co.—11-30-64 to 4-1-74
Philippine Oil Development Co., Inc.—7-19-63 to 11-2-64, 11-24-64 to
    3-31-66 and 5-1-71 to 4-1-74
Philippine Overseas Drilling & Oil Development Corp.—6-29-71 to
    10-30-72
Pioneer Natural Resources Exploration Co., Inc.—7-28-71 to 4-1-74
*Polor LNG Shipping Corp.—4-19-68 to 3-31-69
Premier Consolidated Oilfields, Ltd.—7-19-63 to 6-31-69
Private Investment Company for Asia, S.A.—12-26-68 to 4-1-74
Proyecto Viru Sociedad Anonima—5-17-65 to 4-1-68
P.T. Daralon Textile Manufacturing Corporation—6-28-73 to 4-1-74
P.T. "Djakarta International Hotel"—11-30-72 to 4-1-74
P.T. Indonesian Satellite Corporation—1-19-68 to 4-1-74
Purina Korea Inc.—12-21-67 to 4-1-68
Republic Resources & Development Corp.—7-29-71 to 3-30-72
Resort of the World, N.V.—9-15-70 to 9-28-71 and 2-27-73 to 2-28-74
Rhokana Corporation Limited—7-25-67 to 9-28-70
Roan Consolidated Mines Ltd. (formerly Mufulira Copper Mines, Ltd.)
    —5-29-70 to 9-28-73
Roan Selection Trust Ltd.—1-25-65 to 9-28-70
Rocky Point Development Company Limited (The)—6-3-69 to 5-1-70
Rosita Mines Limited—11-23-65 to 12-29-67
Royal Amsterdam N.V.—10-20-70 to 3-31-71
San Carlos Milling Co., Inc.—7-19-63 to 4-1-74

San Jose Oil Company, Inc.—1-6-65 to 3-30-72
San Miguel Corporation—7-19-63 to 4-1-74
Servicio Pan Americano de Proteccion, C.A. (Venezuela)—10-30-68 to 12-29-73
Servicio Pan American de Proteccion, S.A.—10-25-68 to 9-28-70
Shell Curacao, N.V.—5-31-72 to 4-1-74
Shell Exploratie en Productia Maatschappij, N.V.—5-25-65 to 3-31-66
Shell Finance (Development) Co., Ltd.—5-25-65 to 3-31-67
Shell Quimica de Venezuela, C.A.—5-25-65 to 4-1-74
Shell Nederlandse Antillen Verkoopmaatschappij, N.V.—4-19-73 to 4-1-74
Shell Trinidad Limited—11-30-72 to 4-1-74
*Signess Shipping Company, Inc.—11-30-64 to 3-31-67
Société Hotélière de la Baie de Marigot, S.A.—12-31-66 to 3-31-70 and 10-8-70 to 3-30-72
Société International Financière pour les Investissements et le Développement en Afrique—9-1-70 to 3-31-71
*Space Marine Transport Company—9-23-65 to 3-31-69
St. John d'el Rey Mining Company, Ltd.—11-30-71 to 7-1-74
Standard (Philippine) Fruit Corp.—9-1-66 to 4-3-72
*Sterling Tankers Corporation—10-27-65 to 3-31-67
*TACA International Airlines, S.A.—10-22-65 to 3-30-68
TAW International Leasing Corp.—12-11-68 to 11-29-73
*T. C. Trading Company, Ltd.—12-16-71 to 9-28-73
Takia Resorts, Ltd.—4-19-73 to 9-28-73
"Tefahot" Israel Mortgage Bank Limited—12-16-71 to 6-29-74
Telefonos de Mexico S.A.—4-29-66 to 4-1-74
*Tidal Marine Steamship Co.—1-30-71 to 4-2-73
Tourist Industry Development Limited—7-31-71 to 4-1-74
*Trans-Mediterranean Airways S.A.L.—10-24-67 to 4-1-68
*Trinity Marine Corporation—1-1-64 to 4-1-74
*Trinity Navigation Corporation—11-25-64 to 4-1-74
*Triple Ocean Operation, Inc.—4-11-66 to 3-31-67
Tropical Gas Co. Inc.,—9-16-66 to 4-1-74
*Tropigas Carrier, Inc.—9-16-68 to 6-28-73
*Tropigas Tankers, Inc.—9-28-66 to 6-28-73
Tubos de Acero de Mexico, S.A.—7-19-63 to 4-1-74
Twin Americas Agricultural & Industrial Developers, Inc.—12-21-67 to 12-29-72
*Twin Ocean Operations Inc.—4-11-66 to 3-30-68
Ultrafertil S.A. Industria e Comercio de Fertilizantes—9-14-67 to 4-1-74
*Universal Gas and Oil Company, Inc. (formerly Universal Gas, Ltd.)—12-23-71 to 4-1-74
Urbanizaciones Guacars, C.A.—5-6-65 to 4-1-68
Urbanizaciones Guayance, C.A.—1-17-67 to 3-31-69
Victorias Milling Co., Inc.—6-20-67 to 1-31-70 and 5-28-70 to 1-29-73
West Indies Plantations, Limited—2-29-68 to 12-29-70
*Westwaters Shipping Inc.—1-28-65 to 4-1-68
Zambia Copper Investments Ltd.—9-1-70 to 9-28-73
Zambian Anglo American, Limited—7-25-67 to 9-28-73
Zuari Agro Chemicals Limited—3-10-70 to 4-1-74

Classes of Stock of Foreign Corporations which Satisfy the Requirements of Section 4920 (b) and are Treated as Domestic Issues for Purposes of IET

Alcan Aluminum Limited (formerly Aluminum Limited)—common stock without nominal or par value.

Alliance Tire & Rubber Company Limited—class A Stock.

Allied-Rocana Minerals Limited

Alscope Consolidated Limited—common capital stock.

Asamera Oil Corporation Ltd.—common capital stock.

Avco Delta Corporation Limited (formerly Delta Acceptance Corporation Limited)—first preference share $100 par value, series B 5½ percent cumulative redeemable sinking fund shares; second preference shares and common stock no par value.

Beauty Counselors of Canada, Ltd.—common stock without par value, issued prior to 11/10/64.

Blue Crown Petroleums Ltd.—common stock.

Brilund Mines Limited—common stock.

British-American Insurance Company, Ltd.—common stock.

Cabol Enterprise Limited—common stock without par value.

Calgary & Edmonston Corporation Ltd. (The)—capital stock without nominal or par value.

Canada Costa Rica Mines Limited—common stock, par value $1.00.

Canada Southern Petroleum Ltd.—capital stock and voting trust certificates relating thereto.

Canada Southern Railway Company—common stock.

Canadian Export Gas & Oil Limited—common stock.

Canadian Homestead Oils, Limited—common stock.

Canadian Javelin Limited—common stock without par value.

Canadian Superior Oil Limited—common stock with $1 par value.

Canadian Westinghouse Company, Ltd.—common stock with nominal or par value.

Chemalloy Minerals Limited—common stock, par value $1.

Columbia Cellulose Company, Ltd.—common stock without nominal or par value.

Consolidated Marbenor Mines, Limited—common stock.

Consolidated Panther Mines Limited—common stock.

Continental Research & Development Limited—common stock.

Crow's Nest Industries Limited—common stock (formerly Crow's Nest Pass Coal Company, Limited).

Dome Mines Limited—stock without nominal or par value.

Dome Petroleum Limited—common stock, par value $2.50 and common stock without par value.

Elite Cobalt Mines Limited—common stock.

Exquisite Form Brassiere (Canada) Ltd.—common shares no par value.

Fargo Oil Ltd.—common stock, par value $1.

Ford Motor Company of Canada Ltd.—common stock without par value.

Fruehauf Trailer Company of Canada Ltd.—common stock without nominal or par value.

Glen Lake Silver Mines, Ltd.—common stock.

Wm. Gluckin Company Limited—5 percent convertible preferred stock and common stock, each par value one pound.

Golden Age Mines Limited—common stock (no par value).

Goodyear Tire & Rubber Company of Canada Limited (The)—common stock.
Granby Mining Company Limited (The)—common stock.
Greyhound Lines of Canada Limited—common stock.
Hudson's Bay Oil and Gas Co., Ltd.—capital stock par value of $2.50.
Imperial Oil Limited—capital stock, without nominal or par value.
Indian Mountain Metal Mines, Limited—common stock.
Initiative Explorations Limited—common stock.
International Nickel Company of Canada, Ltd. (The)—common stock without nominal or par value.
James A. Lewis Engineering Co., Ltd.—common stock.
Jefferson Lake Petrochemicals of Canada, Ltd.—common stock.
Jenkins Bros. Limited—common stock.
Kardar Canadian Oil Limited—common stock.
Magellan Petroleum Corporation—common capital stock par value $0.01. and voting trust certificates relating thereto.
Monarch Fine Foods Limited—common stock without par value.
Murphy Oil Company Limited—common stock.
National Malartic Gold Mines Limited—common stock.
* *National Petroleum Corp., Ltd.—capital stock, par value $0.25.
New Cayzor Athabaska Mines Limited (formerly Cayzor Athabaska Mines Limited)—common stock.
North Canadian Oils Limited—common stock, par value $0.25.
Northwest Nitro-Chemicals Limited—common stock.
O'okiep Copper Company Limited—ordinary shares, par value 1 Rand.
Orofino-Mines Limited—common stock.
Pago Mining Limited—capital without par value.
Pancoastal Petroleum Limited—common capital stock voting trust certificates relating thereto.
Pantepec Oil Company, C.A.—capital stock par value on bolivar.
Peel-Elder Limited—capital stock of no par value.
Peruvian Oils & Minerals Limited—capital stock.
Phoenix Canada Oil Company Limited—common stock.
Pompey Oil & Minerals Company Limited—common stock.
Prairie Oil Royalties Company Ltd.—capital stock.
Reeves MacDonald Mines Limited—common stock.
Sailfish Sports Craft Limited—common stock.
Schlumberger Limited—common stock.
Scott Paper Limited—common stock without nominal or par value.
Scurry-Rainbow Oil Limited—common stock.
Sherwin-Williams Company of Canada, Limited (The)—common stock voting, no par value.
Silver Ridge Mining Co., Limited—common stock.
Snowdrift Base Metal Mines Limited—common stock.
Stanrock Uranium Mines Limited—common stock.
St. John D'el Rey Mining Co., Ltd.—shares or ordinary stock.
Syntex Corporation—common stock.
TACA International Airlines S.A.— common stock $0.10 par value.
Teledyne Canada, Limited (formerly Vascan Limited, which formerly was Vanadium-Alloys Steel Canada Limited)—common stock, no par value.

Texaco Canada Limited—common stock without nominal or par value.
Tropical Gas Company, Inc.—common stock and preferred.
Union Carbide Canada Limited—common stock without nominal or par value.
Union Oil Company of Canada Limited—common stock.
United Asbestos Corporation Limited—capital stock, $1 par value.
United Canso Oil & Gas Limited—capital stock par value $1 and voting trust certificates relating thereto.
Western Heritage Properties Limited—common stock.

The Corporations listed below have received ruling letters holding that the described class or classes of their stock are exempt under section 4920 (b) of the Code, but have subsequently issued additional shares which are not exempt, even though they are similar in rights and interest to the exempt shares:
American International Reinsurance Company, Inc.—common stock.
Atlas Consolidated Mining & Development Corp.—common stock.
Banff Oil Limited—common stock and preferred stock. (Corporation underwent voluntary liquidation on December 2, 1970. Acquisition after such date of such "stock" may be subject to tax, unless another statutory exclusion or exemption applies.)
Canadian Curtiss-Wright Limited—capital stock.
Canvil, Limited—common stock.
Coastal Caribbean Oil & Mineral Ltd.—capital stock par value 1 shilling and voting trust certificates relating thereto.
Molybenite Corporation of Canada, Ltd.—common stock with par value $5 (formerly common stock with par value $1) Class "B" shares to be identified as not exempt.
Murky Fault Metal Mines Limited—common stock, issued non-exempt stock.
Pacific Petroleums Ltd.—common stock, par value $1.
Tashota Nipigon Mines Limited—common stock.
Warner Bros. Seven Arts Limited (formerly Seven Arts Production Limited)—common stock without par value.

The stock certificates representing the nonexempt shares should in each case be marked with distinguishing legend.

"Surluga Gold Mines Limited—common stock," "Husky Oil Canada Limited—common stock," and "MacDonald Mines Limited—common stock" were deleted from lists previously published in prior Revenue Rulings. However, if a United States person can establish that his acquisition of shares of common stock of Surluga Gold Mines Limited or Husky Oil Canada Limited are shares which meet the requirements of section 4920 (b) of the Code, such an acquisition will not be subject to the interest equalization tax.

Interest equalization tax will not be imposed upon United States persons with respect to shares of common stock of MacDonald Mines Limited acquired by them prior to the close of August 19, 1968. Furthermore for purposes of a subsequent acquisition of common stock of MacDonald Mines Limited (i.e., after August 19, 1968) by another United States person, any United States person who acquired such stock prior to the close of August 19, 1968, will be considered to have acquired such stock without liability for payment of such tax within the meaning of section 4918(a) (2) (B) of the Code.

**National Petroleum Corp., Ltd. was reinstated by a favorable ruling issued under Section 3(g) of the Interest Equalization Tax. Extension Act of 1971, Public Law 92-9, I.R.B. 1971-19, 79 and 86. The effect of such reinstatement is that section 4920(b) of the Internal Revenue Code of 1954 applies to all shares of the class from July 19, 1963.

2

GOLD IS ALIVE AND WELL

In 1970, before the first dollar devaluation, a British broker visited the United States and tried to sell South African gold mining stocks to American institutional investors. His efforts were in vain.

"Gold?" said an American portfolio manager. "What an anachronism!"

This anachronism tripled in price in terms of dollars between 1970 and 1973, and the prices of many gold stocks doubled and tripled. A very speculative one, *Randfontein,* increased from $1.65 to well over $20 in two years.

Prices of gold and gold stocks had receded to some extent by November 1973, when the United States and several leading European countries announced that they may sell some of their gold from time to time in the open market. This was obviously an effort to "demonetize" gold once and for all, but it did not really fool the true believers in gold, such as the French hoarders of the precious metal, and no panic selling ensued. For the one fact remains unchanged: gold, while not ideal, is by far the most practical yardstick by which to measure the true value of things and money—and as such it will always be an uncomfortable censor of governments that debase their currencies.

What is Money?

Money, after all, is only a standardized token by which the value of goods and services can be measured and which can be used to pay for these goods and services. Throughout history, many different things have been used as monetary tokens and yardsticks—cowrie shells, ax-heads, grains, animal skins, various metals and metal coins, printed paper, and even cigarettes (in the post-World War II era in occupied Germany). The ideal money is one that remains in fairly constant supply relative to the goods and services available. If the supply of money increases faster than the production of goods and services, it loses its value in relation to those goods and services, and prices go up. This is then called "inflation."

Paper money is a perfectly acceptable monetary yardstick as long as its supply is strictly controlled and remains in balance with the available goods and services. However, in the 37 years from 1934 to 1971, money supply in the United States (printed money plus demand and time deposits at banks) rose about three times faster than the gross national product (measured in terms of constant dollars). This meant that the purchasing power of one dollar, as measured by the consumer price index, sank to about 30 cents between 1934 and 1971. During the same time the price of gold remained artificially fixed at $35 per troy ounce (slightly heavier than the regular ounce.) When, on August 15, 1971, the United States declared that it would no longer pay gold for the dollars it owed foreigners, the long-established confidence in the dollar as an international standard of exchange vanished and people turned to what had been a more dependable measure of value since antiquity—gold. Its price tripled within two years, reflecting almost exactly the decline of the purchasing power of the dollar to one-third of its 1933 value. In fact, the average price of a man's suit remained practically unchanged between 1934 and 1973 in terms of gold—about one troy ounce—worth $35 in 1934 and about $100 in 1973.

Many monetary experts maintain that the subject of money in a modern, deficit-ridden economy such as the United States requires volumes of definitions and statistics to put it in its proper perspective. This is probably so. But, as a hackneyed story goes: a fact is when a six-foot statistician drowns crossing a river of an average depth of 4½ feet; and it is a fact that gold has gone from $35 to above $100 in two years, and the people who bought gold or gold shares in 1970 did not drown in the inflation and devaluation of the dollar.

The dollar disaster had been looming throughout the second half of the 1960s. It had been predicted for several years by some Cassandras to whom nobody listened, including some of the now famous gnomes of Zurich. It arrived with some delay. People just couldn't believe that the economically strongest country of the world could be brought to such a pass through fiscal irresponsibility. But then, few Romans realized that currency debasement was a major contributor to their empire's collapse. For most of its last 400 years until its demise in 475 A.D., Rome so inordinately debased its coinage and raised its taxes that its productive citizens found it less and less rewarding to produce. With a declining "gross national product," population began to decline, and finally there were not enough people and resources left to defend the empire against the invading barbarians.

What is the Gold Standard?

Even since the time when man learned to produce and work gold and silver these precious metals have proved to be the most stable and reliable monetary tokens—gold more so than silver because silver has had more erratic production and consumption rates than gold. This made the value of silver less reliable in relation to other goods and services. Gold has the additional advantage of not seriously deteriorating even after centuries of storage under the most unsuitable conditions, such as the bottom of the sea.

Byzantium, which became the successor to Rome in 324 A.D. under Constantine the Great, was one of the longest-lasting empires on the strength of a sound gold currency that retained its face value for 800 years. When debasement started in 1100 A.D. it was downhill until Constantinople, defended by another Constantine, was conquered by the Turks in 1452.

The economic advance of the 19th century was based on the gold standard, which practically all countries of the world had adopted. This meant that they minted gold coins of a specified weight or agreed to exchange paper money for gold at a fixed rate of exchange. In most countries this "golden age" came to an end with World War I; in the United States it lasted a little longer.

The United States went on a *de facto* gold standard in 1834; it fixed the price of gold at $20.67 per troy ounce; and it made the gold standard official in 1900 with the Gold Standard Act. Treasury goldback notes bore the message: "Redeemable in gold on demand at the United States Treasury or in gold or lawful money at any Federal Reserve Bank." Silver also was legal tender in the form of silver coins or silver certificates redeemable in silver dollars.

In 1934 the United States devalued the dollar for the first time in terms of gold—from $20.67 to $35 per troy ounce, and citizens could no longer ask for gold in exchange for paper money or own gold bullion. Foreign central banks, however, could still ask for their dollars to be redeemed in gold.

In 1964 the United States stopped putting silver into coins. The price of silver had risen above the face value of coins and people started hoarding the coins as fast as the government could mint them until the huge government stock of 2 billion troy ounces of silver was completely exhausted. The Federal Reserve also stopped printing on its notes the message that they are "redeemable in lawful money at the United States Treasury or at any Federal Reserve Bank." One-dollar and five-dollar bills with the inscription: "One (or five) silver dollar(s) payable to the bearer on demand" also were withdrawn. In other words, Americans could no longer exchange paper money for real money.

How to Abandon Gold and Sanity

In August 1971, the United States declared that it was no longer prepared to exchange gold for dollars held by foreigners, and in December 1971, it established a new parity of $38 per troy ounce of gold, raised February 10, 1973, to $42.22. This was completely meaningless since neither the Federal government nor any foreign central bank is willing to exchange gold for paper dollars at any price, and the free market price of gold at the end of 1971 was already well above $40 and rose to $65 by February 1973. Thereafter, it doubled in about two months, but came back to somewhat lower levels a few months later.

Trying to halt the rising price of gold at that time was like asking King Canute to arrest the rising tide of the sea. Canute proved to his courtiers, who had asked him to do so to prove his might, that it couldn't be done. Unfortunately the 1971 Canute in the United States seems to have believed his courtiers' counsel that it could be done. (His immediate predecessors apparently never saw the tide even though they helped create it.)

The tide was created by ten years of rapidly increasing deficits in the United States balance of payments and it was artificially shored up during those years by maintaining the fiction that the United States government was willing and able to convert all the dollars it owed foreigners into gold. Most foreign creditors, except de Gaulle, were too polite to call the bluff and upset the apple cart of the "convertible" dollar by actually asking for gold. It would not have helped because there was hardly any left. By 1971, the United States had a foreign debt of about $70 billion while its gold reserves had shrunk to a little over $10 billion (at $35 a troy ounce). When at that time the United States dropped the pretense that it would still convert its debt into gold, the dike burst and the gold price eventually went rampant to find its own proper level (and thereby increased the market value of the United States gold reserve).

The tripling from its 1934 price in terms of dollars merely means that it takes more paper money to buy the same amount of gold—not that gold has become more expensive in terms of real value, such as a man's suit. While it is impossible to predict the future price of gold, the purchasing power of the dollar is likely to continue to be reflected in the price of gold. This means that every percentage point that the dollar loses in purchasing power as a result of inflation is likely to create, on balance, a corresponding increase in the dollar price of gold. Other factors, of course, may also influence the price of gold—increasing industrial consumption, lower production, emotional buying and selling, or massive unloading of central bank gold reserves on the open market.

What is Inflation?

It may be appropriate here to define inflation and its causes. Inflation is not caused by farmers who want more money for their crops, or by the wicked middlemen who want to gorge themselves on the fruits of the farmers' labor, or the nefarious industrialists who fix prices, or the powerful labor unions who strike for higher wages. Throughout history inflation has always been created by the authorities who bloat the money supply and run budget deficits. In the old days, when only metal coins were used as money, the metal in the coins was debased and prices of goods and services rose in relation to the face value of the debased coins. In modern days of paper money, the government simply prints more money than there are goods and services available and expands bank credits. From 1933, the year in which the United States went off the gold standard, to September 1972, the money supply in the United States (paper money plus demand and time deposits) rose more than 13-fold (from about $45 billion to about $600 billion). Gross national product rose at less than half of that rate (from about $141 billion to about $834 billion in constant 1958 dollars—at the end of July 1973). Statistics on money supply, gross national product, and the international balance of payments are difficult to compile and are subject to different methods of compilation, giving the experts many points of disagreement. Nevertheless, in broad general terms all figures agree that the money supply since 1934 rose almost three times as fast as the production of goods and services, and it was continuing to rise in 1973, when at mid-year the money supply was increasing at a rate of over 10% while the gross national product in terms of constant dollars was rising at a real rate of only about 6%.

Inflation appears to make goods and services more expensive but what it really means is that people are getting poorer because their money is worth less; and their money is worth less because they pay for something indirectly that the government will not ask them to pay for directly in taxes. Instead of collecting the necessary taxes, the government simply prints more money or expands the bank credits to pay for its expenditures that are in excess of its income from taxes. This difference is called the budget deficit.

Politicians who praise the justice of the graduated income tax, which makes the rich pay more than the poor, don't seem to be bothered at all by the fact that by issuing more money to pay for budget deficits they are really robbing the poor. For inflation hits the pensioners, welfare recipients, and wage earners hardest. Most of the rich have means of investing their money in real values, such as gold, art treasures, or property. When prices go up as a result of government-created inflation, politicians resort to blaming the gouging manufacturer, middleman, and speculator and slam on price controls in self-righteous indignation. When as a result of price controls production goes down and shortages occur, they start rationing. This is often the beginning of the end. Controls, like a disease, breed more controls, and the end is economic stagnation and eventual decline.

In a freely elected democracy, politicians are not alone to blame for inflation. Ignorance and greed of the voters tend to keep irresponsible officials in office. In a climate where almost everybody wants something for nothing; where it is accepted practice for the public to cheat on every claim against money dispensing institutions, such as insurance companies, welfare agencies, and unemployment offices; where most people want more money for doing less or nothing at all; in such a climate most voters are likely to vote for the candidate who promises bonanzas while keeping taxes down, and not the one who tells them that they must tighten their belts to pay for past monetary sins and having lived beyond their means.

Modern politicians have received additional fuel for their inflationary arson from the theories of the renowned British economist, Lord Keynes, who maintained that the best way to stimulate the economy in a slow period is to increase the money supply, i.e. create inflation; while in boom periods, you deflate, i.e. decrease the money supply. Unfortunately, our politicians have used only the first part of the prescription—even in times of boom—like the psychopath who takes a little alcohol to calm his nerves and then just keeps on taking more and more because it is so effective. Throughout history there is no example of inflation having cured economic ills; healthy economies in the long run have existed only in periods of sound currency when people had an incentive to work and save. Even the Great Depression, during which Lord Keynes developed his theory, was primarily triggered by an abundance of money left over from World War I; not by a lack of it.

Who Pays for Wars?

Inflation is usually worst during times of war. The all-time classic inflation is that of Germany after World War I. The Germans had largely paid for the war through war bonds and other government debts and by printing paper money. Most of the goods produced during a war are, of course, blown up into the air. So when the war was over there was all this paper but no goods to buy with it. The government printed more and more paper, and the more it printed, the more worthless it became, until a loaf of bread cost 100 billion marks. Finally the mark, which before World War I, was exchanged at 4.2 to $1, was stabilized in 1923 at a rate of 4,200,000,000,000 (that is 4.2 *trillion*) to $1. In other words, whoever held nothing but cash or government bonds had paid for the war by being wiped out completely, or very nearly—and those who were wiped out were largely the lower and middle classes who had no property or other solid values.

The United States paid for much of the costs of World War II by inflation. The dollar in terms of 1934 purchasing power declined from about 94 cents in 1939 to about 55 cents in 1948. This is probably a reasonable cost considering the results. The purchasing power of the dollar remained fairly stable during the early 1950s; it then started depreciating slowly in the late 1950s, picking up speed in the late 1960s until it was well below 30 cents in mid-1973. Between 1960 and 1972 alone, the money supply in the United States doubled, growing about 50% faster than the production of goods and services. In addition, the United States ran up its short-term debt obligations to foreigners from about $20 billion to nearly $100 billion in mid-1973.

How to Spread the Disease

Not only have Americans grown poorer from 1960 to 1972 by about 33% in terms of their dollar savings and pensions, but they have also received about $100 billion in goods and services from foreigners for which they have not yet paid in goods and services or other recognized values, such as gold. These dollars have caused inflation in many other countries, too. This money is outside the control of any government; it flows freely from one country to another, increasing the money supply wherever it goes without a corresponding increase in the supply of goods and services. In other words, the United States has carried its disease abroad and contaminated almost the entire free world. In addition, such a huge debt costs a staggering sum of interest that adds to the dollar outflow and in 1973 may have accounted for a major part of the deficit in the United States balance of payments. There are no published accurate statistics available on these interest payments to foreign creditors, but according to an estimate by C. Austin Barker, Vice President-Consulting Economist of *Hornbower & Weeks-Hemphill, Noyes*, interest payments to foreigners on such short-term obligations were running at an annual rate of well over $4 billion in 1973.

One hundred billion dollars—give or take $10 billion—is a staggering amount of money, difficult to visualize. In November 1973, about $7.5 billion would buy a 51% controlling interest in *General Motors* at about $45 per share. About $2 billion would buy the controlling interest of the entire American aerospace industry, consisting of some 20 companies, including *Boeing, McDonald Douglas,* and *Rockwell International.* Buying American companies may, in fact, be the only way for foreigners to get value back for their dollars. And some foreigners have already done so by buying such companies as *Gimbels, Franklin Stores,* and *TraveLodge International* and making bids for *Ronson, Texasgulf,* and *The Signal Companies, Inc.* stock.

No End in Sight?

In the fall of 1973 it was difficult to know whether an end was in sight. The United States payment balance showed its first surplus for a long time. Money supply was rising faster than production of goods and services, but it seemed to be slowing down. Price controls started to create shortages, and the energy crisis threatened economic disaster. The huge overhang of $100 billion in debt to foreigners remained. There was no realization among the public at large about what had really happened. No government leader told the electorate that the country had lived way beyond its means and on borrowed money and time for the last ten years—and that the only way to cure the situation was to pay up, consume less, and produce more for less pay in terms of real money. With human nature being what it is, chances are that timely self-discipline will not be applied. We may have to wait for the hard taskmaster of a depression to restore the true relationship between services rendered and real money received.

Where Will Gold Prices Go?

Throughout history, in times of debased currency people hoarded true values, notably gold and silver. This was again happening at an accelerated pace throughout the world between 1971 and 1973. In the second half of 1973, the gold price per troy ounce seemed to settle at a level of about $100, possibly because interest rates shot up in many countries and investors found it more interesting to buy fixed-income securities or sell gold and lend the money short-term at high interest rates. Both demand and supply seemed to slow down.

Gold and silver have commercial uses—in artisan and industrial applications. Supply comes from mining, scrap recovery, and release from hoards. Demand is governed by commercial and industrial uses plus stockpiling in the form of government monetary reserves and private hoards. During most of this century, supply and demand have been in better balance for gold than for silver. With the recent sharp increase in gold prices one would have expected an increase in production; but surprisingly the opposite was true, and gold production declined by about 10% in 1972 and 1973. The higher gold prices made it economical for the mines to work ores of lower gold content, saving the richer ores for later. As a result, in 1972 world industrial uses of gold outside Russia amounted to about 1,300 metric tons, almost as high as the total supply from mining and release from stockpiles of 1,381 metric tons. Thus, as with some other natural resources, a shortage of gold for industrial uses suddenly becomes a much more imminent possibility than had been expected before 1972.

Is Silver Getting Scarce?

Silver has had a far more erratic supply and demand relationship than gold. In the past, the supply was always ample, and huge amounts of silver were accumulated in private and government hands. India alone is estimated to have a silver treasury of between 2 and 4 billion ounces, mostly in the form of jewelry. The United States Treasury, before 1960, under pressure from the silver lobby, had accumulated about 2 billion ounces of silver. These all disappeared in the wild silver coining spree of 1963-1965.

During the Depression industrial consumption of silver dropped sharply and prices collapsed. (This might well happen again in another depression.) In general, silver prices have fluctuated widely over the years, so that in the recent past silver was not a reliable hedge against inflation.

However, the situation may have changed radically. World silver consumption has increased from about 200 million ounces in 1959 to about 400 million ounces in 1972. Silver is used widely in photographic films, electrical and electronics products, brazing and soldering, jewelry, and medical and dental applications. It is by far the best electric conductor of all metals. For many uses there is no satisfactory substitute. Thus, consumption is likely to increase unless there is a major depression. World production, on the other hand, has remained relatively static at 200 to 250 million ounces per year during the past 20 years. The difference between production and consumption has been made up by salvage from world scrap (about 50 million ounces in 1970) and supply from stockpiles. Silver production is not easily stepped up, since most newly mined silver is a by-product of copper, zinc, and lead mining—and this type of mining depends on the demand for the three metals and is less influenced by the price of silver. Thus, there are predictions that as early as 1974 the demand for silver will have outstripped the combined supply from mining, scrap, and hoards.

Rising silver prices are an illustration of the one other important factor, in addition to inflation, that can boost prices—scarcity. Like inflation, rising prices as a result of scarcity illustrate that we are getting poorer rather than that goods are getting more expensive. Land is the classic example. Its supply on our planet is rigidly limited. As the population increases, we have to share the same pie with more people, and each of us is getting poorer in terms of total land available. This is reflected in higher real estate prices. In the long run, we shall get poorer in relation to all irreplaceable natural resources—and their prices will rise—unless we curb population growth and consumption per capita.

Are Private Gold and Silver Hoards Safe?

Thus, should one hoard gold and silver in anticipation of further inflation and future scarcity? In the United States the actual physical possession has a few drawbacks, including that of safety if one stores it at home and cost if one stores it with a bank. A United States citizen or resident is barred by law from owning gold bullion. At this time he may own gold coins minted prior to 1934, and all silver coins and silver bullion. However, there is no guarantee that the Federal government, in what it will call a "national emergency," will not seize such gold and silver. It has done this in the past. In 1933, the United States demanded the surrender of all gold by private citizens. Treasury officials went so far as to track down people who had made large withdrawals of gold and individually notified them they must turn in their hoards. Nevertheless, anyone wanting to buy gold and silver coins can do so from dealers on the *Pacific Coast Coin Exchange*, which has sales offices in several major cities and from a number of other coin dealers.

It must be remembered, however, that gold and silver coins and bars are not interest bearing. They merely preserve an investor's capital in times of inflation. A safe bond might do the same. Depending on an investor's tax bracket, a bond paying 8% interest before taxes may maintain his capital if inflation runs at about 6% per year and he does not use up his interest income. But in real economic crisis, a bond may not serve as "store value" the way gold has served throughout the ages because the issuer may not be able to meet the interest requirement, and some bonds, as *Penn Central* proved, may even default in relatively good economic times.

Because of the storage problems with gold and silver and the lack of income, many investors seeking inflation protection have looked to gold stocks—less so to silver stocks because there are very few mines predominantly producing silver, and their stock action has been unimpressive in the past.

How to Buy Gold Stocks

During the Depression of the 1930s, most gold stocks did well. *Dome Mines*, a leading Canadian producer, increased in price from about $10 in 1930 to $57 in 1937, in addition to paying substantial dividends. *Homestake Mining Company*, the leading American producer, increased from $83 in 1930 to $430 in 1937, also paying handsome dividends. Many gold stocks have performed equally well in the past few years, and many investors have turned to them as a hedge against inflation and the threat of a depression. Even without this element of a hedge, an investment in a gold mine is an investment in a natural resource for which there is a clearly defined demand and a fairly well established supply picture. In this respect, an investment in gold stocks does not differ from an investment in any mining stock—copper, lead, zinc, etc.,—when commodities are in demand and a free market for them prevails. However, in a period of collapsing commodity prices, only gold retains its "store value."

Gold stocks, both domestic and foreign, are easy to buy in the United States. Most of the important South African gold stocks are actively traded in the United States in the form of American Depositary Receipts and they can be bought from any American broker. However, an investor might get a better price if he buys a gold stock traded over-the-counter from a broker who makes a market for it (see the end of this chapter). Information is readily available. The selection of individual gold stocks is tricky, however, and a specialist in gold stocks is preferable to a generalist as an advisor.

Two key questions about a gold mine are: What are its ore reserves and how rich are its ores? A number of gold mines and holding companies are also in other mining ventures, including platinum, uranium, silver, copper, and lead; and these elements of the operation may have major bearings on earnings and cancel out the results from gold mining. Since many gold mines, like other metal mines, have a relatively short life span, the yield from the investment must repay the invested capital before the mine is exhausted, plus a worthwhile profit to the investors. Finally, it should be observed that gold mining stocks are subject to wide price swings that are exploited by traders. It requires a good deal of insight and restraint, if not inside trading information, to catch a gold stock at the bottom of the swing rather than at the top.

Gold Investment Funds

An investment in a single operating mine has a high element of risk because a mine disaster from fire, flood, explosion, or rock burst can close down a mine for a time. Thus, a seasoned investor will spread his investment over several mines. An investor who cannot afford to buy several gold mining stocks, as well as any beginner, is wise to buy shares of an investment fund specializing in gold stocks. The two leading ones are *International Investors Incorporated* and *ASA Ltd.*

International Investors is a United States-managed fund based in New York. Its asset value more than doubled from about $15 per share in 1971 to about $35 per share before a 3:1 split in September 1973. Shares can be bought directly from the fund or through certain brokers. The buyer pays a "front-end load" commission of 8¾% which is reduced for larger orders. Except for about 4% of foreign industrial and financial common stocks, the entire portfolio of the fund in 1973 consisted of gold stocks. The list of its holdings can serve as a professional guide to gold stocks.

ASA Ltd. is a South African investment fund (formerly *American-South African Investment Company Ltd.*), which can be bought on the New York Stock Exchange in two ways at daily market prices (a higher-priced one that includes Interest Equalization Tax and a lower-priced one on which the tax has not been paid). The shares are also traded on the leading European stock exchanges. The policy of the fund is to invest between 50% and 80% of the assets in South African gold mining companies and up to 20% in companies outside South Africa engaged in mining or related activities or in the holding and development of real estate. In mid-1973 about 75% was in gold, most of the balance in diamonds in the form of *DeBeers* stock.

South African Gold Stocks

South Africa produces about 76% of the total free world production of gold and an estimated 60% of total world production, including Russia, which is probably the second largest producer of gold, followed by Canada and the United States. (Total world production in 1971, including Russia, was estimated at 50 million troy ounces.)

In addition to investing in a mining investment trust, there are two other ways to participate in the South African gold industry—to invest in a mining finance house or to buy stocks of an operating gold mine.

Mining finance houses are large holding companies organized to finance mining ventures of all kinds. Practically all of the more than 40 gold mines in South Africa are partly owned and controlled by one or several finance companies. The leading one among them is *AMGOLD (Anglo American Gold Investment Company, Ltd.)*, representing a 1972 merger between two mining finance companies. Its investments are exclusively in South African gold mines, thus making the stock a pure "gold play." Shares can be bought in the United States on the over-the-counter market in the form of American Depositary Receipts.

AMGOLD should not be confused with *Anglo American Corporation of South Africa Ltd.*, a world-wide finance and holding company with about 25% of its income from gold mining ventures; the balance comes from diamonds, copper, platinum, real estate, coal, and steel. It is a giant organization that controls about 40% of South Africa's gold production and practically the entire world's diamond production (through its control of *DeBeers*). Because of the great diversification, price movement of *Anglo American Corporation* stock has been relatively stable. American Depositary Receipts of the stock are traded in the United States on the over-the-counter market.

An investor who wants to take a greater risk in trying to beat the "averages" of a gold stock investment fund or a finance company has more than 30 American Depositary Receipts of *kaffirs* to choose from. (The South African word *kaffir,* an old term used for the blacks of the country, is a generic term for gold mining stocks, probably because the *kaffirs* are doing most of the physical work.) Shares not available in the United States can be bought in Johannesburg or in London, which maintains the world's most active market in mining stocks.

All South African gold mines must sell their output to the South African government at a fixed price. The government then sells the gold that it does not need as a monetary reserve on the free world market. Profits derived from these free market sales are distributed to the mines on the basis of their deliveries. Thus, the mines benefit from rising gold prices. It must be pointed out in conclusion that some seasoned investors will not buy South African gold stocks, or any other South African stock, because they consider the risk of riots substantial under the *apartheid* system of the country.

Canadian Gold Stocks

Canada, in 1972, produced 2 million ounces of gold or about 4% of world production. Production has been declining steadily over the past few years. Until the recent sharp rise of the gold price, many Canadian gold mines needed government subsidies to stay in business. As in South Africa, the higher gold price has not resulted in higher gold production, but profits have improved. Stock prices of the leading gold stocks rose sharply. *Dome Mines,* listed on the New York Stock Exchange, traded around $60 in 1970 and 1971 and was at about $120 in November 1973. Its affiliate, *Campbell Red Lake Mines*, also listed on the New York Stock Exchange, more than tripled in price from about $20 to $70 between 1970 and November 1973.

The choice among Canadian gold stocks is limited, and the United States investor will find it more convenient to confine himself to those traded in the United States markets.

In addition to the two companies listed on the New York Stock Exchange, two Canadian gold mining issues are listed on the American Stock Exchange—*Giant Yellowknife Mines Ltd.* and *Pato Consolidated Gold Dredging Ltd.* The latter is a Canadian company operating in Colombia, a country that adds an element of risk to investments.

Even though they do not belong in a book on foreign stocks, United States gold and silver mining stocks probably deserve a brief mention to round out the picture. The two leading ones are *Homestake Mining Company*, listed on the New York Stock Exchange, and *Day Mines Inc.*, listed on the American Stock Exchange.

Neither of them is a pure gold producer. In 1972, 5% of *Homestake*'s sales were from gold, 30% lead and zinc, 7% silver, and the balance from building materials and other products. In 1972, lead and zinc accounted for 73% of the operating profits, but in 1973, as the result of higher gold prices, gold became the largest contributor to earnings. *Day Mines* derives about 50% of its revenue from silver, about 20% from gold, and the balance from lead, zinc, and copper. Only the *Homestake* stock price responded to the gold rush, rising from the low $20s to about $50 between 1971 and November 1973. The *Day Mine* stock price has actually shown a declining trend, as have other silver mining stocks.

Two other mining companies with substantial silver production until mid-1973 have had a relatively uninspiring stock performance— *Hecla Mining Company* and *Sunshine Mining Company*, both listed on the New York Stock Exchange. *Sunshine* has diversified somewhat into manufacturing operations.

Sources of Information

With the renewed interest in gold came a veritable flood of information on gold and gold stocks, mostly in the form of articles and seminars. There is no way of doing justice to all of them here. But a good deal of material is available from a few leading United States brokerage houses. Good information is also available from leading British brokerage houses (see the end of Chapter 10).

The classic book on the subject is *How to Invest in Gold Stocks* by Donald J. Hoppe. It makes highly informative reading even for someone who is not an investor in gold stocks or any other stocks. For those who are, Mr. Hoppe also reviews all major gold mining stocks of the world.

All gold stocks listed on the New York and American Stock Exchanges, and several of those traded over-the-counter, are covered at regular intervals by *Standard & Poor's* service.

Weekly charts on South African *kaffir* gold stocks are available in the United States from *Indicator Chart Service, Inc.*, Palisades Park, New Jersey.

The *Mining Journal* in London, England, publishes an excellent

Quarterly Review of South African Gold Shares and covers the entire gold scene extensively in its editorial pages. The daily *Financial Times*, London, publishes detailed annual and interim reports on South African gold mining stocks and an index of share prices. Canadian mines are covered in the *Northern Miner*, published in Toronto, as well as in the *Financial Post*, Toronto, investment information service.

Most South African gold mines and finance companies produce outstandingly informative annual reports which are sent to investors on request.

Major South African Finance and Investment Companies in Gold and Precious Metals

Asterisk (*) indicates stocks traded as ADRs on the over-the-counter market

*Anglo American Corporation of South Africa Ltd.**
*Anglo American Gold Investment Company, Ltd.**
Anglo-Transvaal Consolidated Investment Company Ltd.
Barlow Rand
Charter Consolidated
Consolidated Gold Fields Ltd.
*DeBeers**
General Mining and Finance Corporation Ltd.

*Gold Fields of South Africa Ltd.**
Johannesburg Consolidated
Lydenburg Platinums
Middle Wits
*Potgietersrust Platinums**
Rand Selection Corporation Ltd.
Sentrust
T.C. Land
U.C. Investments
Union Corporation Ltd.
Union Platinums
Waterval Platinums

South African Gold Mining Companies

Asterisk (*) indicates stocks traded as ADRs on the over-the-counter market

*Blyvooruitzicht**
Bracken
*Buffelsfontein**
Doornfontein
East Driefontein
Elsburg
*Free State Geduld**
Grootvlei
Harmony
Hartebeestfontein
Kinross
*Kloof**
Leslie
Libanon
Marievale

*President Brand**
*President Steyn**
Randfontein
*Saint Helena**
Southvaal
*Vaal Reefs**
Venterspost
Vlakfontein
*Welkom**
*West Driefontein**
Western Areas
*Western Deep Levels**
*Western Holdings**
Winkelhaak

Gold Investment Funds

International Investors Inc. / 420 Lexington Avenue / New York, New York 10017
ASA Ltd. (traded on the New York Stock Exchange) / 54 Marshall Street / Johannesburg, South Africa

Canadian Gold Stocks

TSE: Toronto Stock Exchange; CSE: Canadian Stock Exchange; NYSE: New York Stock Exchange; ASE: American Stock Exchange; MSE: Montreal Stock Exchange; VSE: Vancouver Stock Exchange

Agrico Eagle (TSE)
Aunor Gold Mines Ltd. (TSE)
Camflo Mines Ltd. (TSE, CSE)
Campbell Red Lake Mines Ltd. (NYSE, TSE)
Dickenson Mines Ltd. (TSE)
Dome Mines Ltd. (NYSE, TSE, CSE)
Giant Yellowknife Mines Ltd. (ASE, TSE)
Kerr Addison Mines Ltd. (TSE)
Madsen Red Lake Gold Mines Ltd. (TSE)
Pamour Porcupine Mines Ltd. (TSE, CSE)
Sigma Mines (Quebec) Ltd. (TSE)
Pato Consolidated Gold Dredging Ltd. (ASE, TSE, MSE, VSE)

Investment Information and Advisory Services

Kaffir Chart Service published weekly by *Indicator Chart Service* / Indicator Digest Building / Palisades Park, New Jersey 07650
Quarterly Review of South African Gold Shares published by *The Mining Journal Ltd.* / 15 Wilson Street / London, England
The Financial Post (on Canadian mining industry) published by *Maclean-Hunter Limited* / 481 University Avenue / Toronto, Canada and 625 President Kennedy Avenue / Montreal, Canada

Book

How to Invest in Gold Stocks by Donald J. Hoppe, published by *Arlington House* / New Rochelle, New York

Publications

Mining Journal, Ltd. (weekly, by airmail) / 15 Wilson Street, Moorgate / London, England
The Northern Miner (weekly) / Circulation Department / 77 River Street / Toronto, Ontario, Canada
The London Financial Times (daily, except Sunday, by airmail) / Bracken House, Cannon Street / London, England
(Next day delivery to New York area may be arranged through their office at 551 Fifth Avenue, New York, New York)

A Partial List of United States Brokerage Houses that have Published Information on Gold and Gold Stocks

Delafield Childs, Inc. / 770 Lexington Avenue / New York, New York 10021 (Mr. Joseph Kelly)
Fahnestock and Co. / 110 Wall Street / New York, New York 10005 (Mr. Peter Kiernan)
Harris, Upham & Co. Inc. / 120 Broadway / New York, New York 10005 (Mr. Deson Sze)
P. R. Herzig & Co. / 1 State Street Plaza / New York, New York 10004 (Mr. William Tehan)

Hornblower & Weeks-Hemphill, Noyes, Inc. / 8 Hanover Street / New York, New York 10004 (Mr. C. Austin Barker)

David A. Noyes & Co. / 208 South LaSalle Street / Chicago, Illinois 60604 (Mr. William L. Graham, Jr.)

James H. Oliphant & Co., Inc. / 61 Broadway / New York, New York 10006 (Mr. Joseph Gellart)

Piper, Jaffrey and Hopwood / 120 Broadway / New York, New York 10005 (Mr. William L. Roberts)

Smith, Barney and Co. Inc. / 20 Broad Street / New York, New York 10005 (Mr. Adolphe J. Warner, author of the widely read article "Gold is Dead')

Partial Listing of Investment Advisory Letters Covering Gold From Time to Time

American Institute for Economic Research / Barrington, Massachusetts

The Dines Letter / 18 East 41st Street / New York, New York 10017

The International Reports / 200 Park Avenue South / New York, New York 10003

Investment Guideline / McConnell Craig Capital Advisors Ltd. / Suite 408, 200 Bay Street / Toronto, Ontario, Canada

The Lynch International Investment Survey / 120 Broadway / New York, New York 10005

The Powell Monetary Analyst / Reserve Research Limited / 63 Wall Street / New York, New York 10005

Partial List of United States Brokers Making a Market in Over-the-Counter Gold Stocks

Arnhold and S. Bleichroeder Inc. / 30 Broad Street / New York, New York 10004

Carl Marks & Co. Inc. / 77 Water Street / New York, New York 10005

Drexel-Burnham & Co. Inc. / 60 Broad Street / New York, New York 10004

Goldman Sachs & Co. / 55 Broad Street / New York, New York 10004

Hornblower & Weeks-Hemphill, Noyes, Inc. / 8 Hanover Street / New York, New York 10004

Loeb, Rhoades & Co. / 42 Wall Street / New York, New York 10005

Merrill Lynch, Pierce, Fenner & Smith Inc. / 1 Liberty Plaza / New York, New York 10006

Market makers for all over-the-counter stocks are published daily in the so-called "pink sheets" which are available at every brokerage office.

Decline in United States Treasury Gold Stock
Short-Term Liabilities to Foreigners

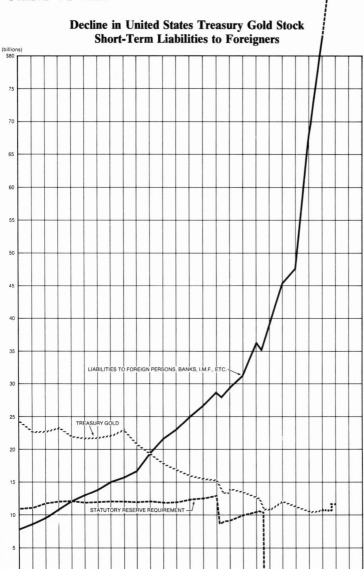

Courtesy, C. Austin Barker, *Hornblower & Weeks-Hemphill, Noyes, Inc.*

3

CANADA
THE RESOURCEFUL NEIGHBOR

The relationship between U.S. "Americans" and Canadians has a few touchy aspects. Canadians often are shocked by the complete ignorance about their country among Americans who have no business or social relations there. On the other hand, Canadians often feel overwhelmed by more news coming from their neighbor to the south than they care to know. The high percentage of American ownership of Canadian enterprises has become a serious political issue. To the most sensitive Canadians, the United States in the days of the dollar debacle and Watergate looked like an inebriated giant who, bleary-eyed, stumbled from one political morass into another via the quicksands of economic crises, irresponsibly throwing his money away, madly flailing his arms in his efforts to repair the damage only to get himself into deeper trouble, while unwittingly landing some hard blows on the heads of innocent bystanders.

To Canadians and Americans doing business with one another, however, the picture is different. American investors for a long time have found the Canadian economy one of the most rewarding areas for portfolio investments. Responsible Canadians recognize that the huge Canadian resources could not have been developed without the massive direct investments of American corporations and financial institutions. And American companies operating in Canada go out of their way to be good citizens.

On October 3, 1973 the Canadian dollar (C$) was valued at U.S. 99.3¢.

74

Going Its Own Way

The hackneyed phrase "when the United States sneezes, Canada catches cold," is only a half-truth in 1973, if still true at all. Canada's economy and stock markets, since 1972, have begun to go their own ways, and the majority of Canadian stocks are considered "foreign" enough by the Internal Revenue Service to make them subject to the Interest Equalization Tax. While still doing about 70% of its foreign trade with the United States, Canada's gross national product in 1972 and 1973 grew faster than that of its giant neighbor (about 8% vs. less than 4% in terms of constant dollars). The Canadian stock markets performed considerably better in 1972 and 1973 than the United States markets. The floating Canadian dollar appreciated from 93 cents in 1969 to 103 cents in 1972.

The Canadians have begun to reverse the tables in across-the-border acquisitions. Instead of being on the acquired side, Canadians in the summer of 1973 made tender offers for the shares of two large United States corporations. The *Canada Development Corporation,* a relatively young government agency formed to encourage Canadian investments in the development of Canadian resources, made a tender offer for 10 million shares of *Texasgulf, Inc.,* a New York-based multinational metals and sulphur producing company which owns large mines and processing plants in Canada. A group of Montreal investors made a tender offer for 1 to 1.5 million of the 19.7 million outstanding shares of *The Signal Companies, Inc.,* a California-based conglomerate with large oil interests.

In addition to setting up the *Canada Development Corporation,* the Canadian government has taken several other steps to reduce the percentage of United States ownership in the Canadian economy and raise the percentage of Canadian ownership. (United States money, in 1973, still controlled about 50% of three key Canadian industries—petroleum and natural gas, mining and smelting, and pulp and paper. The Canadian automobile industry is 86% United States-owned.) A bill has been passed by Parliament that would empower the national government to prevent the take-over of Canadian-owned companies by non-residents if it feels the take-over is not in the best interest of the country. Already on the books is a regulation that certain key industries—including banking, broadcasting, and uranium mining—may not have more than 25% non-resident stockholders.

Two regulations have encouraged greater investment in Canadian securities by Canadian institutional and individual investors. First, Canadian pension funds, which are growing at the same fast rate as United States pension funds, must invest at least 90% of their funds in Canadian securities. Second, individual Canadian investors pay lower taxes on dividends received from Canadian companies than on those received from foreign investments.

At the same time, the Canadian government has given a tax break to industry. The general corporate tax is being reduced by 1% a year, from 50% in 1972 to 46% in 1976. To give further impetus to manufacturing and processing enterprises in Canada (in contrast to the extracting industries), companies pay only a 40% corporate tax on that part of their activities that can be clearly identified as manufacturing and processing.

All these measures are likely to spur the Canadian economy and make it less dependent on the political vagaries and economic roller coaster trips of its neighbor.

Why Invest in Canada?

Canada's increasing independence from the United States economy makes it well worth while to take a look at the Canadian investment market, divorced from American stock markets. Here are a number of factors which, according to the economist of a leading Canadian brokerage house, make Canada different from the United States and other investment markets:

1. Canada is the only industrial nation in the world that has within its own borders all the known energy sources in ample supply: oil, natural gas, coal, uranium, and hydroelectric power;

2. In addition, Canada has other valuable resources, including nonferrous metals, iron ore, forest products, and grain. With shrinking resources in many parts of the world, Canada is sitting in the driver's seat in a seller's market as far as supplies and prices are concerned;

3. Canada's economy is growing faster than that of the United States;

4. The economy is freer than that of the United States—no price and wage controls; less government interference;

5. There are no social problems as in England (the political problems with the French-speaking Canadians seem to have simmered down), no racial problems as in the United States, no economic imperialism as with *IT&T*, and not so much self-righteousness as in France.

Allowing for only a modest level of Canadian pride, most of these reasons are no doubt based on sound fact.

Recommended Industry Groups

When asked what the most interesting Canadian stocks for the non-resident investor are, most Canadian brokers will mention the natural resources—oil, natural gas, mining, pulp and paper, and real estate.

The Canadian metal and mining stocks best known to American investors are *Alcan Aluminium Ltd.*, *International Nickel Company of Canada Ltd.*, and *Hudson's Bay Mining and Smelting Company.* Since the start of the recent gold rush on the investment scene, gold mining stocks may be added to this list—*Campbell Red Lakes Mines Ltd.* and *Dome Mines Ltd.* These five are among the 19 Canadian stocks that are traded on the New York Stock Exchange. Another 49 Canadian companies are listed on the American Stock Exchange, and 41 Canadian issues traded over-the-counter are quoted on the NAS-DAQ system of the National Association of Securities Dealers (see the end of Chapter 1 for complete lists). On the over-the-counter list, the most actively traded Canadian mining stock is *Noranda Mines, Ltd.*, a major producer of copper.

When recommending mining stocks, a reputable broker will not include the penny stocks that gave the Toronto Stock Exchange such a bad name in the 1960s. Since then the Ontario Securities Commission and the Toronto Stock Exchange have tightened controls over disclosure and trading practices considerably. Nevertheless, there are still many cheap Canadian mining stocks traded over-the-counter or on the smaller Canadian exchanges for gamblers. An investor should beware of unregistered Canadian stocks which he may never be able to sell again.

The group that outperformed all others on the Toronto Stock Exchange in 1972 was the oil refining group. Refinery production rose by 13% in 1973, while crude oil production in the key province of Alberta rose by 15%. The largest Canadian oil company is *Imperial Oil Limited*, 70% owned by *Exxon*, followed by *Gulf Oil Canada Limited*, 69% owned by *Gulf Oil* (both Canadian companies are traded on the American Stock Exchange).

Rising crude oil prices and the shortage in the United States have focused attention on a huge untapped Canadian oil reserve—the *Athabasca* tar sands, with an estimated 280 billion barrels of recoverable oil. Formerly, the gap between world crude oil prices and recovery costs was too wide to bridge, but with improved recovery methods bringing costs down and rising world market prices for crude oil, recovery has become an economic proposition. In the meantime, active exploration in the Canadian Arctic and off the Eastern Coast of Canada resulted in major new oil and gas discoveries.

One of the steadiest advances in the Toronto Stock Exchange Index over a period of several years was actually not produced by any natural resource group, but by the bank group. The ten chartered Canadian banks occupy a somewhat unique position. In contrast to the United States where commercial banks can operate only within a limited geographical area (and in some cases, such as Texas, not have any branch offices at all), the Canadian chartered banks can operate nation-wide. Their extensive network of branches have put the leading Canadian banks among the largest banks of the world. Canadian chartered banks provide roughly the same services that American commercial banks provide, except for trust services. Trusts are managed by specialized trust companies which also handle savings accounts. The most actively traded bank stocks in 1972 were the *Bank of Montreal*, 32nd among the world's largest banks, and the *Royal Bank of Canada*, the 17th largest bank in the world.

Steel stocks were another popular group in contrast to the United States where, as one broker said, "you can't give them away." Canada's rapid growth makes the steel industry a growth industry. The three leading steel companies are *Steel Company of Canada, Dominion Foundries and Steel* and *Algoma Steel Corporation*.

Investors can get a double play on two foreign economies—Brazil and Canada—by buying *Brascan, Ltd.,* a Canadian holding company. Its main holding in Brazil is the *Brazilian Light & Power Company* which, together with the Brazilian economy, has grown at a rapid rate. In Canada, *Brascan* holds 33% of *John Labatt Co.*, a leading brewery, and in 1973 it acquired the *Great Lakes Power Corporation,* a utility.

The forest products and paper industry has benefitted from the tight supply situation in the United States and other parts of the world, and it is likely to continue to do so. The largest Canadian forest products company is *MacMillan Bloedel,* followed by *Domtar Ltd.* and *Abitibi Paper Company.*

The real estate industry in 1972 also performed well on the Canadian stock markets. Largest in this group are *Trizec Corporation, Cadillac Development,* and *Markborough Properties Ltd.*

Interest Equalization Tax

When selecting a Canadian stock, the investor should determine whether the stock is subject to the Interest Equalization Tax or not. (See Chapter 1 for details on the tax.) Many Canadian stocks are exempt on application to the IRS if the company is at least 65% owned by United States investors. A list of stocks traded on the Toronto Stock Exchange that were exempt in 1973 is found at the end of this chapter. The list may change from time to time if the composition of the ownership changes. The stocks are not automatically exempted. The company involved must apply to the Internal Revenue Service for exemption with evidence of ownership.

Once the tax has been paid on a stock that is not exempt, the stock becomes American-owned and it can be sold to another United States resident without the tax becoming due again. If a United States-owned stock is sold back to a Canadian, the tax cannot be recovered. Thus, if an investor buys an American-owned stock on which the tax has been paid by a previous owner, he should make sure that the stock has a ready market in the United States (which is not always the case with lesser-known issues traded on the smaller Canadian exchanges or over-the-counter).

Some brokers selling a Canadian stock to United States investors on which the tax is due will take care of the payment and charge the investor a total price that includes the tax. In such cases, and in fact with all Canadian stocks that are not actively traded in the United States, it is advisable to leave the stock certificates in the custody of the brokerage house. This simplifies matters when the stock is sold and also assures that the investor's interests are properly taken care of in the case of rights offerings, stock dividends, and other matters affecting stock ownership.

Rights Issues

If a Canadian company issues rights to its shareholders for the purchase of additional shares, these rights cannot be offered to a United States resident investor unless they are registered with the United States Securities and Exchange Commission (which they rarely are). If they are not registered with the SEC the rights are usually sold in Canada on behalf of the owner, who receives the proceeds from the sale. If the owner finds out about the rights offering himself and, at his own initiative, informs the Canadian distributor that he wants to exercise his rights, he can legally do so.

New Issues

What applies to rights also applies to new equity issues offered in Canada. Unless registered with the SEC, new Canadian issues cannot be offered in the United States. Moreover, Canadian brokers will let the issue "settle" in a regular trading pattern on Canadian exchanges for at least 90 days before selling it to United States residents. It is then no longer considered a "new issue." Such stock would then normally be subject to the Interest Equalization Tax. However, if a new Canadian issue is offered wholly or partly in the United States, the stock sold in the United States is exempt from the Interest Equalization Tax. The tax will become due on the newly issued stock after 90 days unless it is American-owned at that time. Very few new Canadian equity issues have been offered in the United States in recent years, and in view of the efforts of the Canadians to own their own industries, even fewer are likely to be offered in the future.

Fixed-Income Securities

Canadian fixed-income securities are more frequently offered in the United States than equity issues. For a United States resident only the new issues offered here, or old issues that are American-owned, are of interest. On securities sold and traded in Canada he would have to pay the Interest Equalization Tax.

As a natural resources supplier, not only for its own rapid expansion but also for the increasing needs of the world at large, Canada will require a tremendous amount of new financing during the next two decades. It is estimated that the energy industries alone will need more than $100 billion of new capital in the next 15 years. This includes some $10 billion for a number of new oil and gas pipelines to connect the Arctic fields with the population centers of Canada and several billion dollars more for huge hydroelectric projects, such as the James Bay and Nelson River developments, each of them larger than the Aswan Dam.

The general policy is to use debt as much as possible in the construction and development stage, and then try to retire these debt issues with equity issues when the projects begin to operate and produce income. Such huge financing cannot, at this time, be done in Canada alone. Part of the money will no doubt be raised in the United States, but the Canadian authorities are also likely to look increasingly at other capital markets in Europe and Asia, which in the last few years have gained considerable ground *vis-à-vis* Wall Street.

There are four main types of fixed-income securities in Canada— Federal government, provincial governments and agencies, municipal, and corporate. The interest rates for these different types of bonds rise in the same order, with a spread of 1 to $1\frac{1}{2}$ percentage points between Federal government and corporate bonds. Interest rates in Canada usually follow those of the United States with a slight time lag. There are no tax exempt bonds in Canada.

Withholding Tax

There is no withholding tax on interest received by the non-resident investor from Federal, provincial, and municipal government bonds. All bonds, including corporate bonds, issued between December 20, 1969, and April 15, 1966, are also exempt from withholding tax. Withholding tax on other bonds, as well as on common stock, is generally 15%. For certain common stock, at least 25% Canadian owned, the withholding tax may be reduced to 10%, and there are other exceptions, which an interested investor would have to ascertain from a broker.

Canada recently introduced a capital gains tax. Fifty percent of net capital gains is added to the taxable income of the resident and is then taxed at his regular income tax rate. The tax applies irrespective of the length of time the security was held. Losses may be written off in full against the capital gains. If there is a net loss, the taxpayer may deduct up to $1,000 from his taxable income during one year and carry the balance forward indefinitely until used up or wiped out against capital gains.

An investor with his residence outside Canada pays capital gains tax, where applicable, according to the tax laws of the country in which he files his income tax return.

Investment Funds

Canada has a thriving investment fund industry. In 1973 there were some 150 open-end funds with assets well in excess of $3½ billion plus about 30 closed-end funds with assets of more than $700 million.. To a United States citizen or resident, they are of relatively minor interest since they are all subject to the Interest Equalization Tax. However, there is a United States-based fund available with a predominantly Canadian portfolio, the *Canadian Fund Inc.*, which can be bought without payment of the Interest Equalization Tax.

To an investor not subject to the Interest Equalization Tax, Canadian funds offer a convenient way to invest broadly in Canada or in specific sectors of the Canadian economy. There are funds specializing in securities of the metal and mining, oil and gas, utility and paper industries, for instance. Many Canadian funds have broad international portfolios. Canadian trust companies recently began to offer investment funds which are sold through their own offices, at a relatively low commission charge. However, asset values are established only once a month, which means that shares can only be bought or sold once a month. Life insurance companies have begun to offer pension plans based on common stock funds. Such funds must consist of at least 90% of Canadian securities.

Where to Buy Canadian Securities

All Canadian stocks actively traded on American stock exchanges or on the United States over-the-counter market can be bought through any registered United States broker. The purchase of a Canadian security traded only in Canada may prove a little more difficult, at least for the individual investor.

Canadian brokers established in New York (see the listings at the end of this chapter) will accept business from institutional investors and United States brokers, but practically none of them are set up to handle retail business unless it involves a sizable portfolio. Six American brokers have their own subsidiaries in Canada, which are members of the Toronto and Montreal Stock Exchanges. This enables them to carry on retail business both in Canada and the United States. Also, the American brokers listed in Chapter 1 as handling retail business in foreign stocks accept retail orders for Canadian stocks. If an American broker has to go through a Canadian broker to buy Canadian shares for a customer he will often add an "override" to the regular commission charged by the Canadian broker.

Some American investors have accounts with Canadian brokers in Canada. In this case it is the investor's obligation to pay the Interest Equalization Tax on the purchase of Canadian securities that are subject to the tax.

Some of the larger Canadian brokers have a United States correspondent brokerage house. Correspondent brokers reciprocate in their business referrals and exchange their research materials.

Stock Exchanges

The services provided by Canadian brokers are comparable to those provided by American brokers. The range of services includes institutional and retail business, research, and investment banking. (However, they must call themselves investment dealers rather than investment bankers because the chartered banks object to the use of the word "banker" by the brokerage houses.)

Canadian brokers also operate as floor brokers on their stock exchanges. There are no floor specialists who make a market in a certain number of stocks as is customary on the United States stock exchanges. The Canadian exchanges are auction markets where the sale is made to the highest bidder.

Many Canadian stocks have multiple listings on at least two of the Canadian exchanges—usually Toronto and Montreal—and often also on one of the American exchanges. An astute Canadian broker will execute the order on whatever exchange he gets the best price. Arbitrage usually keeps the prices of a multiple-listed stock pretty much in line on all exchanges.

With the shift of the financial center from Montreal to Toronto over the last two decades, Toronto has become by far the largest stock exchange in Canada. Value of all trades in 1972 was $6.2 billion, as compared with $160 billion on the New York Stock Exchange and $21 billion on the American Stock Exchange.

At the end of 1972, there were 1185 listings on the Toronto exchange, about 74% of them industrial shares, underscoring the increasing importance of the Toronto Stock Exchange in the industrial development of Canada.

Second is the combined Montreal and Canadian exchange, merged in 1973, with a total trading volume of $2 billion. Before Toronto took the lead, Montreal was the largest stock exchange in Canada. Its relationship to the Canadian Stock Exchange, also located in Montreal, was comparable to that of the New York to the American Stock Exchange. The Canadian Exchange was the "curb" exchange for less seasoned issues.

The third largest exchange is Vancouver, with a 1972 trading volume of $784 million. At the end of 1972, 622 companies were listed on the Vancouver Stock Exchange, many of them oil and mining stocks that would not meet the listing requirements of the Toronto Stock Exchange. Smaller exchanges of local significance are in Calgary and Winnipeg.

Sources of Information

All leading Canadian brokerage houses provide investment research services for their customers and make them available in the United

States through their New York offices or their correspondent brokerage houses.

By far the leading independent investment information service, comparable to *Standard & Poor's*, is the *Financial Post Corporation Service*. It provides complete information on most of the publicly traded Canadian companies, plus special supplements, dividend records, new issue reports, and warrant reports.

A somewhat more limited information service is provided by *Canadian Business Service*, Toronto. *Moodies Services Ltd.*, in London, England, publishes information on Canadian stocks.

There are two Canadian chart services—one published by *Canadian Industrial Stock Charts,* Vancouver, and the other by the *Canadian Analyst Ltd.*, Toronto.

The leading English-language financial papers in Canada are the *Financial Times of Canada* and the *Financial Post. The Globe and Mail* has a special financial section which can be subscribed to separately. *Investor's Digest of Canada* is a bimonthly financial publication.

The Toronto Stock Exchange publishes an excellent annual report, as well as monthly reports which provide valuable information on the activities of the exchange and the Canadian economy.

Canadian Brokers Established in New York

A. E. Ames & Co., Inc. / 2 Wall Street / New York, New York 10005
Bell, Gouinlock & Company, Inc. / 74 Trinity Place / New York, New York 10006
Burns Bros. & Denton, Inc. / 37 Wall Street / New York, New York 10005
The Dominion Securities Corporation Harris & Partners, Inc. / 100 Wall Street / New York, New York 10005
Equitable Canada Incorporated / 27 William Street / New York, New York 10005
Fry Mills Spence Inc. / 115 Broadway / New York, New York 10006
Greenshields & Co., Inc. / 64 Wall Street / New York, New York 10005
McLeod, Young, Weir, Inc. / 63 Wall Street / New York, New York 10005
Midland Canadian Corporation / 140 Broadway / New York, New York 10005
Nesbitt, Thomson & Co., Ltd. / 1 Battery Park Plaza / New York, New York 10014
Pitfield, Mackay & Co., Inc. / 30 Broad Street / New York, New York 10004
Richardson Securities, Inc. / 40 Wall Street / New York, New York 10005
Wood Gundy, Incorporated / 100 Wall Street / New York, New York 10005

United States Brokers with Canadian Affiliates Members of the Toronto and Montreal Stock Exchanges

Bache & Co. / 100 Gold Street / New York, New York 10038
Baker Weeks & Co., Inc. / 1 Battery Park Plaza / New York, New York 10004
Dominick & Dominick / 14 Wall Street / New York, New York 10005
du Pont Walston Inc. / 77 Water Street / New York, New York 10005
Laidlaw-Luggeshall Inc. / 20 Broad Street / New York, New York 10005
Merrill Lynch, Pierce, Fenner & Smith Inc. / 1 Liberty Plaza, 165 Broadway / New York, New York 10006

A complete directory of all brokers in Canada is included in *Security Dealers of North America*, published by *Standard & Poor's Corporation* / 345 Hudson Street / New York, New York 10014. Many brokerage offices in the United States and major reference libraries have a copy of this directory.

Sources of Information on Canadian Securities

The Financial Post Corporation Service (also publishes the *Financial Post Survey of Investment Funds*) / *Maclean-Hunter Limited* / 481 University Avenue / Toronto, Ontario
Canadian Business Service / Suite 1205, 55 York Street / Toronto, Ontario

Canadian Daily Stock Charts (weekly) / and *Graphoscope* (bimonthly) /
  The Canadian Analyst Ltd. / 32 Front Street, W. / Toronto, Ontario
Canadian Mining & Oil Stock Charts (weekly) / *Canadian Industrial
  Stock Charts* / *Independent Survey Co. Ltd.* / 1706 West First Avenue /
  Vancouver, B. C.
The Toronto Stock Exchange / 234 Bay Street/ Toronto, Ontario

Canadian Financial Publications

Financial Post / 481 University Avenue / Toronto, Ontario
Financial Times of Canada / 10 Arundel, Place Bonaventure / Montreal,
  Quebec
Globe & Mail Report on Business / 140 King Street, W. / Toronto,
  Ontario
Investor's Digest of Canada / 481 University Avenue / Toronto, Ontario

Stocks that Make up the Indeces of the Toronto Stock Exchanges

Bank
Bank of Montreal
Bank of Nova Scotia
Cdn. Imperial Bank
Royal Bank
Toronto Dominion Bank

Beverage
Canadian Breweries
Crush International Ltd.
Distillers Corp.-Seagrams
John Labatt Ltd.
Molson Industries
H. Walker-Gooderham

Chemical
Cdn. Industries
Celanese Can.
DuPont of Canada
Union Carbide Canada

Communications
Maclean-Hunter Ltd.
Selkirk Holdings Ltd.
Southam Press Ltd.
Standard Broadcasting Corp.
Thomson Newspapers
Western Broadcasting Co. Ltd.

Construction and Material
Canada Cement Lafarge
Dominion Bridge Co. Ltd.

Lake Ontario Cement
St. Lawrence Cement

Food Processing
Atlantic Sugar
B. C. Sugar Refinery
Burns Foods Ltd.
Canada Malting Co.
Canada Packers Ltd.
Federal Industries Ltd.
Redpath Industries
Weston George

General Merchandising
C.A.E. Industries Ltd.
Canron Ltd.
Cdn. Corp. Management
Cdn. Marconi
Emco Ltd.
Ford Motor of Can.
Hayes-Dana Ltd.
Interprovincial Steel & Pipe
I.T.L. Industries Ltd.
Leigh Instruments
MLW-Worthington
Versatile Manufacturing
Westinghouse Canada

Industrial Mines
Alcan Aluminium Ltd.
Brunswick Mining
Cominco Ltd.

Denison Mines
Falconbridge
Hudson's Bay Mining & Smelting
International Nickel Co. of Can.
Mattagami Lake Mines
Noranda Mines Ltd.
Rio Algom Mines Ltd.
Sherritt Gordon

Merchandising
Canadian Tire Corp.
Dominion Stores Ltd.
Hudson's Bay Co.
Koffler Stores Ltd.
Loblaw's
Loeb, M. Ltd.
Metropolitan Stores
Oshawa Group
Silverwood Industries
Simpson's Ltd.
Simpsons-Sears Ltd.
Steinberg's Ltd.
Woodward Stores Ltd.
Zellers Ltd.

Oil Refining
Gulf Oil Canada
Imperial Oil
Petrofina Canada
Shell Canada
Texaco Canada

Paper and Forest Products
Abitibi Paper Co. Ltd.
B.C. Forest Products
Consolidated-Bathurst Ltd.
Domtar Ltd.
Fraser Companies Ltd.
Great Lakes Paper Co.
Maclaren Power & Paper
MacMillan Bloedel
Price Co. Ltd.

Pipeline
Alberta Gas Trunk Line
Interprovincial Pipeline
Pembina Pipeline Ltd.
TransCanada PipeLines Ltd.
Trans Mountain Pipe Line
Westcoast Transmission
Westcoast Petroleum Ltd.

Real Estate
Block Bros Industries Ltd.
Bramalea Cons. Devel. Ltd.
Cadillac Development
Campeau Corp. Ltd.
Markborough Prop. Ltd.
Peel-Elder Limited
Trizec Corp.

Steel
Algoma Steel Corp.
Dominion Foundries & Steel
Steel Co. of Canada

Trust and Loan
Can. Permanent Mortgage
Guaranty Trust
Huron & Erie Mortgage
IAC Ltd.
Investors Group
Laurentide
Montreal Trust
National Trust
Royal Trust
Victoria & Grey Trust

Utility
Bell Canada
B.C. Telephone
Brinco
Calgary Power
Consumers' Gas
Great Lakes Power
Inland Natural Gas
Maritime T & T
Northern & Central Gas
Union Gas

Miscellaneous Industrial
Acres Limited
A.G.F. Management
Algoma Central Railway
Argus Corp.
Cdn. Cablesystems
Cdn. General Investments
Cdn. Pacific
Crain, R. L.
Dominion Glass
Dominion Textile Co. Ltd.
Genstar Ltd.
Great-West Life Assur.

Greyhound Lines of Can.
Harding Carpets
Hawker Siddeley
Imasco Limited
IU International Corp.
Kaps Transport
Massey-Ferguson Ltd.
McIntyre Porcupine Mines Ltd.
Moore Corp. Ltd.
Neonex Int'l Ltd.
OSF Industries
Power Corp. of Can. Ltd.
Reed Shaw Osler Ltd.
Rothmans of Pall Mall Canada
Slater Steel Industries Ltd.
United Corp.
White Pass & Yukon Corp.

Gold
Camflo Mines Ltd.
Campbell Red Lake Mines
Cochenour Willans Gold Mines
Dickenson Mines Ltd.
Dome Mines Ltd.
Giant Yellowknife Mines Ltd.
Little Long Lac Mines Ltd.
Madsen Red Lake Gold Mines
Pamour Porcupine Mine Ltd.
Sigma Mines (Quebec)
Upper Canada Resources

Base Metal
Advocate Mines Ltd.
Agnico-Eagle Mines Ltd.
Asbestos Corp. Ltd.
Bethlehem Copper Ltd.
Campbell Chibougamau Mines
Cassiar Asbestos Corp. Ltd.
Conwest Explorations
Craigmont Mines Ltd.

Dynasty Explorations
East Sullivan Mines Ltd.
Falconbridge Copper
Gibraltar Mines
Granduc Mines Ltd.
Hollinger Mines Ltd.
International Mogul Mines
Kerr-Addison Mines Ltd.
Labrador Mining & Exploration
Northgate Explorations Ltd.
Orchan Mines Ltd.
Patino N. V.
Pine Point Mines
Placer Development
Roman Corporation Ltd.
Steep Rock Iron Mines
Teck Corp.
United Asbestos Corp.
United Keno Hill Mines
United Siscoe Mines
Yellowknife Bear Mines Ltd.

Western Oil
Alminex Ltd.
Aquitaine Co. of Canada
Bow Valley Industries
Cdn. Export Gas & Oil Ltd.
Cdn. Hydrocarbons
Cdn. Occidental Petrol.
Cdn. Superior Oil
Dome Petroleum
Great Plains Development
Home Oil
Hudson's Bay Oil & Gas
Husky Oil Canada
Pacific Petroleums
PanCanadian Petroleum
Scurry Rainbow Oil Ltd.
Union Oil Co. of Canada
United Canso Oil & Gas Ltd.
Western Decalta Petroleum

For stocks also traded in the United States on the New York or American Stock Exchanges, or over-the-counter, see appendix to Chapter 1.

4

MEXICO
RETIREMENT NEST EGG

Most "packaged" tourists who jet in and out of Acapulco, the "Miami on the Rocks," and catch *la tourista,* a dysentery also known as "Montezuma's Revenge," do not suspect that there is another, more idyllic side to Mexico where content retirees sit on their shaded patios in picturesque hill towns while the Mexican "money trees" shower a steady and generous income into their laps that allows them to live in much greater comfort than they could have in the United States. Many of them started to build and nurture their Mexican nest eggs long before they actually retired, with a guaranteed fixed income of 10% net per year (after Mexican taxes) being par for the course; and that means doubling your money every seven years.

Investments Easy and Rewarding

Even for those who do not intend to retire "south of the border," investments in Mexico for over two decades have been safe and profitable, and there is no indication at this time that they will be less so in the foreseeable future. The Mexican peso is fully convertible, and dividends and interest from investments, as well as the principal if the investor wants to withdraw from the Mexican market, can be taken out of the country without any formality. Moreover, for a United States resident it is much simpler to invest in Mexico than in practically any foreign country, and it is much easier to keep in-

On October 3, 1973 the Mexican peso was valued at U.S. 8.01¢.

formed about the investments. All leading Mexican banks and brokers are set up to handle foreign investment accounts, and a number of them publish informative investment newsletters. All will correspond and send regular statements in Spanish and quite a few banks will correspond in English, although their statements will be in Spanish. Brokers specializing in handling United States and Canadian clients, on the other hand, correspond in English, and their booklets, brochures, and accounting statements are in English.

A foreign investor can ask his Mexican bank or broker to send his statements to any address of his choice, or he can give instructions for the statements to be held until he can pick them up. The foreign investor can also leave standing instructions for the reinvestment of interest and dividends earned. In order to do this, as well as to execute buy and sell orders, Mexico's banks and brokers almost always require a limited power-of-attorney making them *"mandatarios,"* or authorized representatives of their investment clients. This is a simple thing to arrange, involves no legal fees, and can be revoked at any time without penalties.

Peso Pegged to the Dollar

Mexican investments did not provide a protection against the two dollar devaluations as did investments in other foreign countries whose currencies rose in relation to the dollar. The Mexican peso is rigidly pegged to the dollar at the official rate of $1.00=12.50 pesos (12.49 pesos to the dollar at the actual bank rate of exchange) and it devalued together with the dollar in relation to other currencies. Nevertheless, the peso is considered a very strong currency in international banking circles; in fact, it has been the only strong and fully convertible currency among all currencies of so-called developing countries.

Economy Grows Fast

The Mexican economy during the past decade has grown at a compounded annual real rate of about 7%—that is, about twice as fast as that of the United States. For 1973 and 1974 an even higher rate has been predicted. Between August 1972 and August 1973, the gross national product rose 9.1%.

Inflation in the past has been kept under control. Wholesale price increases were held to 3.7% in 1971, and consumer price increases in 1971 and 1972 were 5.5% and 4.9% respectively. However, a higher rate of inflation arrived in 1973 as a result of the world-wide inflationary forces set loose by the huge pool of dollars held outside the United States. During the first five months of 1973, for instance, wholesale prices in general climbed by 9.5% and, on a few specific items, went up as high as 12% or more, Mexico's private and public sectors are both greatly concerned about this trend, and a series of programs have been created to combat this inflation. However, as *Lloyd's Mexican Economic Report* points out, "The discovery of a permanent and complete way to stop inflation is no more in sight in Mexico than it is in the United States and most other nations of the world. In short, it looks as if Mexico, like other countries, will have to accept a 'controled' inflation as a fact of life, and learn to live with it."

No Equalization Tax

A United States resident investing in a Mexican bank or in Mexican industry does not have to pay the Interest Equalization Tax which he must pay on the purchase price of most other foreign securities bought in the United States. (This tax is currently 11.25% on the purchase price of foreign common stock.) However, a Mexican federal tax is automatically deducted from interest and dividend income. The current Mexican tax rate on common stock dividends held in bearer form is 21%. This same rate also applies to interest earned on fixed-income securities, such as Time Deposit Contracts with banks. Foreign investors who can qualify as permanent residents (*inmigrados*) *and* who are willing to register their securities, can reduce the tax on both stocks and fixed-income securities to 15%, as can Mexicans who are willing to register their securities.

Because of this, it is important to know whether a Mexican bank or brokerage firm is quoting gross yields on registered securities (as most do), or is giving the potential foreign investor the net yield, after Mexican taxes, on non-registered investments.

The Mexican tax can be claimed as a deduction from United States taxable income (using Form 1116). There is no inheritance tax in Mexico, and no probate fees have to be paid for the transfer of funds to heirs.

Government Stable

Democracies come in all shapes and sizes. The Russians think they have a democracy; so do the Americans; and so do the Mexicans. To the Anglo-Saxon purist, a one-party system is not a democracy. Yet the Mexicans have had the same party in power for the past 50 years. It is indeed surprising that such a one-party system has not degenerated into a dictatorship. The Mexicans have preserved all key features of a democracy: free movement of people inside the country and across its borders; a free press; free admission of all foreign news media; free flow of money in and out of the country; and a rule of law, even if its application may sometimes appear harsh or capricious.

Probably the secret to the Mexican political system is the fact that a balance of power exists within the ruling party, which includes representatives of major national interests, such as labor unions, business, and the military. The presidential candidate of the party is nominated by an internal election process within the party. Once nominated, his election by the electorate is assured. Nevertheless, he appears to run even harder for office than American presidential candidates. For several months before the election he visits almost every hamlet from the Yucatán to the Rio Grande. This campaign does not change the election results, but it serves the useful purpose of giving the president a face-to-face acquaintance with many of his people and their problems.

The president is elected for one term of six years. He cannot run for re-election. Each president and his cabinet implant their special stamp on the economy. The current president, Echeverría, whose term expires in 1976, is trying to curb direct foreign domination of production facilities, but he does everything possible to stimulate the economy and to encourage investments by individual foreigners through Mexican financial institutions.

The Mexican political system, instituted after 100 years of much bloody turmoil, seems to be the most workable for the Mexican people. Nevertheless, like many living bodies after 50 years, the Mexican government does show signs of sclerosis in some of its "limbs," and its future course, like that of practically all governments, injects an unpredictable element into the investment picture. However, on balance, the Mexican government continues to demonstrate strong regenerative powers and there is no indication that sweeping changes are in the wind.

Stock Market Tiny

Compared to the New York Stock Exchange, the Bolsa de Valores in Mexico is a doll's house where one can't always be sure who moves the puppets and the fixtures. Average *monthly* trading volume is about 1 million shares, worth about $650,000, compared with an average *daily* trading volume on the New York Stock Exchange of some 13 million shares, worth several hundred millions of dollars. About 400 stocks are listed, but only about 40 to 50 are actively traded. Most others are closely held by family or other inside groups. A large percentage of the trading occurs off the floor (which means that it is not reported in the stock reports and is known only to the two trading partners involved).

Such a market has its dangers, of course. A financially strong individual or group can manipulate the price of a stock. An investor may find it difficult to sell a stock when he wants to. Except for some operations in which American corporations have a stake, Mexican companies do not divulge much information for the benefit of their stockholders. Certain types of stocks cannot be bought by foreigners, including mining, cement, aluminum, and petrochemical stocks.

As a result of the thin market, it is not surprising that the Mexican stock market did not go anywhere in particular for many years. The 30-stock price index hovered between 140 and 177 from 1965 through 1970. In 1971, when the Mexican economy briefly faltered, it went as low as 127. However, the Echeverría government has made efforts to strengthen the stock market and make it a useful tool for the raising of capital. As a result the index went from its low of 127 to a high of 205 on March 15, 1973. Other indications of increased stock market activity can be found in *The Mexican Investor,* a bi-monthly investment advisory letter written by Sidney T. Wise, which regularly publishes a model Mexican portfolio. Between January 1, 1966, and March 15, 1973, this portfolio grew by 290%.

Stock Registration Required

Until 1973, all stocks were issued on a bearer basis, which means the owner was not identified. This is still the custom for stocks purchased and held by Mexicans although, as mentioned earlier, they may choose to register their holdings in order to pay less federal taxes. Now, however, all foreigners who own stock must register their holdings with an agency of the federal government. This is somewhat of a bother even for foreigners who speak Spanish fluently; and it is just about an impossibility for non-Mexicans who are not familiar with Spanish. Any Mexican bank or brokerage firm, however, will perform this service.

Some Popular Stocks

One of the most popular, and probably also one of the safest stock investments are the shares of *Telefonos de Mexico,* the government-controlled Mexican telephone service, called *Telmex* for short. These shares usually yield about 10% and often more as a result of a complex early stock retirement plan which, on the other hand, has the effect of keeping the stock price within a narrow range. *Telmex* can also be bought over-the-counter in the United States in the form of American Depositary Receipts, which have yielded an average of 9% after the withholding of the 21% Mexican dividend tax.

Another popular stock is *Banco de Cédulas Hipotecarias,* which in past years has yielded an average of 12%.

Among investors who prefer the more informative reporting of American affiliates, *Celanese Mexicana* has been popular. It had a low of 134 and a high of 165 during the 12-month period November 1972 to November 1973. The yield at the high price was about 7%.

Investment Funds

Three Mexican investment funds are actively traded on the Bolsa—*Firme, Fimsa,* and *Fondo de Inversiones Banamex.* They offer a diversified portfolio with a high percentage of government securities. They are operated under strict government regulations. Sales charges are limited to a maximum of 5% but *Banamex* charges only 1%. The trusts are exempt from Mexican income tax and there are no custodial charges. Yields are somewhat lower than those of many common stocks, but fund shares, in contrast to many stocks, can usually be sold instantly at the quoted prices. *Fimsa* pays only stock dividends.

Fixed-Income Securities

The Mexican businessman, as one Mexican investment counsellor has said, prefers to pay a high interest on debt to build his business rather than have stockholders poke their noses into his affairs and tell him what to do. The shoe may also be on the other foot. Investors may prefer a safe income to a speculation on the uncertain fate of shares in a company that does not tell them what is going on.

Whatever the case may be, the overwhelming majority of investment opportunities in Mexico in the past has been in fixed-income securities, and this still holds true today. Receiving average net yields of from 9% to 12% a year between 1968 and 1973, the investor in Mexican fixed-income securities has done considerably better than practically every amateur and professional investor in the American stock market during the same time.

Very little expertise is needed. The leading banks and brokers offer a choice of sound investment opportunities and take care of all of the purchase details. Not all banks and brokerage firms, however, audit and collect interest for their foreign clients; nor do all send their foreign clients monthly statements in English. In other words, some of the institutions act as straight commission sales agents only and, once the transaction is completed, it is up to the foreign investor to personally manage the details of his investment. Because of this, most American and other foreign investors in Mexico have found it convenient to select banks or brokerage firms which have administrative and custodial services, and report to their clients monthly in English.

High-Liquidity Investments

Mexico offers the foreign investor two classes of highly liquid securities which, although called (legitimately) "bonds," actually function like call-money. By far the most popuar of these are the *Bonos Financieros* or "liquid bonds." These are issued in minimum units of 100 pesos ($8) by all of Mexico's industrial development banks, and by *Banco Nacional Financiera* (the huge, government-owned, industrial development bank). Net interest, after Mexican taxes, currently runs from 9% to 10%, depending upon the amount of money invested, and these bonds can be cashed by the investor, or his Mexican representative, in a matter of minutes. Furthermore, the investor may take out all, or part, of his investment at any time, with no questions asked, and will be paid full par value at all times. (Interest in "liquid bonds" is paid quarterly.) Less popular, but still highly liquid, are *Bonos Hipotecarios* which are a form of mortgage bond. These pay 8.25% per year after Mexican taxes, with interest payable monthly. As in the case of "liquid bonds," all or part of the investment can be withdrawn at any time without penalty and at par. Most banks and brokerage firms handle these bonds, or they can be purchased directly from the issuing mortgage banking institutions. And, of course, the interest earned from both "liquid bonds" and "mortgage bonds" may be re-invested (compounded) for greater yields or, at present, around 9.50% to 10%.

Bank Time Deposit Contracts

By far the most popular form of investment with both foreigners and Mexicans are the Bank Time Deposit Contracts, or, as they are frequently called in the United States, Certificates of Deposit. As in the case of "liquid bonds," Time Deposit Contracts are issued by all Mexican industrial development banks (*financieras*), and by *Banco Nacional Financiera.* The time period covered by these contracts used to run up to five years and, in some cases, as long as twelve years. Because of fluctuating world interest rates, however, plus other considerations, the *Bank of Mexico* (the Republic's central or "Federal Reserve" bank) has currently limited almost all Time Deposit Contracts to a period of one year. Net interest, after Mexican taxes, runs from 9% to 10% per year as of this writing, depending upon the amount of money initially invested. Most brokerage firms require an initial investment of 50,000 pesos ($4,000) to open an account for a foreign investor. After that, the investor may increase his holdings by any amount he finds convenient. Interest on Time Deposit Contracts is paid monthly, and may be either taken out or reinvested to bring the net yearly yield close to 10% or more on these bank securities.

No Investor Losses

It is well worth noting that although Mexico has no equivalent of the American Federal Deposit Insurance, no depositor in a Mexican bank, or investor in the debt obligations (such as Time Deposit Contracts) of a Mexican bank, has lost a dime over the last 45 years. Banks have failed, of course, just as they have in other parts of the world. But when this happens in Mexico, the Mexican National Banking Commission takes over the institution, re-organizes it, and gets it back on its feet. During this time the stockholders of the bank may lose money, but the depositors and investors in the bank's debt securities are protected to the last cent, and the bank's doors are never closed.

Minimum Risk Plus a Raffle Chance

Among Mexicans, one of the most popular long-term, fixed-income securities are Mexican government bonds, which are comparable to United States Savings Bonds. Their popularity stems partly from the fact that the government holds a raffle every three months with every number of every bond sold participating. There is one winner for each series of 4,000 bonds, and each winner receives, tax free, ten times the amount he paid for his bond. An investor who buys all of the 4,000 bonds in a single series can, therefore, increase his income by 1%. Without the winnings, an investor will receive exactly double his investment after ten years, when the bond matures. If he cashes it before expiration, he receives about 7% interest, prorated for each three-month period the bond was held. Redemption values of the bonds are printed on the back of the certificate. Mexican government bonds cannot be purchased by Americans within the United States, but any North American visiting Mexico may invest any amount in these securities without getting into trouble back home.

Government Promissory Notes

The highest yields available in Mexico today are through investment in promissory notes issued by the various Mexican states to finance internal projects such as roads, schools, hospitals, etc. These notes are sold on a discount basis and, at maturity, currently are yielding from about 11% to 15% a year net, depending upon the length of time until maturity. Since Mexico does not have any reference books such as *Moodies* or *Standard & Poor's* to rate the notes of various states, the prudent investor is well advised to purchase them only through a reliable brokerage firm which has screened them before offering them for sale. Another factor worth mentioning is that many of these notes have a clause on their face which, in Spanish, says that it is not legal for foreigners to own them. Some Mexican brokerage firms have told their clients that this clause is meaningless and have convinced the purchaser to go ahead with the deal. This is unfortunate, to say the least, because in the case of any serious problem with the broker or the issuing state the foreign investor doesn't have a legal leg to stand on, and will almost certainly lose his initial investment and his yield. It is also important to note that, at the federal level, there is a definite attitude to the effect that state promissory notes cannot be held by foreigners. The answer to this, from the banks and brokerage firms, is that the state promissory notes they are selling go into the hands of Mexican custodial banks, and not directly into the hands of non-Mexicans. There has been no official ruling to date regarding these conflicting points of view, and Mexican state promissory notes are being sold like the proverbial hot-cakes to Americans as well as other foreigners around the world.

How to Retire in Mexico

For Americans there is no other foreign country where the investment climate and the retirement climate are equally favorable, and any American considering retirement in Mexico will soon also consider investments there, and vice versa. Thus, even though this book is not about retirement, a word about it in this chapter seems appropriate.

There are many features that attract American retirees to Mexico —the climate (pleasingly moderate at most altitudes, with practically no rain from October to April in most parts of the country), a breathtaking scenery, picturesque towns, pleasing people, relatively low living costs, availability of household help, and colonies of compatriots in certain popular retirement spots, such as Guadalajara, Cuernavaca, San Miguel de Allende, and along Lake Chapala.

Deep-sea fishermen congregate along the Pacific opposite Baja California and, lately, in rapidly developing Baja California itself—particularly around Cabo San Lucas, where the Sea of Cortez (formerly called the Gulf of California) meets the Pacific. These American colonies assure good company and common interests among like-minded fellow retirees and good communications even for those who are not talented or inclined to learn Spanish. Besides, trips back home are relatively inexpensive and fast.

For retirees who shun their fellow countrymen and prefer to immerse themselves in local life and color there are a number of attractive communities where few retirees so far have settled; among them Patzcuaro, Uruapan, Oaxaca, Puebla, as well as many smaller ones. Taxco, while usually crowded with day tourists, regains its Mexican flavor in the evenings. It is generally loved as the most picturesque city in all of Mexico; it has an excellent climate and its main architectural features are protected by law.

Mexico City, one of the most fascinating and dynamic cities of the world, has unfortunately been rendered unsuitable for retirement because of a frightening air pollution problem. The Gulf Coast is the least desirable area because of water pollution and a poorer climate, with sticky heat in the summer and frequent rains in the winter. On the other hand, the Pacific Coast still has literally thousands of miles of undiscovered and underpopulated pure beaches. Foreigners can lease real estate inland under a trust arrangement, and can now also use the Mexican trust or *Fideicomiso* to obtain land along the coasts of Mexico to build their vacation or retirement homes.

An excellent road system offers the opportunity to shop among a multitude of potential retirement places many years before the actual event. An appealing place can be tested by staying for a few days or a few weeks to absorb the local atmosphere and gather pertinent information.

Mexico also offers a few exotic and stimulating hobbies aside from deep-sea fishing and hunting in remote mountain areas and the shrubbery of the Yucatàn. There is archeology, pre-Colombian art collecting, butterfly chasing, orchid hunting, or just plain gardening in a rewarding climate and soil.

Finally, if one really does not like it after a time, one can easily pull up one's stakes, including all investments, and take them elsewhere without impediment.

Any Mexican consulate will provide information on immigration for retirement in Mexico. For shorter visits of up to six months a simple Tourist card obtainable from Mexican tourist offices is all that's needed.

Major Mexican Banks

(Headquarters only; most of them have many branch offices)

Banco Comercial Mexicano, S.A. / Calle Victoria No. 14 / Chihuahua, Chihuahua

Banco de Comercio, S.A. / Venustiano Carranza No. 44 / Mexico City

Banco Internacional, S.A. / Reforma No. 156 / Mexico City

Banco de Londres y Mexico, S.A. / Bolívar and 16 de Septiembre / Mexico City

Banco del Pais, S.A. / Torre Latino Americano / Mexico City

Banco Mexicano, S.A. / 5 de Mayo No. 35 / Mexico City

Banco Nacional de Mexico, S.A. / Isabel la Católica No. 44 / Mexico City

(New York Office: 45 Wall Street)

The Largest Industrial Development Banks

(Financieras)

Credito Minero y Mercantil, S.A. / Reforma No. 144 / Mexico City

Financiera del Atlantico, S.A. / Venustiano Carranza No. 48 / Mexico City

Financiera Banamex, S.A. / Isabel la Católica No. 39 / Mexico City

Financiera Bancomer, S.A. / Venustiano Carranza No. 44 / Mexico City

Financiera Comermex, S.A. / Uruguay No. 55 / Mexico City

Financiera Industrial, S.A. / Monterrey, Nuevo Leon

Financiera International, S.A. / Reforma 156 / Mexico City

Financiera del Norte, S.A. / Morelos 110 (corner of Reforma) / Mexico City

Nacional Financiera, S.A. / Isabel la Católica No. 51 / Mexico City

The Five Largest Mortgage Banks

Banco de Cédulas Hipotecarias, S.A. / Paseo de la Reforma No. 364 / Mexico City

Banco Hipotecario Azteca, S.A. / Paseo de la Reforma No. 107 / Mexico City

Banco Nacional de Mexico, S.A. / Isabel la Católica No. 44 / Mexico City

General Hipotecaria, S.A. / Paseo de la Reforma No. 195-ler piso / Mexico City

Hipotecaria Bancomer, S.A. / San Juan de Letran No. 13 / Mexico City

Mexican Investment Trusts

(Comparable to closed-end mutual funds)

Fondo Industrial Mexicano, S.A. ("Fimsa") / Paseo de la Reforma 45 / Mexico City

Fondo de Inversiones Banamex, S.A. / Isabel la Católica 44 / Mexico City

Fondo de Inversiones Rentables Mexicanas, S.A. *("Firme")* / Venustiano Carranza 54 / Mexico City

Government Savings Bonds (Bonos del Ahorra Nacional)

Information office: Paseo de la Reforma 77 / Mexico City
Nacional Financiera, S.A. (Liquid Bonds and Time Deposit Contracts) /
Isabel la Católica 51 / Mexico City

Brokerage Firms in Mexico

Hughes de Mexico, S.A. / Padre Mier 134 Oriente / Monterrey, Nuevo
Leon
Impulsora de Inversiones Internacionales, S.A. / Insurgentes Fur 682 /
Mexico City
(Branch office in Cuernavaca.)
Inversiones Alba S.A. / Paseo de la Reforma 336 / Mexico City
Allen W. Lloyd y Asociados, S.A. / Priscilinao Sanchez 220 / Guadala-
jara, Jalisco
(Branches in Tijuana, San Miguel de Allende, Chapala, Puerto Vallarta,
Mexico City, Nogales, Ensenada, and Nuevo Laredo.)
Valores de Capital, S.A. / Paseo de la Reforma 116 / Mexico City
(Branches in Guadalajara, Monterrey, and Cuernavaca.)

Sources of Information

The Basic Facts for Investing in Mexico by Donovan P. Samuels, pub-
lished by *Ammex Asociados, S.A.* / Lago Silverio No. 224 / Mexico
City
Business Mexico, published by *American Chamber of Commerce of
Mexico* / Department X, Lucerna 78 / Mexico City
Business Trends / Homero 136 / Mexico City
Establishing a Business in Mexico, available from *United States Govern-
ment Printing Office* / Washington 25, D.C.
Invest and Retire in Mexico by Sidney T. Wise, published by *Doubleday
& Company* / Garden City, New York.
Lloyd's Mexican Economic Report, published by *Allen W. Lloyd y Asoci-
ados, S.A.* / Priscilinao Sanchez 220 / Guadalajara, Jalisco
Making Money in Mexico by Betty and Don Gilmore, published by *Haw-
thorne Books, Inc.* / New York, New York
The Mexican Investor, published by *Mexican Financial Advisory Service* /
Reforma 398-203 / Mexico City
Mexletter S.A. / Hamburg 159 / Mexico City

Active Issues of the Bolsa de Valores

Aguila (tobacco)
Agusa (printing)
Altos Hornos (steel)
Aluminio (aluminum)
And Clay (agricultural food)
A. P. Green (refractories)
Apasco (cement)
Aviamex (airline)
Bacardi (liquors)

Banamex (bank)
Banco Ced. (bank)
Bimex (bicycles)
Campos (tools)
Cannon (hosiery)
Carbide (chemical)
Cechisa (cellulose)
Celanese (synthetics)
Cenmalt (malt)

Eaton (automotive)
Ecatepec (steel)
Fibanco (bank)
Fimsa (investment fund)
Firme (investment fund)
Fondo BNM (investment fund)
Frisco (mining)
Fundidora (steel)
Gen. Electric (electric)
IEM (electric)
Indetel (telecommunications)
Ind. Resistol (chemical)
Kimberly (paper)
Lamosa (construction items)
Liverpool (department store)
Loreto (paper)
Metalver (tanks)
Moctezuma (brewery)
Moderna (tobacco)

Moresa (automotive)
Nafin (government bank)
Negromex (chemical)
Pal. Hierro (department store)
Paris Londres (department store)
Peñoles (mining)
Reynolds (aluminum)
Sanborn (department store)
San Cristobal (paper)
San Luis (silver)
San Rafael (paper)
Spicer (automotive)
Tabacalera (tobacco)
Tamsa (steel pipe)
Telmex (telecommunications)
Tepeyac (steel)
Teziutlán (iron alloys)
Tolteca (cement)
Tremec (automotive)

5

BRAZIL
A GIANT STIRRING

Except for Mexico, Latin America at this stage would not appear to be a suitable playground for the portfolio investor. Most Latin American countries are plagued by political instability, and for most of them much agony is likely to lie ahead before they can reach a political climate that permits a healthy and stable growth of their economies from which all their people can benefit, not just a privileged few. The unfortunate feudal heritage and attitudes left by Spain at its departure in the early 19th century still survive today in many of the Latin American countries. The blindness that the ruling groups display towards the masses of hapless poor may well be the kind of blindness about which the Ancient Greeks said it strikes those whom the Gods would destroy. The tragic events of the downfall of President Allende of Chile in September 1973, show that even a country with a respected democratic tradition is not immune to the built-in social stresses that prevail in most Latin American countries. Cuba demonstrates that radicalism in the other extreme is not a road to riches either; rather a scaring away of the geese that can lay edible eggs. Unless an understanding and a union between those who have the know-how and money and those who must learn to use the modern tools of production is reached there is not much hope for a country to improve the economic lot of all its people and enjoy living in peace. So far, in most countries, the tradition of the upper few to take their earnings to Switzerland rather than reinvest them in their own country still continues. Why then should a foreign investor—

On October 3, 1973 the Brazilian cruzeiro was valued at U.S. 16.6¢.

either directly or through portfolio investments—put his money into such countries?

Rich in People and Resources

The one exception—and the one country to watch—is Brazil. Being of Portuguese rather than Spanish descent in their traditions and attitudes, the Brazilians have shown a great tolerance towards other races and creeds, and they have kept their doors wide open to immigrants from all parts of the world. Portuguese, Africans, American Indians, Italians, Germans, Japanese, and others have come to blend into a nation of more than 100 million in a country that is larger than the Continental United States without Alaska, a country that has more farmland than the whole of Europe, more forests than any other country except Canada and Russia, a third of the world's known iron ore deposits, and many other natural resources, including bauxite, manganese, limestone, diamonds, gold, silver, nickel, and chromium.

In the course of its history Brazil has gone through a number of economic boom periods based on single commodities, notably cotton, rubber, and coffee. These were usually accompanied by erratic production and price swings, so typical for most commodities, and ended in depressions. In the late 1950s and early 1960s, Brazil was a country in economic chaos that couldn't pay its bills and had a runaway inflation which sometimes reached almost 100% a year.

In the late 1960s a radical change took place. A new economic boom started—but this one was based on solid industrial development and sound finance. Manufacturing and mining passed agriculture as the main contributor to the gross national product. Brazil became almost overnight an important producer of steel, automobiles, chemicals, pharmaceuticals, cement, and paper. Automobile production increased from 225,000 vehicles in 1967 to over 600,000 in 1972, many of them made for export. Brazil has become practically self-sufficient in manufactured consumer goods. Foreign investments have poured in from all parts of the world, with the United States leading, followed by West Germany, Canada, Japan, and Switzerland. The Japanese, who over the past century have settled there as farmers, are now coming as big investors, planning to build steel mills and other heavy industry for which they can no longer find suitable locations in their crowded homeland.

Sound Growth

Brazil has begun to run a solid surplus in its balance of payments with foreign countries—$2.5 billion in 1972, up from $555 million in 1971. Foreign currency reserves rose from an all-time low of $199 million in 1967 to more than $4 billion in 1973, and they were expected to reach $6 billion by the end of 1973. However, there was still a foreign debt of $10 billion in 1973, including accumulated earnings of foreign companies and investors that haven't been repatriated. Inflation was still running relatively high in 1973, but had come down to more manageable levels below a 20% annual rate in 1973. Gross national product in real terms was increasing at an annual rate of around 10% in 1971, 1972, and 1973—one of the highest rates in the world. Employment was rising at a rate of almost 1 million new jobs a year, and per capita income had almost doubled from about $360 in 1969 to more than $600 in 1973. The newly-won wealth was seeping down to all levels of the "economically active," but with the rapid population growth, the "economically inactive" were gaining on the "economically active." In 1973, well above 50% of the population was under 20, and Brazil still has fairly large groups of people in huge jungle areas untouched by the new economic boom.

What is perhaps of some concern to strong believers in democracy or in liberally inspired, state directed redistribution of wealth is the fact that Brazil's economic miracle of the past five years was accomplished under a military regime, which took the reins through a coup in 1964. In spite of some vague promise of eventual restoration of civilian rule, there was no evidence of it actually being imminent in 1973, when the new military president to take office for a five-year term beginning in March 1974, had already been named. Possibly Brazil's present rulers are thinking in terms of a one-party system comparable to the one in Mexico which has given that country stability over the past 50 years and provided the foundation for solid economic growth.

Stock Exchanges with a Future

The Brazilian government has taken steps to develop the two leading stock exchanges of the country—one in São Paulo and the other in Rio de Janeiro—into useful sources for new capital by providing a number of incentives to Brazilians to invest in stocks and bonds. As a result of this policy, there was a wild speculative fever on the two stock exchanges in 1971, sending stock prices to giddy heights, but they all came to sobering levels again, where they still were in 1973. Nevertheless, a beginning has been made to encourage Brazilians to invest their savings at home rather than send them abroad, and there is a good possibility that the Brazilian stock markets in the next few years will offer investors some of the last few growth investment opportunities in the world. In 1973, however, it was too soon for the foreign portfolio investor to send his money to Brazil. A number of restrictions were in force that made investments by non-residents difficult and uninteresting, including major ones applying to the repatriation of realized profits and of the original capital. Judging by the comment of a Brazilian government information officer, the Brazilian authorities had not fully grasped the fact that free profit taking provides the trading volume that is essential for floating new issues. He said: "We don't really want foreign portfolio investments; all that a foreign investor does is take his profits and run."

There are more than 300 issues listed in São Paulo and more than 200 in Rio de Janeiro. Information is hard to come by. There is none available from Brazilian information offices and banks in New York, and even the two stock exchanges in Brazil provide very little information. *Bank of Boston International,* in its *Newsletter Brazil,* includes a general stock market report, and the daily *Journal do Brasil,* available on some newsstands in New York, reports on the Brazilian stock markets.

A simple way to participate in Brazil's economic development is to buy shares of *Brascan Ltd.,* a Canadian holding company heavily invested in Brazil whose shares are traded on the American Stock Exchange.

An illuminating report on the Brazilian stock markets appeared in an article by David M. Darst of *Goldman Sachs & Co.* in the September 10, 1973, issue of *Barron's* magazine.

The Two Leading Brazilian Stock Exchanges

Bolsa de Valores / Rio de Janeiro
Bolsa de Valores / 4 rua Alvares, Penteado 151-65 / São Paulo

General Information in English

Newsletter Brazil published by *Bank of Boston International* / 2 Wall Street / New York, New York 10005

Security Firm Specializing in Brazilian and Other Latin American Stocks

Deltec Securities Corporation / 1 Battery Park Plaza / New York, New York 10004

6

ISRAEL
THE BLOOMING DESERT

There is probably nothing that shiftless incompetents and other grandiloquent nonperformers of all denominations hate more among their midst than a hard-working, intelligent man who keeps his nose to the grindstone. He remains a permanent thorn of reproach in their sides, and they will pounce on him at every given opportunity unless they can be appeased by force, flattery, or bribes.

Such a resentment may perhaps play a part in the Israeli-Arab conflict, more so than the dubious legality of the origins of the Israeli state (for what country has not had a bit of dubious legality in its history?). It must be an insufferable leak to an inflated pride to see 3 million people make a non-oil producing miniature piece of desert bloom while 100 million of one's own brethren with several hundred times as much desert at their disposal can do little more for their own economic well-being than extort the skills and efforts of foreign treasure hunters on their soil.

Shortly before the 1973 war, Israel was one of the brightest new stars on the international investment firmament. It may shine even brighter if the war leads to a permanent peace agreement, and for anyone having faith in the eventual safety of the Israeli state, the time to invest in it is before the announcement of the good news. Interestingly enough, in contrast to Wall Street, where mass hysteria sets in when King Faisal sneezes, there was no panic selling in Tel Aviv when the

---

On October 3, 1973 the Israeli pound (I£) was valued at 23.81¢.

war started, and the market index at the time of the truce was only a few percentage points below its high.

If there is no peace settlement, on the other hand, and blackmail and extortion is allowed to prevail, Jehovah and Allah may have mercy upon all of us—and what follows here has only a very limited historical appeal.

Like many other foreign stock markets, the Tel Aviv market came to life at a time when Wall Street was in distress. Average daily trading volume increased from Israeli £ 1.6 million ($353,000) in 1970 to I£ 6.7 million ($1.6 million) in 1972, while the general share index increased from 115.51 in 1970 to 156.96 at the end of 1971 and to 306.59 at the end of 1972. Many Israeli common stocks doubled and tripled in price.

In addition, Israel offers an inflation-proof investment in bonds that is almost unique in the world. The price of many Israeli government development bonds is linked to the cost-of-living index. If, as happened in 1972, the official consumer price index rises by 12%, the price of an I£ 1000 bond rises to I£ 1120 (and can be sold at this price). With a 5% yield, this is a 17% return on the investment during one year.

What's most important, an American investor does not pay Interest Equalization Tax on the purchase price of Israeli securities (which on most other foreign common stocks amounts to 11.25% of the purchase price). By definition of the Internal Revenue Service, Israel is an underdeveloped country, and United States investments in such countries are exempt from the tax. Dollars or other foreign currency invested in Israel, plus dividends and interest earned, can be freely taken out of the country again.

Unique Economy

Three features make Israel's investment climate unique so that it cannot be judged by the standards that apply to investment markets of mature industrial countries:

- a patriotic, even religious attitude towards work;
- a continuing influx of immigrants;
- a constant unilateral inflow of money from abroad.

All three are major factors affecting the economy. Productivity in plants can, of course, be measured by the output produced per worker employed; but in advanced industrial countries this productivity is largely the result of labor-saving machinery. The worker himself is in most cases controlled by the speed with which machinery runs and he can do very little to speed up output (but he can, of course, "go slow"). In less mechanized industries, in artisan occupations, in professional and office work, and in agriculture the dedication and enthusiasm that a worker brings to his job can do much to increase his productivity even if it cannot always be measured in exact quantitative terms. By all accounts, the work input beyond the call of work rules and paychecks in Israel is far above that encountered in any other country. Based on patriotic and religious ideals, this work attitude is perhaps the secret to Israel's phenomenal economic and military successes. And there is no reason to believe that it will not continue in the future, even stronger if Israel comes out of its present dilemma.

The work ideal is partly fed by continuing immigration. In 1971, 42,000 people immigrated and in 1972, 55,000, while the total population increased from 3,046,000 in 1971 to 3,147,000 in 1972. Initially, a good many of the new immigrants are a burden to the economy, but once integrated they no doubt add to the spirit of work dedication.

In addition to the influx of people, Israel continues to have a unilateral influx of money, partly outright contributions from Jewish sources, and partly restitution payments from West Germany. In 1971, these contributions amounted to I£ 800 million ($192 million), and in 1972, to I£ 945 million ($225 million), almost as much as the long-term capital inflow of I£ 1,103 million ($265 million) in 1971 and I£ 1,160 million ($278 million) in 1972. Long-term capital inflow must, of course, one day be repaid, whereas the unilateral receipts represent a net addition to the capital resources of the country which, properly applied, add to the gross national product. One day, these unilateral payments are likely to slow down, or cease completely.

Investment Channels

For this reason Israel is interested in promoting regular investments of all kinds in the country, including stock market investments by individuals and institutions. The recent attractions of the Tel Aviv stock market have not remained unnoticed, and while most of the investment interest has probably come from Jewish investors in all parts of the world, gentiles have also added Israeli securities to their portfolios.

In the United States, the Israeli stock market boom led to the rapid spawning of Israeli investment clubs. There were about 200 in mid-1973, with one new one being founded about every week. About 50 of the clubs are in the New York metropolitan area, 40 in the Washington, D.C. area, 40 on the West Coast, and the balance scattered throughout the rest of the country. Anyone interested in joining such a club need only telephone the nearest B'nai B'rith office for a few names and addresses.

For many club members, investment in Israel has had the additional fillip of planning for retirement there. Living costs so far have been considerably lower than in the United States (although housing prices have climbed steeply); the cost-of-living linkage bonds offer protection against inflation—the worst enemy of all retirees; human involvement opportunities are high; and the climate is excellent—sunny and dry in Jerusalem, the most popular retirement city, and a little hotter and more humid along the coast for those who like their daily dip in the sea.

It is very simple to invest in Israeli securities, even in those traded only in Israel, from the United States. Any broker will handle orders for Israeli securities traded on the American Stock Exchange and on the over-the-counter market. For Israeli securities not actively traded in the United States an investor would have to go to one of the brokerage houses specializing in foreign securities (listed at the end of Chapter 1) or to the only Israeli security dealer established in the United States, *Leumi Securities Corporation*, New York, a subsidiary of *Bank Leumi le-Israel B.M.*, the largest Israeli bank, with assets of over I£ 21.9 billion ($522 million) on June 30, 1973. In Israel itself, about 70% of the brokerage business is in the hands of the banks that are members of the Tel Aviv Stock Exchange (listed at the end of this chapter), but banks cannot sell securities in the United States. The balance of the business in Israel is done by other members of the exchange.

Information

Leumi Securities distributes investment information prepared by the *Bank Leumi* and does not itself make any stock market recommendations. Other Israeli banks also prepare investment information. Two consulting firms in Tel Aviv provide independent investment information: *Stock Exchange Information Service, Halevi & Co. Economic Counselling Ltd.,* Jerusalem, which publishes data on individual companies similar to the *Standard & Poor's* sheets, and *National Consultants Ltd.*, Tel Aviv. Two financial newspapers with stock market information are published in Tel Aviv: *Shaar* and *Yom-Yom*.

The larger Israeli companies, and especially the banks and investment companies, produce excellent annual reports in English. However, many of the smaller companies are less informative and provide no information in English. Annual reports are often not published until six months after the end of the fiscal year, and the Tel Aviv Stock Exchange, in 1973, did not require that listed companies release quarterly earnings.

Risks

Limited information obviously increases the investment risk. So does the small "float'" of many Israeli companies. Small "float" means that the number of shares available for trading is small, leading to wide swings of a stock under relatively small buying and selling pressure.

The greatest risk of all is Israel's precarious position with its neighbors. In addition, the fiscal situation of the country has two major elements of risk—devaluation and inflation—that can adversely affect the economy and the value of investments.

Since 1954, when $1 was equal to I£ 1.80, the Israeli pound was devalued five times—to I£ 3 per dollar in 1962, I£ 3.5 in 1967, to I£ 4.20 in 1971, and then in tandem with the dollar twice more in relation to many other currencies. Such devaluation can play havoc in certain industries heavily dependent on imports; and it can mean a substantial loss to an investor in a country whose currency is revalued in relation to the Israeli pound. (There are, however, certain Israeli bonds that are linked to the dollar, protecting the investor against another devaluation of the Israeli pound against the dollar.)

Continuing weakness of the dollar may also create a major dilemma for Israeli monetary authorities in the future. If, through further inflationary policies in the United States and continuing loss of dollars abroad, the dollar on the "floating" exchange markets of the world continues to lose in value, should the Israeli pound continue to follow the dollar and lose further in value in relation to stronger world currencies, or should it cut itself loose? Both courses may create problems. To cut itself loose from the dollar will reduce, in terms of the Israeli pound, the investment and other contributions received from the United States, as well as the restitutions received from West

Germany. Further devaluation in relation to European currencies, on the other hand, may do major damage to many industries and boost the cost-of-living index beyond bearable limits. Of Israel's total 1972 imports of I£ 1.880 billion ($450 million), I£ 1.201 billion ($286 million), or 60%, came from Europe.

Inflation running rampant can undermine the economy of a country and distort all values. One of the main causes of inflation, as explained earlier, is a money supply that rises faster than the amount of goods and services produced. In 1972, Israel's money supply rose by 28%, from I£ 4.341 billion ($1.04 billion) to I£ 5.519 billion ($1.32 billion). The gross national product, in constant money terms, rose only by 9.5%. This discrepancy caused a rise in the consumer price index from 119 in 1971 to 134 in 1972 (1969 = 100), or about 12%. There is one redeeming feature in these figures: a part of the increasing money supply was created by the influx of unilateral contributions from abroad, which raised the foreign currency reserves from I£ 576 million ($138 million) in 1971 to I£ 1.070 billion ($255 million) in 1972. Such money can, of course, be applied against goods and services to be imported from abroad. On the other hand, the war footing, if it is not terminated soon, is likely to drive inflation to exorbitant levels.

A growth in gross national product of 9.5% in constant money terms is outstanding. (In the United States the real growth in 1973 was about 6%.) And there are many other positive factors in the Israeli economy. (Excellent economic statistics are available from Israeli government sources and the leading Israeli banks. The figures used in this chapter were taken from materials published by *Bank Leumi le-Israel*.) Nevertheless, the Israeli government is aware of the risks of inflation and took steps in 1973 to curb the money supply.

The Stock Market

Activities and prices on the Tel Aviv Stock Exchange in the past seem to have been boosted rather than curbed by devaluation and inflation. After being in the doldrums from about 1964 to 1969, when the consumer price index rose only in small increments (it was the lowest in 1967 with an increase of 1.62%), the market suddenly came to life in 1971 and 1972, when the consumer price index rose by about 12% each year, and after the Israeli pound had been devalued from 3.5 to the dollar to 4.2. Total trading volume increased from I£ 389.8 million ($93 million) in 1970 to I£ 624.8 million ($160 million) in 1971 and I£ 1.671 billion ($397 million) in 1972. This rise in trading volume was particularly dramatic for common stocks which represented I£ 52.3 million ($12.4 million) of the total in 1970 and I£ 763.0 million ($182 million) in 1972. The annual average price index rose from 122.1 in 1970 (1960 = 100) to 207.8 in 1972 with a high in 1972 of 306.78.

Ordinary and preferred shares of a total of 83 companies are listed on the Tel Aviv Stock Exchange, with a total market value of about I£ 2.8 billion ($665 million) at the end of 1972. Government and corporate bonds traded on the exchange had a market value of about I£ 9 billion ($2.14 billion).

As in Switzerland and Germany, the banks fulfill the manifold financial functions that in many other countries are separated—commercial banking, investment banking, brokerage business, stock exchange trading, and management of investment funds. Only a handful of Tel Aviv Stock Exchange members are not banks. Much of the stock trading is done outside the exchange, and only those trades that cannot be matched directly among the members are executed on the floor of the exchange. It is estimated that the volume traded off the exchange is at least as much as that traded on the exchange. Investors normally do not take delivery of their stock certificates. They are left in custody of a central clearing house, and stock transfer is by bookkeeping entry.

Investment Companies and Funds

Israeli banks also own major portions of Israeli industry. An investor who wants to have a diversified participation in the Israeli economy can buy shares of one of the bank investment and holding companies. Leading among them are the *Bank Leumi Investment Company Limited* and the *Discount Bank Investment Corporation Limited,* both traded on the Tel Aviv Stock Exchange. In addition, *Bank Leumi* manages five open-end investment funds, with different investment objectives, and the *Israel Discount Bank* manages three.

In the United States, two American-based funds with Israeli security portfolios can be bought—the *Israel Development Corporation* and the *Israel Investors Corporation,* both closed-end funds. *Israel Development Corporation* is part of the *AMPAL-American Israel Corporation,* a group of financial companies founded in 1942 to help finance the development of Israel. *AMPAL* debentures and preference ares are traded over-the-counter in the United States. *AMPAL's* annual report includes capsule reviews of the results of the Israeli orporations in which the group has major investments.

Individual Stocks

Among individual stocks, most banks themselves (as distinguished om the bank investment companies) have done well. The common ock of the largest bank, *Bank Leumi le-Israel,* and of the third rgest, *IDB Bankholding Corporation, Ltd.,* are traded in the United ates over-the-counter in the form of American Depositary Receipts.

Maritime Fruit Carriers, an Israeli shipping company carrying pro- uce and meat all over the world, and planning to go into oil and gas ansport, is an Israeli company that offered its stock to the American ublic without listing on the Tel Aviv exchange. Much of its earnings omes from international business rather than Israel, and purchase of s stock is subject to the Interest Equalization Tax.

Another Israeli stock, very actively traded over-the-counter in the nited States in the form or original shares, rather than American epositary Receipts, is that of a small company—*Elscint Ltd.,* a high-technology" firm making radioisotope scanning and image stor- ng equipment. *General Electric* markets some of *Elscint's* medical quipment in the United States. *Elscint's* United States underwriters ld 400,000 shares in September 1972, on the United States new is- ue market, at $8 per share. After an immediate run-up, the share rice by mid-1973 had dropped back close to its offering price.

Three Israeli issues are actively traded on the American Stock Ex- hange—*Alliance Tire and Rubber Company Ltd.,* Israel's only tire anufacturer, *American Israel Paper Mills Ltd.,* the largest paper anufacturer, and *Etz Lavud,* a wood products manufacturer. Stock rices of all three in mid-1973 had come down considerably from eir highs. *Alliance Tire* had been suffering from higher raw material rices (crude rubber prices went out of sight in the first half of 1973), s well as from a labor shortage; *American Israel Paper* stock, which ad been driven up by the company's stake in the Wankel engine, ame down again when it became apparent that the Wankel engine as taking its time to bloom; and *Etz Lavud,* too, suffered from higher nport prices.

Among Israeli shares traded only in Tel Aviv that found investor nterest in the United States are *The Electro Wire & Cable Company f Israel Ltd.,* a manufacturer of power and telephone wire and cable,

Property and Building Corporation Ltd., a large real estate development firm, and *"Koor" Industries Ltd.,* an industrial holding and
development company.

New Issues

"Koor" is one of the Israeli companies that has been reported to
consider offering new shares in the United States; and the same is true
of *Clal Industries Ltd.,* another industrial holding company. In Israel
itself, the new issue market has come to life as a result of the higher
trading volume on the Tel Aviv Stock Exchange. Convertible notes of
IDB Bankholding Corporation Ltd. offered early in 1973 reportedly
were 30 times oversubscribed, demonstrating a pent-up demand for
sound Israeli securities.

Two new issues came out in the fall of 1973—*Polygon,* a textile
dyeing firm, and *Elite Ltd.,* a famous manufacturer of chocolates and
candies. Others were reportedly waiting in line to go public or to offer
additional shares to the public. Moreover, the Minister of Finance
was quoted to the effect that the government was considering selling
government holdings in industry to private investors.

New issues in Israel are sold directly to the public by subscription
rather than through an underwriting team. This means that an investor
can send his check and subscription order directly to the selling agent
rather than having to buy it through a broker or bank. Like all foreign
new issues, Israeli new issues cannot be offered in the United States
unless they are registered with the SEC. After the issue has been
sold, a certain time must elapse until the new issue can be considered
"settled" and the shares sold in the United States. About 90 days are
usually considered adequate (there is no specific regulation about the
time limit).

Inflation and Devaluation Protection

One of the most interesting features of the Israeli investment scene
are bond issues that protect the investor against a cost-of-living increase or against a devaluation of the Israeli pound *vis-à-vis* the dollar, or both.

The Government of Israel and major banks offer, on a regular
monthly basis, five-year bonds in Israeli currency that are protected
against inflation. As explained at the beginning of this chapter, if the
cost-of-living index increases by 12%, and the yield of the bond is
5%, the investor has a 17% return on his investment—12% appreci-

ion of the bond price and 5% interest. An Israeli citizen will pay come tax on the interest received, but no capital gains tax on the preciation of the bond.

He can do even better than this by not collecting the interest and lling the bonds to a pension fund before redemption including accmlated interest. Pension funds pay no income tax on the interest these bonds. As a result, they are willing to pay a private holder the bonds more than he would get if he redeems the bonds himself d pays taxes on the interest at redemption time. The deal becomes creasingly interesting as redemption approaches, and active trading sually starts when the bonds still have about two years to go. It takes me higher mathematics to figure out what the bonds are worth at a ven moment, but with the help of computers Israeli banks and funds ake these calculations daily.

A United States resident can also buy these bonds, and if he holds em at least six months he can treat the cost-of-living increase in the ond as long-term capital gains but he pays regular income tax on the terest income. However, he runs the risk of seeing the Israeli pound evalued. Devaluation protection can be bought by "half and half" onds that offer a combination of protection against devaluation and st-of-living increases. There are also bonds that offer protection nly against devaluation. And finally, there are straight bonds that fer no protection at all. The more protection there is, the lower the terest rates. Straight bonds pay the highest rate—about 9% in mid-973.

Taxes

Israelis pay income taxes on dividends and on interest from most onds up to a maximum rate of 25% (which may be considerably less an some Israelis pay under a graduated income tax schedule). Some sues of companies operating in areas that are designated by the raeli government as "less developed" have a lower withholding tax te. The income tax is withheld by the paying organization. A foreign vestor may claim exemption from this tax provided the investment as paid from the proceeds of the sale of foreign currency or of ertain State of Israel Bonds. A United States citizen or resident who as paid the tax can set it off against his taxable income on his Federal come tax return. Even though there is no capital gains tax in Israel, United States citizen or resident must pay capital gains tax to the RS on the profits made from the sale of Israeli securities.

Israel Investment Companies and Funds Traded in the United States

AMPAL American Israel Corporation / 30 East 42nd Street / New York, New York 10017

Israel Development Corporation / 30 East 42nd Street / New York, New York 10017

Israel Investors Corporation / 850 Third Avenue New York, New York 10022

Mutual Funds Traded in Israel

Managed by *Bank Leumi*:
  Vygdal (100% common stock)
  Bedolach (75% common stock; 25% cost-of-living-linked bonds)
  PIA (100% common stock)
  Gavish (25% dollar-linked bonds; 45% cost-of-living linked bonds; 30% common stock and cash)
  ZAMID (50% cost-of-living-linked bonds; 50% dollar-linked bonds)
Managed by *Discount Bank Investment Corporation*:
  Alon Linked Unit Trust
  Dekel Cumulative Fund
  Brosh Unit Trust

Partial List of Brokers Accepting Orders for Israeli Securities Traded Only in Israel

Leumi Securities Corporation / 18 East 48th Street / New York, New York 10017

Oscar Gruss & Son / 80 Pine Street / New York, New York 10005

Brager & Co., Inc. / 787 Fifth Avenue / New York, New York 10022

  Other United States brokerage houses accepting orders for foreign securities not traded in the United States are listed at the end of Chapter 1.

  All United States brokerage houses will accept orders for Israeli securities actively traded in the United States.

Investment Information Services

Stock Exchange Information Service published by *Halevi & Co. Economic Counseling Ltd.* / 54 Haneviim Street / Jerusalem

National Consultants Ltd. / Hadar Dafna Building, 39 Shaul Hamelech Boulevard / Tel Aviv

Financial Newspapers

Shaar / 15 Hatzfire Street / Tel Aviv
Yom-Yom / 34 Itzchak Sade Street / Tel Aviv

Israeli Securities Traded on the American Stock Exchange

Alliance Tire and Rubber Company Ltd.
American Israel Paper Mills Ltd.
Etz Lavud Ltd.

Israeli Securities Traded Over-the-Counter (in New York)

Bank Leumi le-Israel B.M.
Elscint Ltd.
Israel Discount Bank Ltd.
IDB Bankholding Corporation Ltd.
Industrial Development Bank of Israel Ltd.
Israel Bank of Agriculture Ltd.
"Isras," Israel Rassco Investment Company Ltd.
Maritime Fruit Carriers
"Rassco," Rural and Suburban Settlement Company Ltd.
Real Estate Participation
Tourist Industry

Companies with Shares Listed on the Tel Aviv Stock Exchange

Commercial Banks and Bankholding Companies

Bank Hapoalim B.M.
Bank Leumi le-Israel B.M.
IDB Bankholding Corporation Ltd.
Israel British Bank Ltd.
Israel Discount Bank Ltd.
Otzar Hityashvuth Hayehudim B.M.
Union Bank of Israel Ltd.
United Mizrahi Bank Ltd.

Mortgage Banks

Bank Adanim Mortgage and Loans Ltd.
Carmel Mortgage and Investment Bank Ltd.
General Mortgage Bank Ltd.
Housing Mortgage Bank Ltd.
The Israel Development and Mortgage Bank Ltd.
Mortgage and Investment for Building Ltd.
"Tefahot" Israel Mortgage Bank Ltd.
Unico Investment Company Ltd.

Specialized Financial Institutions

Gazit Incorporated, Panama
Industrial Development Bank of Israel Ltd.
The Israel American Independent Development Bank Ltd.
Israel Bank of Agriculture Ltd.
Otzar Hashilton Hamekomi B.M.
Otzar La'taasiya Ltd.

Insurance

"Aryeh" Insurance Company Ltd.
Hassneh Insurance Company of Israel Ltd.
"Sahar" Insurance Company Ltd.
"Zur" Insurance Company Ltd.

Commercial Services and Utilities
"Delek" The Israel Fuel Company Ltd.
The Israel Cold Storage and Supply Company Ltd.
The Israel Electric Corporation Ltd.
Israel Lighterage and Supply Company Ltd.
The Motor House Ltd.
Zim Israel Navigation Company Ltd.

Land, Building, Development, and Citrus
Africa-Israel Investment Ltd.
Anglo-Israel Investors Ltd.
Azorim, Investment Development and Construction Company Ltd.
I.C.P. Israel Citrus Plantation Ltd.
The Israel Land Development Company Ltd.
"Ispro," The Israeli Properties Rental Corporation Ltd.
"Isras," Israel Rassco Investment Company Ltd.
Mehadrin Ltd.
Neot Aviv Ltd.
Pri Or Ltd.
Property and Building Corporation Ltd.
"Rassco," Rural and Suburban Settlement Company Ltd.
Solel Boneh's Building and Public Works Company Ltd.

Industrial
Alliance Tire and Rubber Company Ltd.
American Israel Paper Mills Ltd.
"Arad" Quarries and Roads Ltd.
The Argaman Textile Dye Works Ltd.
"Ata" Textile Company Ltd.
Chemicals and Phosphates Ltd.
Dubek Ltd.
Elco Israel Electro Mechanic Industries Ltd.
Electra (Israel) Ltd.
The Electro Wire and Cable Company of Israel Ltd.
Elite Ltd.
Enterprises of Assis and Bejerano Brothers Ltd.
Israel Glass Works "Phoenicia" Ltd.
E. Lewin-Epstein Ltd.
Moller Textile Ltd.
Nechustan Wholes and Manufacturers Ltd.
Polygon Ltd.
Shemen Industries Ltd.
Taal Manufacturing of Plywood Ltd.
"Teva" Pharmaceutical & Chemical Works Ltd.

Investment and Holding Companies
"Amissar" American Israel Investment Mortgage Ltd.
Bank Leumi Investment Company Ltd.
Chevra Lahashkaot Miyissoda Ampa B.M.
Clal Industries Ltd.
"Clal" Israel Investment Company

Discount Bank Investment Corporation Ltd.
Elgar Investment Ltd.
Ellern's Investment Corporation Ltd.
"Export" Investment Company Ltd.
Hassuta-Foreign Trade, Industrial
Investment Company of Bank Hapoalim Ltd.
Investment and Development of Paz Ltd.
Investment Trust "Piryon" Haifa Ltd.
Investment United Mizrahi Bank Ltd.
The Israel Central Trade & Investment Company Ltd.
The Jordan Exploration Company Ltd.
"Koor" Industries Ltd.
Oz-Investment Company Ltd.
Pama Investment and Property Company Ltd.
Wolfson Clore Mayer Corporation Ltd.

List of Tel Aviv Stock Exchange Members

Banks & Banking Institutions

Bank Hapoalim B.M. / 50 Rothschild Boulevard / Tel Aviv
Bank of Israel / 37 Lilienblum Street / Tel Aviv
Bank Leumi le-Israel B.M. / 28 Yehuda Halevi Street / Tel Aviv
Bank Barclays Discount Ltd. / 103 Allenby Street / Tel Aviv
Bank Japhet Ltd. / 11 Rothschild Boulevard / Tel Aviv
Israel British Bank Ltd. / 20 Rothschild Boulevard / Tel Aviv
Israel Discount Bank Ltd. / 27 Yehuda Halevi Street / Tel Aviv
Israel Finance Bank Ltd. / 14 Rothschild Boulevard / Tel Aviv
Israel General Bank Ltd. / 28 Ahad Haam Street / Tel Aviv
Kupat-Am Bank Ltd. / 13 Ahad Haam Street / Tel Aviv
Kupat Milwe Vehisachon Le-Olei Irak Cooperative Society Ltd. / 19 Ahad
   Haam Street / Tel Aviv
United Mizrahi Bank Ltd. / 48 Lilienblum Street / Tel Aviv
Otsar Ha-Hayal Ltd. / 84 Hashmonaim Street / Tel Aviv
The First International Bank of Israel Ltd. / 38 Rothschild Boulevard /
   Tel Aviv
The Israel Industrial Bank Ltd. / 13 Montefiori Street / Tel Aviv
Trade Bank Ltd. / 42 Lilienblum Street / Tel Aviv
Union Bank of Israel Ltd. / 6 Ahuzat Bait Street / Tel Aviv

Financial Institutions and Brokers

Africa-Israel Investments Ltd. / 13 Ahad Haam Street / Tel Aviv
F.I.T. Financial, Industrial and Trade Company Ltd. / 5 Ahuzat Bait
   Street / Tel Aviv
Haron & Lavy Ltd. / 113 Allenby Street / Tel Aviv
Unitrust Securities and Investment Corporation Ltd. / 9 Ahad Haam
   Street / Tel Aviv
Moritz and Tuchler Ltd. / 41 Lilienblum Street / Tel Aviv
Salzmann, Julius / 112 Allenby Street / Tel Aviv
Suesskind, Danziger and Company / 12 Rothschild Boulevard / Tel Aviv
Securities and Investments Ltd. / 70 Ahad Haam Street / Tel Aviv
The Central Securities Corporation Ltd. / 29 Lilienblum Street / Tel Aviv

7

JAPAN

THE SWARMING HONEY BEES

Anyone who had picked a Japanese stock in 1968, shortly before the New York stock market collapsed, would have had an excellent chance of tripling or quadrupling his money by 1972 if he had done only as well as the averages. The Tokyo Dow Jones average of 225 selected blue chip stocks ranged between a low of 1266 and a high of 1851 in 1968 to reach a high of 5207 in December 1972, peaking out at 5359.74 on January 24, 1973. It wasn't until later in 1973 that the Japanese stock market seemed to run out of steam and in November the index was at about 4300.

Many individual Japanese stocks did far better than the average—the best known among them that of *Sony Corporation*, the consumer electronics company that rose like a rocket from $77 million in sales in 1963 to $796 million in 1972, showering its excellent products on all parts of the globe. The *Sony* American Depositary Share traded on the New York Stock Exchange, which equals two *Sony* shares on the Tokyo Stock Exchange, rose from the equivalent (after splits and rights issues) of about $7 in 1968 to above $50 in early 1973. Many other Japanese stocks have also performed far better than average. The stock of *Nomura Securities Co., Ltd.,* the largest Japanese brokerage house, benefitting from the Japanese stock market boom, rose by 413% in a single year—1972. In the same year, *Nikko Securities Co., Ltd.,* the second largest brokerage house, saw its stock rise by 440%.

On October 3, 1973 the Japanese yen was valued at U.S. 0.376¢.

The stock of *The Sumitomo Bank, Ltd.*, the second largest bank, went up 330%, and that of *Sumitomo Marine and Fire Insurance Co.*, a large insurance company, climbed 263%. *Nissan Motor Co., Ltd.*, which makes Datsun cars, had a sharp rise of 317%. An American investor would have gained another 30% in terms of dollars as a result of the revaluation of the yen. In 1973, most of the Japanese stocks receded from their all-time highs.

Where to Buy Japanese Stocks

There are more opportunities to buy Japanese stocks in the United States than stocks of any other foreign country except Canada. In September 1973, about 85 Japanese common stocks were available in the United States in the form of American Depositary Receipts or shares. Many of them trade quite actively so that there is no problem of buying and selling shares close to the quoted prices. This is not always the case with many other foreign stocks. Practically all American brokers are willing to execute orders for ADRs, but for an ADR traded over-the-counter an investor might get a somewhat better price from a broker who is making a market in a specific ADR (market makers are listed in the so-called "pink sheets" which are published daily and are available at every American brokerage office).

Japanese ADRs are registered either under Form S-1 or S-12. Registration under Form S-1 conforms to American accounting principles and regulations of the Securities and Exchange Commission. Form S-12 is a simpler registration, accompanied by the latest financial report of the foreign company, and it is not registered with the SEC.

The easiest way to participate in the Japanese market on a broad, diversified scale under professional management is to buy shares of *The Japan Fund*, which are traded on the New York and Pacific Stock Exchanges, either American-owned, that is, including the Interest Equalization Tax, or foreign-owned, excluding the tax. The fund has an average of 60 Japanese securities in its portfolio, including a good number not available in the United States in American Depositary Receipts. It publishes quarterly reports to shareholders with current portfolios and balance sheets, and its portfolio is a good guide to Japanese securities selection.

An investor who wants to buy a Japanese stock that is not traded in the United States will have to go to one of the American brokers specializing in foreign stock trading (listed at the end of Chapter 1), or to a Japanese broker represented in the United States (listed at the end of this chapter). While initially Japanese brokers opening offices in the United States were not equipped to handle business of individual investors, they were more and more willing to do so in 1973, and the eventual objective of some is to provide truly international portfolio management for customers. Japanese brokerage houses receiving business from an American brokerage house will often "negotiate" the commission, so that an investor will not necessarily pay a higher commission on a Japanese stock if he goes to an American brokerage house. But his information service from a Japanese brokerage house is likely to be better. An investor buying Japanese stock not traded in the United States and not American-owned will have to pay the Interest Equalization Tax of 11.25% on the purchase price of the stock. This may have seemed inconsequential in the past when the Japanese market was rising at a rapid rate, but with a less buoyant market, the tax would obviously be a consideration.

Where is the Tokyo Market Headed Now?

After the spectacular performance of the past, the question is: What can the Tokyo market do for an encore? This, of course, will depend to a large extent on what the Japanese economy will do.

In the years 1951 to 1970 the gross national product grew by 510% (unadjusted for inflation). Between 1970 and 1971, the Japanese annual gross national product rate grew from Yen 73.213 trillion to Yen 81.141 trillion ($270 billion to $305 billion), or about 11%; to Yen 97.336 trillion ($363 billion) in 1972, an increase of about 20%; and to Yen 108.193 trillion ($403 billion) by the end of June 1973, a growth of more than 11% in half a year. The annual growth rate in 1973 in real terms was still about 10%, and it was expected to be about 9% in 1974. In other words, while the stock market had slowed down in 1973, the economy continued to rise.

The assumption was widespread that the yen revaluation would hurt Japanese exports, and thus the economy in general. Exports were running at a considerably higher rate than imports during the years 1970 to 1972 so that Japan's foreign currency reserves had jumped from about $4.3 billion in 1970 to $15.2 billion at the end of 1971 and to $18.3 billion at the end of 1972. They reached an all-time high of $19 billion at the end of February 1973, but then receded to $15 billion by the end of August 1973. The Japanese were fast to spend their newly earned money, not necessarily in increased imports, but by swarming abroad for pleasure and business travel, opening offices in all parts of the world, and investing in many new international ventures. Exports actually constitute only about 11% of the gross national product, much lower than in most countries of Europe where they range from about 20% of gross national product in West Germany to more than 40% in Belgium. Thus, a modest reduction in exports is unlikely to have a major impact on the Japanese economy, while investments abroad may in the long run add considerably to the country's earnings.

Japanese firms have three main incentives to invest abroad—(1) soaring labor costs in Japan; (2) government pressure to reverse the influx of foreign currency (and when the Japanese government gives a signal, usually everyone follows it); and (3) tariffs and other import restrictions in many countries against products imported from Japan which induces Japanese firms to start manufacturing abroad.

With the lifting of the bamboo curtain, Mainland China may become by peaceful means what the Japanese in the 1930s tried to take by military invasion—a promised land of 700 million customers. The first companies that are likely to benefit most from this international expansion are the large Japanese trading companies—*Mitsubishi Corporation, Mitsui & Co., Ltd., C. Itoh & Co., Ltd.,* and *Marubeni,* and the larger banks with overseas involvement such as *The Mitsubishi Bank, Ltd., The Mitsui Bank, Ltd., The Fuji Bank, Ltd.,* and the *Bank of Tokyo.*

Internal Fat

Japan has a reputation for efficient manufacturing practices. But major improvements in the over-all productivity of the economy and of the profitability of many companies may still be possible through modification of some of the traditional business practices. The two features that strike a Western businessman as particularly inefficient are the distribution system and the lifetime job security of Japanese employees.

In distribution, century-old channels still exist that include up to four intermediaries between the producer and the ultimate consumer. Even department stores buy through a chain of wholesalers rather than go directly to the manufacturer. In addition, department stores are hamstrung by a law, intended to protect the small retailer, which limits the expansion of their floor space and restricts their operating hours. (This law was to be revised in 1973.) When the law was passed, self-service supermarkets did not exist and thus were not covered by the law. This omission made is possible for self-service chain stores to come into existence and grow at a rapid rate. By far the largest among them is *Daiei Inc.*, which started as a cut-rate drug store in Osaka in 1957 and grew to an operation of almost 100 combined food, clothing, and discount stores by the end of 1972, with a total sales volume of more than Yen 300 billion ($112 million). In 1972 alone, sales grew by about 40%, while earnings grew by more than 70%. For about 20% of its supplies, *Daiei* goes directly to the producer, bypassing all middlemen, and it has also cut out such Japanese frills as kimono-clad, smiling and bowing elevator dispatchers. Another supermarket chain growing at a rapid pace is *Ito Yokado*. Neither *Daiei* nor *Ito Yokado* was available through ADRs in the United States in 1973 (but *Daiei* had about 9% foreign stockholders).

As the practice of eliminating middlemen spreads, and as the increasing shortage of labor in Japan makes the protection of labor-intensive small operations less and less desirable, the larger companies in the distribution sector should greatly benefit.

Labor shortages may eventually also cut into the lifetime job security that practically all Japanese companies still offer today. This high-school-to-grave job security, a Japanese businessman said, saddles him with a rigid cost for a labor force consisting of 20% dead wood, 60% who coast on their jobs, and 20% who carry the company. An American businessman retorted that this percentage is par for the course of an American business, too, where there is no comparable job security. In a recession, American management can immediately lay off hourly workers not needed for the reduced production level, and if things don't improve outright dismissals of white collar workers up to the executive suite are not uncommon.

In a Japanese recession, on the other hand, fixed labor costs may wipe out a manufacturer's profit entirely within a very short time. Since World War II, no severe test has been put on the lifetime job security practice. The most drastic step so far was taken by *Hitachi, Ltd.* when after the first yen revaluation it did not hire its usual yearly contingent of high-school graduates. This job stability may have been part of the secret of Japan's economic success, creating loyalty and effort beyond the call of duty. And it may remain so in the future, perhaps with certain modifications that may make it easier for employees to leave their companies for others needing their services more urgently.

When all is said and done, however, the Japanese economic "miracle" remains somewhat of a mystery considering the lack of most natural resources in the country and the perpetuation of traditions that would seem to preclude "efficiency" in the Western sense. One answer to the mystery seems to lie in the astonishing discipline of the Japanese, both as individuals and in groups, and the homogeneity of purpose of the entire nation, which makes partners of government, business, and labor.

High Leverage Risk

Another two-edged factor in the profitability of Japanese business is the high debt carried by most companies. In Europe and the United States publicly owned manufacturing companies, on the average, borrow about 40% of the money they need to operate. (The balance is equity financing, which means sale of common stock or bonds convertible into common stock.) Japanese companies often borrow up to 80%, helped by credit rules of the Central Bank of Japan that are far more liberal than those under which American banks operate. In times of growing business and profitability this means that the total capital can produce substantial earnings in relation to the relatively few common shares outstanding. Thus, earnings per share may increase very rapidly. In times of recession, the high costs of borrowing money may rapidly wipe out earnings already reduced by a lower business volume. This high debt ratio is called "high leverage," and a highly leveraged stock may fluctuate in price to a far greater extent than the economy itself.

Additional volatility to stock prices is added by the Japanese investors who are inveterate traders, often buying and selling on the same day. Many act as impulsively and emotionally on the basis of rumors and poorly digested news as investors endowed with a gambling instinct almost anywhere else in the world. (And below their polite, disciplined manners, most Japanese are highly emotional people.)

Other Risks

A number of negative factors have appeared within Japan that may impair economic growth in the future. They are all connected with the fact that on the small islands the population and production facilities are rapidly running out of space. Air and water are seriously polluted. Land is getting scarce. Traffic is crawling in Tokyo and other big cities. Farmland is being lost. Fishing grounds are being exhausted and polluted. Energy supplies are getting scarcer and more expensive.

And Japan is heavily dependent on imports of raw materials, some of which are in short supply, and most of which have risen steeply in price. Like an army that has swept a continent, Japanese business may have to call a halt to secure the hinterland and build up its supply base before making another thrust. Plans include dispersal of population to new model towns from the overcrowded population centers, radical pollution control, the procurement of new energy and raw material resources, and the building of new production capacity abroad.

Thus, as on any other stock market, the investor must keep a watchful eye on his Japanese stock, as well as on the economy in general, and he must learn to distinguish between erratic temporary swings on the Tokyo market and genuine declines and advances.

How Does the Japanese Stock Market Operate?

There are eight stock exchanges in Japan. Tokyo accounts for about 75% of the trading volume; Osaka for 21%; and Nagoya for 3%. The other five represent the balance. For the foreign investor only Tokyo is of practical interest.

At the end of June 1973, there were 1355 issues listed on the Tokyo Stock Exchange—820 in the "first section" and 535 in the "second section." The 1355 issues represent about 138 billion shares. The "first section" has somewhat stricter listing requirements than the "second section" and represents more seasoned companies. This difference is comparable to that existing between the listing requirements of the New York and American Stock Exchanges.

Trading volume until February 1973, was extremely high. During 1972 it averaged 327 million shares a day in the first section, with peak trading days of more than 1.8 billion shares. With six trading days per week, this added up to more than 100 billion shares per year. In 1973, the average daily trading volume of both sections combined declined from a high of 635 million in January to a low of 110 million in June. The yen value of all trades converted into dollars in 1972 represented more than 30% of the dollar volume traded on the New York Stock Exchange.

The Tokyo Stock Exchange is the first in the world in the number of shares traded and second only to New York in the value of shares traded (but The Stock Exchange, London, also claims the latter honor). It is also a highly liquid stock market—at times even more liquid than New York—and this gives it an attraction to institutional investors in all parts of the world that many European stock markets have not yet fully developed. (Liquidity of the market means that it is relatively easy to buy or sell most listed stocks in fairly large quantities without excessive effect in the price of the stock.)

Japanese individual investors still account for about 75% of all shares traded on the Tokyo Stock Exchange; the balance is filled by institutional investors, business corporations, and foreign investors. In New York, more than 60% of the trading is done by institutional investors.

The high trading volume of Japanese individual investors is particularly surprising considering that individuals, in 1973, owned only about 33% of all the shares listed in the "first section" of the Tokyo Stock Exchange. Banks and other financial institutions owned 37%, business corporations 23%, and the balance was spread among foreign investors, securities companies, investment trusts, and government and local bodies. The percentage of individual ownership has come down over the years from 50% in 1966 to 33% in 1973. The number of total shares held by individuals decreased during that time, reaching a level of about 47 billion in 1971 and about 45 billion in 1972.

In spite of the great advance of the Japanese stock market, the market prices of Japanese stocks are still very low, most of them lying within a range of Yen 100 (about 37 cents) to Yen 100 ($3.70). The average price on September 14, 1973, was Yen 300 ($1.11). Minimum trading unit for shares of Yen 50 par is usually 1000 shares, and for the Yen 500 par, 100 shares.

New Issues

In the past it was common practice for Japanese companies to raise money by offering additional shares to existing shareholders at par value, which was usually well below the market price. This sometimes gave stockholders a handsome profit. More and more companies have gone over to selling additional shares close to market price—usually a few percentage points below it—but others have continued the practice of selling new shares at par. One of the better known among the latter is *The Tokio Marine and Fire Insurance Co., Ltd.*, the largest Japanese insurance company, actively traded on the United States over-the-counter market in the form of American Depositary Receipts. In August 1973, the company offered its shareholders rights to 26 million new shares at the par value of Yen 50 (18.7¢) on the basis 0.45 shares for each share held. In the United States, where each

American Depositary Receipt represents 50 underlying Japanese shares, the rights entitled a holder of 100 ADRs to buy 45 additional ADRs at a price of $9.50 each, plus $1.07 Interest Equalization Tax. He could also sell the rights. This confronted the shareholder with highly complex mathematics. To make matters more complicated, shareholders had received a stock dividend of three shares per 100, but these shares were not eligible for rights. Before their expiration date, the rights were selling below the price at which, theoretically, the ADRs would sell into which they could be converted. At the end of July 1973, at the time of the rights announcement and before issuance of the stock dividend, a *Tokio Marine and Fire* ADR was selling at about $170. With the addition of 45 new ADRs to 100 old ADRs, plus the stock dividend of 3 new shares, a holder of a total of 148 ADRs should have found the price of an ADR share adjust to about $112 ($170 divided by 1.48 = $115, minus the cost of 45 rights at $10.57 each, that is $475.65, divided by 148, or $3.21). However, in practice this does not always work that way. Recipients of new shares from a rights issue often sell them immediately, and in anticipation of this the stock price often declines. In the case of *Tokio Marine and Fire*, the ADR price declined to about $95 on the day of the expiration of the rights on September 21, 1973, a good deal more than the Tokyo market average during the same time. Thus, apart from the arithmetical headache he gets, a stockholder is not necessarily well served by a rights offering at an apparently very low par price.

Foreign rights can be offered in the United States only if they are registered with the SEC. Except for the Japanese ADRs very actively traded in the United States, this is not usually done; and it is never done for Japanese stocks traded in Japan. Nevertheless, if the investor finds out about the rights offering he can give his broker instructions to exercise them. Otherwise they will be sold on his behalf and he will be credited with the proceeds.

Placing an Order

A non-resident foreign investor will have to be guided in his purchases by the brokerage houses that execute his order, but here are a few technicalities that may be worth knowing: As in the United States, stock can be bought and sold at the best market price prevailing when the order reaches the Japanese broker in Japan or at a price limit set by the investor. There are no floor specialists on the floor of the Tokyo Stock Exchange as there are on the American stock exchanges. Markets are made by the Japanese brokerage firms. Stop-loss orders are not permitted. (A stop-loss order is an instruction to the broker to sell a stock when the price has come down to a specific level.) Japanese can buy stocks on margin—that is they put up only 30% to 40% of the cost of the purchased stock, the balance is lent to them by their broker. However, non-resident foreigners cannot buy on margin.

Foreign Ownership Liberalized

Until May 1973, the number of shares of any company that foreigners could own was limited to 25% of the total outstanding in non-restricted industries, to 15% in certain restricted industries. Under new regulations, all but five industries will eventually be open to 100% foreign investment, but for 17 industries the decontrol is postponed from one to three years.

Sectors that will remain subject to case-by-case screening are agriculture, forestry and fisheries, petroleum refining and distribution, and leather and leather goods. Mining will be restricted to 50%. Retail establishments with more than 11 outlets are still subject to screening; those with fewer outlets remain open to 50% foreign investment.

Industries in which 100% investment has been postponed until May 1, 1975, are meat processing, tomato products and cooked foods for restaurants, manufacture and marketing of clothing, manufacture of pharmaceuticals and agricultural chemicals, production of ferro-alloys, manufacture of hydraulic machinery, manufacture of packing and crating machinery, manufacture of electronic precision machinery, manufacture of phonograph records, and real estate. The manufacture, marketing, and rental of electronic computers will be decontrolled on December 1, 1975; the information processing industry April 1, 1976; processing of fruit juice and fruit drinks, and the manufacture of sensitized photographic materials on May 1, 1976.

An increase in the ratio of foreign investment in an established firm is subject to the consent of the Ministry of Finance. By late 1973, only a handful of Japanese companies had been given such "consent," including *Sony Corporation*, which increased its maximum of foreign ownership to 47%.

When foreign ownership of a Japanese stock has reached the maximum, and the stock is also traded in the form of ADRs in the United States, the ADR may sell at a premium above the underlying stock in Japan. The *Sony* ADRs in 1973 were selling at a premium of about 35% above the stock price in Japan.

Compare Prices

In any case, whenever American Depositary Receipts of a Japanese stock are available in the United States and the underlying stock in Japan can still be bought, it is a good idea to compare the price of the ADR with that of the Japanese stock, plus the Interest Equalization Tax of 11.25%. Different demand and supply situations in Japan and the United States may create price differences big enough to be considered by the investor. If the total cost of the Japanese stock plus the tax is much lower than the price of the ADR, obviously it makes sense to buy the stock, even if it is more complicated and may cost more in commissions. If the ADR cost is lower or roughly the same, obviously the ADR should be bought. Arbitragers are usually quite active in Japanese ADRs, taking advantage of these fluctuating price differentials, with the result that the differentials never get much out of hand except for the Japanese stocks that can no longer be bought by foreigners in Japan.

Proxy and Custodian

In order to trade in Japanese shares, a non-resident must appoint a Japanese standing proxy—generally the Japanese broker. This proxy is authorized to act on the investor's behalf, as far as buying, selling, and dividend disposition is concerned. It is also advisable to appoint the broker custodian of the share certificates since it is impractical and risky to have them delivered outside Japan. Besides, the certificates are printed only in Japanese, and even foreign brokers usually leave their certificates in Japan since they usually are not able to read and handle them. There are no street name accounts in Japan in which a broker can hold the shares in his own name on behalf of his customers. If Japanese shares are bought through an American broker they are often left in the custody of an American bank established in Japan.

Dividends and Taxes

Dividends for non-resident investors are paid to the Japanese custodian who can either remit them or reinvest them. Most Japanese companies pay dividends twice a year—about two months after the record date. Dividends on common stocks have traditionally been expressed as a percentage of the par value of the stock, but stock tables published in the financial pages usually show the actual yen amount per share, plus the yield.

A 15% tax is withheld in Japan on dividends due non-resident investors. A United States resident may claim the tax against his own Federal income tax. There is no capital gains tax in Japan, but of course capital gains made on the sale of Japanese stocks must be reported on the Federal income tax form.

Japanese Brokers

As in the United States, the securities business in Japan is separated from the commercial banking business. Only brokers can deal in securities.

There are more than 250 securities firms in Japan, but the business is dominated by the "big four"—in the order of their size: *Nomura Securities Co., Ltd., Nikko Securities Co., Ltd., Daiwa Securities Co., Ltd.*, and *Yamaichi Securities Co., Ltd.* Together they account for about one-half of all stock transactions, up to 80% of all bond trading, and for practically all of the underwriting management of new issues. All four are represented in the United States and in many other countries of the world. Three of the smaller ones opened offices in New York in 1973—*New Japan Securities International Inc., Nippon Kangyo Kakumaru Securities Co. Ltd.*, and *Sanyo Securities Co. Ltd.* This makes the Japanese the largest foreign fraternity of brokerage houses in the United States.

Unlike American brokerage houses, the big four have been enormously profitable in the past few years—partly a result of the rapid expansion of the business overseas, but partly also because they seem to be far more efficiently operated than most American firms. They can handle billion-share days without a hitch thanks to advanced computerization.

The shares of *Nomura, Nikko,* and *Daiwa* are listed in the "first section" of the Tokyo Stock Exchange, and their ADRs are traded in the United States over-the-counter. *Yamaichi, New Japan, Nippon Kangyo Kakumaru*, and *Sanyo* shares are listed in the "second section" (no ADRs were available in 1973).

There are bright spots also in the future of Japanese brokerage firms. It is expected that many Japanese corporations will reduce their debt financing and raise money by selling more common shares. This will boost the underwriting business of the big four brokerage houses. In addition, Japan has become a major source of capital for foreign corporations and government organizations, and the Japanese brokerage houses are participating in substantial financing operations outside

Japan. On the other hand, declining trading volume on the Tokyo Stock Exchange is likely to depress earnings. Reportedly, 250 million shares a day must be traded for the domestic brokerage business to break even.

Banks

An even brighter picture applies to the Japanese banking industry. The largest among the Japanese banks are the so-called "city banks," headquartered in major cities but operating branch offices throughout the country. Most of them have also spread world-wide, financing the expanding foreign trade and investments of Japanese industry and participating in international financing operations, such as Eurodollar loans. In Japan they provide all regular commercial and private banking transactions, including savings accounts. Most of their funds are derived from deposits—demand, time, and saving.

The four largest Japanese banks are among the top 12 in the world, according to the July 31, 1973 tabulations of *American Banker* magazine—*Daiichi Kangyo Bank, Ltd.,* Tokyo, No. 5; *The Sumitomo Bank, Ltd.,* Osaka, No. 8; *The Fuji Bank, Ltd.,* Tokyo, No. 9; and *The Mitsubishi Bank, Ltd.,* Tokyo, No. 12. The ranking is based on total deposits on December 31, 1972, converted into dollars at the then prevailing exchange rates. All four Japanese banks had gained two or three places in the ranking as compared with the previous year. The next largest bank, *The Sanwa Bank, Ltd.,* Osaka, No. 15, had moved up four places on the list, followed by *The Mitsui Bank, Ltd.,* Tokyo, No. 25, seven places ahead. The fast internal growth of Japan, plus the rapid expansion of the Japanese banks on the international scene combined to give the Japanese banks the fastest growth rate of all banks in the world—and in some other countries banks also had outstanding growth records during the same year. *The Bank of Tokyo, Ltd.,* which had concentrated particularly on overseas business, advanced 18 places, reaching No. 33. According to a Japanese broker's opinion in 1973, the Japanese financial institutions, notably banks and insurance companies, were likely to have a better growth rate near term than most manufacturing companies whose profit margins were expected to be hurt by rising labor costs, higher money rates, and the energy crisis.

Insurance Companies

Life insurance companies are mutual companies—owned by policy holders and not by stockholders. However, casualty companies are publicly owned and their growth rate in the early 1970s has been exceptional. In addition to insurance writing, they also engage in loan and investment activities. The four largest, roughly in the order of their size, are *The Tokio Marine and Fire Insurance Co., Ltd., The Yasuda Fire and Marine Insurance Co., Ltd., Taisho Marine and Fire Insurance Co., Ltd.,* and *Sumitomo Marine and Fire Insurance Co., Ltd.*

Heavy Industry

Among industrials, steel companies and shipbuilders were popular in 1973. The steel industry was operating at maximum capacity and with such a large backlog that it was expected to remain profitable for a long time to come. Among the more actively traded Japanese steel stocks are *Nippon Steel Corporation, Nippon Kokan, K.K.* (also shipbuilding), *Kawasaki Steel Corporation,* and *New Japan Iron and Steel Corporation.*

The shipbuilding industry of Japan has built up a world-wide reputation for price and quality, and in 1973 most shipyards had orders for many years in advance, with prices that allowed for inflation projections. Three shipbuilders recommended by a leading brokerage house were *Hitachi Shipbuilding and Engineering Co., Ltd., Ishikawajima-Harima Heavy Industries Co., Ltd.,* and *Mitsui Shipbuilding and Engineering Co., Ltd.*

Zaibatsu

An investor who wonders about the frequent recurrence of the same name in companies in different industries (there is *The Sumitomo Bank, Sumitomo Marine and Fire Insurance Co., Ltd., Sumitomo Chemical Co., Ltd., Sumitomo Metal Industries, Ltd.,* etc.) should know that these all originally belonged to huge family enterprises, called *zaibatsu,* which engaged in practically every type of business activity in the country—manufacturing, trading, banking, shipping, mining, insurance, etc. Before World War II, about 80% of the Japanese economy was controlled by the *zaibatsus.* After the war the *zaibatsus* were dismantled and the individual units set up as independent companies, most of them publicly held. Over the years, however, the old family ties revived. There are now interlocking stock ownerships among many of the old families, informal over-all policy meetings among the managements of the independent companies, mutual financial aid where needed, and reciprocal business "favoritism."

The largest of the old *zaibatsu* groups is Mitsubishi, which includes *The Mitsubishi Bank, Ltd., The Tokio Marine and Fire Insurance Co., Ltd., Mitsubishi International Corporation* (trading), *Mitsubishi Heavy Industries, Ltd.* (aerospace, shipbuilding, industrial plants), *Mitsubishi Mining Co., Kirin Brewery Co., Ltd., Nippon Yusen Kaisha* (the largest shipowners in the world), and about 40 others in different industries. *The Mitsubishi Bank, Ltd.* holds shares in all of the publicly owned Mitsubishi companies—usually less than 10%, but it provides often 20% and more of the commercial loans these companies borrow. Other large *zaibatsu* groups are Mitsui, Sumitomo, and Yasuda.

These groups have some positive aspects of conglomerates—financial resources can be directed wherever they are most effective, the interchange of business intelligence from various industries, and business referrals among the members. At the same time they have the advantage that each member has independent management exposed to the cold eyes of security analysts and the harsh realities of the stock market.

Investment Trusts

Practically all Japanese mutual funds are managed and sold by brokerage firms, and the name of the firm is usually identified in the name of the fund. Some Japanese trusts have a limited lifetime, with a fixed number of shares which, when redeemed, are retired. On maturity the trust is liquidated and replaced by a new trust. Other Japanese investment trusts are comparable to American mutual funds, and their shares are always redeemable. Foreign investors need approval from the Ministry of Finance to buy Japanese investment trust shares, but this is usually a formality undertaken by the management company. The foreign investor must also commit himself not to redeem the shares for at least six months.

Japanese investment trusts cover a variety of different investment objectives, including growth, balanced portfolio, and fixed income. A number of Japanese funds have international portfolios.

Performance of most Japanese funds with Japanese stocks portfolios has been at least as good as that of the market in general.

Fixed-Income Securities

In an effort to stem the inflow of foreign currency, the Ministry of Finance, in October 1972, no longer permitted foreign investors to buy Japanese fixed-income securities unless paid for with the proceeds of a sale of other Japanese fixed-income securities. In the second half of 1973, it appeared that this restriction might be lifted in the face of a reversal of the foreign currency flow and a reduction of Japanese foreign currency reserves.

Corporate and government bonds in Japan have traditionally paid good yields, with a rate of about 7% to 8% during the second half of 1973 when the government had increased the cost of money to combat inflation. For an American investor these rates are, of course, not interesting enough as long as the Interest Equalization Tax is in force. And in 1973 the yen seemed slightly overvalued in relation to many other currencies rather than undervalued, so that another yen revaluation seemed remote.

In 1973 there was an upsurge in new convertible issues as the stock market had stopped its rise and new common share issues declined as a result. Yields of new convertible issues were slightly above 5% at that time.

Sources of Information

Some Japanese companies, especially those involved in international business, are publishing annual reports in English, but most Japanese annual reports are in Japanese and thus not accessible to the non-Japanese-speaking foreign investor. Moreover, Japanese accounting principles vary greatly from those applied in all other countries. For instance, Japanese corporations do not consolidate their financial statements, reporting earnings of only the parent company, excluding those of wholly or partly-owned subsidiaries. This often understates true earnings. However, the leading Japanese brokerage houses have stepped up their investment information tremendously, and a great deal of it is available in English. The research units of the leading Japanese brokerage houses are far larger than those of their United States counterparts of comparable size. The largest among them, *Nomura Research Institute of Technology,* organized in two subdivisions, *Japan Industry and Economic Division* and *Life Scientific Division*, employ together about 300 security analysts. In addition, *Nomura* has set up a special unit to interpret Japanese accounting principles for foreign investors, the *Overseas Institutional Research and Advisory Department,* which in September 1973, employed 15 security analysts who were all graduates of United States business schools. *Nikko,* the second largest brokerage house, has set up the *Nikko Research Center, Ltd.,* serving customers throughout the world.

The leading reference work in English on the larger Japanese publicly owned companies is *Diamond Japan Business Directory.* The directory includes financial data for each company.

The *Oriental Economist,* a monthly magazine, publishes a yearly *Japan Company Directory,* as well as the *Japan Economic Yearly.*

Two Japanese financial weeklies are published in English, and an investor in any part of the world can subscribe to their air mail editions—the *Japan Stock Journal* and the *Japan Economic Journal.*

Japanese Brokerage Houses in the United States

Daiwa Securities Co. America, Inc. / 100 Wall Street / New York, New
 York 10005 / and 250 East 1st Street / Los Angeles, California 90012
New Japan Securities International Inc. / 80 Pine Street / New York,
 New York 10005 / and 235 East 2nd Street / Los Angeles, California
 90012
Nikko Securities Co. International, Inc. / 1 Chase Manhattan Plaza /
 New York, New York 10005 / and 555 California Street / San Fran-
 cisco, California 94104 / and 250 East 1st Street / Los Angeles, Cali-
 fornia 90012
Nippon Kangyo Kakumaru Securities Co. Ltd. / 1 State Street Plaza /
 New York, New York 10004
Nomura Securities International, Inc. / 100 Wall Street / New York, New
 York 10005 / and 523 West 6th Street / Los Angeles, California
 90014 / and P.O. Box 3857 / Honolulu, Hawaii 96813
Sanyo Securities Co. Ltd. / 100 Wall Street / New York, New York 10005
Yamaichi International America, Inc. / 1 World Trade Center / New
 York, New York 10048 / and 321 East 2nd Street / Los Angeles, Cali-
 fornia 90012

Japanese Stocks Traded in the United States in the Form of American Depositary Receipts

Asterisk (*) denotes ADRs traded on the New York Stock Exchange;
all others are traded over-the-counter

Registered With S-1 Form
Canon, Inc. (photographic equip-
 ment)
Hitachi, Ltd. (electrical and elec-
 tronic equipment)
Honda Motor Co., Ltd. (automo-
 biles)
Kansai Electric Power Co., Inc.
 (electric utility)
Komatsu, Ltd. (earthmoving and
 construction machinery)
*Matsushita Electric Industrial Co.,
 Ltd.** (radio, TV, appliances)
Mitsubishi Heavy Industries Ltd.
 (aerospace, shipbuilding, indus-
 trial plants)
Mitsui & Co., Ltd. (trading com-
 pany)
Nippon Electric Co., Ltd. (elec-
 tronic equipment)
Sony Corporation* (radio, TV, ap-
 pliances)
*The Tokio Marine and Fire Insur-
 ance Co., Ltd.* (insurance)

Toshiba (electrical and electronic
 equipment)

Registered With S-12 Form
Ajinomoto Co., Ltd. (food prod-
 ucts)
Akai (tape recorders)
Asahi Glass Co., Ltd. (glass, chem-
 icals)
Bridgestone Tire Co., Ltd. (tires
 and rubber)
The Calpis Food Industry Co., Ltd.
 (soft drinks)
Daiichi Kangyo Bank, Ltd. (bank-
 ing)
Daiwa House Industry Co., Ltd.
 (prefabricated houses)
Daiwa Securities Co., Ltd. (stock-
 brokerage, investment banking)
Eisai Co., Ltd. (pharmaceuticals)
The Fuji Bank, Ltd. (banking)
Fuji Photo Film Co., Ltd. (photo-
 graphic film, Xerography)

Fujitsu Ltd. (telecommunication equipment, computers)

Hitachi Koki (industrial machinery)

The Industrial Bank of Japan, Ltd. (banking)

Japan Air Lines Co., Ltd. (airlines)

Kajima Corporation (construction, civil engineering)

Kao Soap Co., Ltd. (soap and detergents)

Kashiyama & Co., Ltd. (textiles, apparel, shoes)

Kawasaki Steel Corporation (steel)

Kirin Brewery Co., Ltd. (brewery)

Kobe Bank Ltd. (banking)

Kubota, Ltd. (agricultural and industrial machinery)

Kyowa Bank Ltd. (banking)

Marui Co., Ltd. (retailing)

Matsushita Electric Works Ltd. (lighting equipment, wiring devices)

The Mitsubishi Bank, Ltd. (banking)

Mitsubishi Corporation (trading companies)

Mitsubishi Estate Co., Ltd. (real estate)

The Mitsui Bank, Ltd. (banking)

Mitsukoshi, Ltd. (retailing)

Nikko Securities Co., Ltd. (stockbrokerage and investment banking)

Nippon Kangyo Bank, Ltd. (banking)

Nippon Optical (photographic cameras)

Nissan Motor Co., Ltd. (automobiles)

Nomura Securities Co., Ltd. (stockbrokerage and investment banking)

Pioneer Electronic Corporation (radio, TV, appliances)

Ricoh Co., Ltd. (office machines)

Saitama Bank Ltd. (banking)

Sanko Steamship Co., Ltd. (shipping)

The Sanwa Bank, Ltd. (banking)

Sharp Corporation (radio, TV, appliances, calculators)

Shiseido Co., Ltd. (cosmetics)

Shizuoka Bank (banking)

The Sumitomo Bank, Ltd. (banking)

Sumitomo Electric Industries, Ltd. (cables)

Taisei Construction Co., Ltd. (construction)

Taisho Marine and Fire Insurance Co. Ltd. (insurance)

Teijin Ltd. (synthetic fibers)

Tokai Bank Ltd. (banking)

Toray Industries, Inc. (synthetic fibers)

Toto Ltd. (sanitary equipment)

Toyota Motor Co., Ltd. (automobiles)

Yokohama Bank Ltd. (banking)

A Selection of Some Popular Japanese Stocks Not Available in the United States as ADRs

The Bank of Tokyo, Ltd. (banking)

Daiei Inc. (retailing)

Ishikawajima-Harima Heavy Industries Co., Ltd. (shipbuilding)

Ito Yokado (retailing)

Mitsui Shipbuilding and Engineering Co., Ltd. (shipbuilding)

New Japan Iron and Steel Corporation (steel)

Nippon Kokan, K. K. (steel and shipbuilding)

Nippon Musical Instruments Manufacturing Co., Ltd. (pianos, organs)

Toyo Kogyo Co., Ltd. (automobiles and rotary engines)

Sources of Information

The leading Japanese brokerage houses provide investment information in English.

Directory

The English language *Diamond Japan Business Directory* includes financial information on each company. It is available from:

Diamond Lead Co. / 4-2 Kasumigaseki 1-chome / Chiyoda-ku / Tokyo / and *OCS America Inc.* / 27-08 42nd Road / Long Island City, New York 11101

Japan Company Directory published by *Oriental Economist* / Nihon-bashi / Tokyo

English-Language Financial Publications

Japan Economic Journal / 9-5, 1-chome, Otemachi / Chiyoda-ku / Tokyo
Japan Stock Journal / C.P.O. Box 702 / Tokyo

8

AUSTRALIA
DOWN UNDER UPBEAT

A schoolboy joke considered risqué in 1930 posed the question: "How's a woman's love at her various ages?" Answer: "At 20, as hot as Africa; at 30, as wild as Asia; at 40, as technically accomplished as America; at 50, as shopworn as Europe; at 60, as remote from all traffic lanes as Australia."

There was a grain of truth in it when Australia, a country as large as the then 48 States of the Union, had only about 6 million people and was highly selective in the choice of her immigrants. Today the joke is passé. Foreigners are lining up at Australia's doorstep to leave their money for her goods and participate in her industries.

By 1973 Australia's population had reached about 13 million, growing at an annual rate of 2%, including more than 100,000 immigrants per year, and with plenty of space and resources to continue growing at a rapid rate. Australia is in the fortunate position of having many natural resources far in excess of her own needs, and some of them are in short supply elsewhere. The country is a major exporter of wool, wheat, meat, coal, iron ore, nickel, bauxite, and other minerals. From being almost completely dependent on imports of crude oil, Australia in 1973 became about 80% self-sufficient in petroleum products. Together with huge coal deposits, these new oil reserves make Australia relatively immune to the energy crisis.

On October 3, 1973 the Australian dollar (A$) was valued at U.S. $1.49.

Per capita, Australia has accumulated more foreign currency reserves than probably any other country in the world, except the Arab oil sheikdoms—more than U.S. $6 billion in mid-1973. After the longest time of being pegged to the American dollar, the Australian dollar (A$) was finally revalued *vis-à-vis* the American dollar, making it worth about U.S. $1.49 in 1973.

Loosening United States Ties

The divorce from the American dollar was more than a fiscal act—it was a visual evidence of the fact that Australia, like several other former American camp followers, had decided in the crucial years of the decline of the American dollar to loosen its ties to the American fiscal and political systems. It was also one of the first, almost symbolical acts of a newly elected Labor government which, after 23 years out of power, had run its election campaign on the promise to "buy Australia back for the Australians."

Discovered relatively late in the course of European exploratory travels after Columbus, Australia was first settled late in the 18th century by small numbers of Britishers. It is now governed as a Federation of States with a constitution fashioned after the British parliamentary system.

Until World War II, Australia, limiting its immigration mostly to Anglo-Saxons, remained glaringly underpopulated in an increasingly overcrowded world. As Japan started its expansionary thrust in the 1930s, Australians became increasingly concerned about their relative population vacuum and the 10,000 miles between themselves and the arms of their mother country, England. They began to form closer ties to the United States, and throughout World War II, the Korean War, and the Vietnamese War, Australia remained the United States's staunchest ally and supporter in the Pacific political and military theater.

Americans also began to play an increasingly important role as private investors in Australia's industrial and natural resource developments. These American investments accelerated greatly in the late 1960s and the early 1970s until by 1973 they reached an estimated total U.S. $5 billion, or about 42% of an estimated total of U.S. $12 billion in foreign direct investments. This put British investments, for the first time, in second place, a few percentage points behind the United States. In 1973 about 63% of the Australian mining industry was foreign owned, and about 22% of the manufacturing industries.

A New Broom

The new Labor government has announced that it will reverse this trend and reduce foreign investments in Australia. Newspapers, broadcasting, and domestic airline companies are closed to foreign investments. Foreign ownership in life insurance companies and uranium mines has been limited to specific percentages. Other industries, including the finance industry, may be added to this list. Foreign controlling interest in an Australian company always needs government approval. Land purchases by foreigners may be restricted (large tracts have already been bought by Americans for cattle raising).

In 1973, it was difficult to know how the new government and its measures would affect the Australian stock markets over the next few years. No matter where an investor's personal sympathies lie in the choice between a government labeled socialist and one labeled conservative, he must allow for the fact that the former often has a dampening effect on stock prices, and this has been the case in Australia in 1973. If it is more concerned with redistributing wealth than creating new wealth, a socialist government may even depress the economy. The Australian Labor Party, however, since its previous tour of duty in the late 1940s when it tried unsuccessfully to nationalize the banking industry, may have changed its pholosophy somewhat. Its proposed "national capitalism" does not seem to include state ownership of any now private industry. In fact, Australian banks may be the main beneficiaries of the new "buy back Australia" program since they will have to raise much of the money needed. Reportedly, some bankers, brokers, and businessmen concerned with the easy-going attitude of the former Liberal government towards foreign control of Australian resources and finance lent a hand, or funds, to elect the Labor government.

Banks and Bank Stocks

Australian banks occupy a particularly strong position in the economy. Like the banks in Canada, but unlike United States banks, they are not restricted in their geographical range of operations. They may have nation-wide branch systems. This resulted in the emergence of only five publicly owned Australian "trading" banks, plus one government owned commercial bank, the *Commonwealth Bank*. Together, the six handle more than 90% of the country's commercial and checking account deposits and about 75% of the savings accounts. The largest of the publicly owned banks, *The Bank of New South Wales,* has more than 1200 branch offices inside and outside Australia. The other four are the *Australia and New Zealand Banking Group Ltd., The National Bank of Australasia Ltd., The Commercial Bank of Australia Ltd.,* and *The Commercial Banking Company of Sydney Ltd.* Australian banks offer a wide range of services, including commercial and private deposit and savings accounts, commercial and consumer finance, merchant banking, mutual fund management and sales, portfolio management, investment services, and even travel services. Their excellent earnings from 1968 to 1973 were even better than reported because Australian banks have developed the practice of allocating substantial unspecified amounts to reserve every year. Their stock prices went counter to the general trend of the Australian market during 1970 and 1971, when many mining and industrial stocks depressed the combined stock averages. All five bank stocks are traded in London as well as on the main Australian markets. There are no restrictions for portfolio investments in banks by foreigners, as distinct from buying a controlling interest.

Stock Exchanges

The combined Australian market index advanced strongly in 1967 and 1968, carried away by new oil, gas, and nickel discoveries and some exuberant speculation in natural resources stocks. It lost half of its gains again in 1971, and was at about the same level in August 1973, following the second Australian dollar revaluation that year. Between 1945 and 1972, the combined stock market index increased fivefold from about 100 to 500; trailing, however, the rise of the gross national product. In 1972-1973, the gross manufacturing product was rising about $3\frac{1}{2}\%$ in real terms; and farm production was rising at about the same rate, after having lost ground for several years because of ample world supply and falling prices—a situation that was drastically reversed in 1973.

The two leading Australian stock exchanges are Melbourne and Sydney. There are smaller exchanges in Adelaide, Brisbane, Hobart, and Perth. All of them operate under the same trading procedures established by the Australian Associated Stock Exchanges. Following a decision in January 1972, to adopt common listings, all listed Australian companies can be traded on any one of the exchanges. At the end of September 1973, listings on the Melbourne Stock Exchange included 1156 industrial common stocks, 419 mining stocks, 293 preferred issues, and some 2300 fixed-income securities, with a total market value of A$ 32.5 billion (U.S. $49 billion). The total market value of the industrial common stock issues was A$ 14.7 billion (U.S. $22 billion), and that of the mining issues A$ 4.8 billion (U.S. $7.2 billion).

After a record number of 107 new issues in 1970, there were only 27 new listings with a nominal value of A$ 97 million in the 1973 business year, plus new share issues of already listed companies with a nominal value of A$ 859 million (U.S. $1.288 billion). It is expected that under the new government policy of Australian ownership the new issue market will increase.

By United States standards, the Australian stock markets are very narrow. Only perhaps 30 to 50 of the common stock issues are traded actively enough to be of interest to the foreign investor who is not actually on the scene. Relatively inactive issues always involve the rist of excessive price movements or of not easily finding buyers or sellers at any price.

Where to Buy Australian Stocks

Most of the investment business in Australia is handled by brokerage houses which deal directly with individual and institutional investors and banks and trade with each other on the floor of the exchanges. Some of the Australian banks provide investment advisory and portfolio management and custodial services for investors. Probably the most active in this area is *The National Bank of Australasia Ltd.,* which has published an excellent booklet on portfolio investments in Australia. The bank has an office in New York, which cannot directly execute investment orders but which will refer an interested investor to its Melbourne office and provide him with published investment information. Other Australian banks with representative offices in New York are *The Bank of New South Wales, Australia and New Zealand Banking Group Ltd.,* and *Commercial Banking Company of Sydney Ltd.*

In 1973, there were no Australian brokers established in the United States and an American investor would have to contact them directly in Australia (see listing at the end of this chapter). A few Australian brokers have offices in London. Some Australian shares, especially mining shares, can be traded in London.

A United States investor can also buy Australian shares through one of the American brokerage houses trading in foreign stocks (see listings at the end of Chapter 1).

Australian Stocks Traded in the United States

In 1973, at least four Australian issues were traded on the United States over-the-counter market in the form of American Depositary Receipts, including American-owned shares on which the Interest Equalization Tax has been paid. They were *Woodside-Burmah Oil N.L.,* a mining company, *G. J. Coles & Co. Ltd.,* and *The Myer Emporium Ltd.,* two retail operations, and the largest of all Australian companies, *The Broken Hill Proprietary Co. Ltd.*

Originally a mining company, *Broken Hill Proprietary* now makes practically all the steel used in Australia; in a joint venture with *Esso* it produces a large portion of the oil and natural gas consumed in Australia; it mines all the iron ore, manganese, and coal it needs; it owns large bauxite deposits and has access to other minerals; it does heavy manufacturing, including shipbuilding and the fabrication of mining equipment; and, finally, it is involved in the development of a new internal combustion engine together with its inventor, Ralph Sarich, who claims that his engine, as is being claimed for the Wankel engine, will one day make the reciprocating engine obsolete. *Broken Hill Proprietary,* like many publicly owned Australian companies, publishes no sales figures, but earnings peaked out in 1973 as the result of a number of pricing problems created by the government price regulations for steel and oil, as well as a result of the revaluation of the Australian dollar which cut into export earnings. Nevertheless, long-range, *Broken Hill Proprietary* is likely to remain a leading factor in the development of Australia's industry and natural resources.

Oil Production

After many decades of search, Australia finally made sufficient oil discoveries in the late 1960s to reduce its dependence on foreign crude oil supplies from 90% in 1969 to only about 30% in 1973. Refinery capacity has also been increased to such an extent that practically no petroleum products are imported in refined form. In addition to *The Broken Hill Proprietary Co. Ltd., Ampol Petroleum Ltd.* is an Australian owned petroleum company, with a sales volume in 1972 of A$ 164 million (U.S. $245 million). It has an interlocking ownership with *Ampol Exploration Ltd.,* an oil exploration company, with about A$ 5 million (U.S. $7.5 million) reported revenue. The other listed petroleum distributor, *H. C. Sleigh, Ltd.,* is 23% owned by *Caltex Petroleum* of the United States. Other Australian oil activities are carried on by foreign oil companies.

Mining Stocks

Mining stocks, once of primary interest to investors in Australian securities, were the main depressants on the combined Australian stock index in 1970 and 1971; and many of them also performed poorer than the market in 1972 and 1973, with the metals and minerals index declining, while most other indices advanced. Many mining companies, like many other Australian companies, do not report sales figures, but on the basis of earnings, here are some of the larger ones: *Conzinc Riotinto of Australia Ltd.* (iron ore, aluminum, lead, zinc), 81% owned by *British Rio Tinto Zinc Corporation Ltd.; MIM (Holdings) Ltd.* (silver, lead, copper, zinc); *Western Mining Corporation Ltd.* (nickel, gold, aluminum); *Peko Wallsend Ltd.* (copper, coal mining); *NBHC Holdings Ltd.* (lead, silver, zinc); and *Broken Hill South Ltd.* (copper).

The most notorious Australian mining stock is *Poseidon Ltd.* It caused a world-wide investment sensation when in 1968 its price shot up from A$ 1 to A$ 250 on the news of large nickel discoveries, but it came all the way down to A$ 4 again by 1973 as operating losses piled up. There is no question that many of the Australian mines contain riches that will be much in demand in the years to come, but to evaluate their returns in terms of their stock price is a specialist's game.

Industrial Stocks

A far steadier growth picture can be found among the Australian industrial stocks, representing now about 75% of the capitalization of all Australian common shares. The growth of the population has enlarged the market for industrial products to such an extent that it has become economical to manufacture products locally that formerly were imported. In 1973, there were about 64,000 plants in Australia in 200 different industries. Manufacturing contributed about 30% of the gross national product and employed about 30% of the working population. Distribution and service industries also perked up. Many of the industrial and consumer companies outperformed the market in the years 1970 to 1973, among them: *Allied Mills Ltd.,* (flour milling, bakeries, edible oils); *Australian Consolidated Industries Ltd.* (glass, plastics, engineering); *Carlton and United Breweries Ltd.* (brewery); *G. J. Coles & Co. Ltd.* (retail), *F & T Industries Ltd.* (floor coverings, fibers); *Hooker Corporation Ltd.* (real estate, building, mutual funds, hotels); *The Myer Emporium Ltd.* (retail); *Pio-*

neer Concrete Services Ltd. (pre-mixed concrete); and *Thomas Nationwide Transport Ltd.* (freight transportation).

Investment Trusts

Although somewhat limited in their portfolio selections because of the narrowness of the Australian stock market, both closed-end and open-end funds (unit trusts) have achieved a certain success in Australia. While operated by management companies, many of the investment trusts are associated with Australian trading banks, which actively sell the shares. Unit trusts have a particular attraction for Australian investors because income, including capital gains, is not taxable in the hands of the trust, which can thereby distribute the maximum of earnings. The unit trust shareholders must, of course, pay taxes on the dividends received. There is no capital gains tax in Australia on any securities held longer than the tax year, which runs from July 1 to June 30. Many of the unit trusts have a substantial portfolio of high-yielding fixed-income securities.

Fixed-Income Securities

One of the more interesting features of the Australian bond market, especially for the smaller investor, are Commonwealth bonds whose rates of interest and redemption prices rise at stated intervals during the life of the issue. Rates are usually marginally better than the current short-term bond rates. An investor is limited to a maximum holding of A$ 50,000 per issue. Together with the firmness of the Australian dollar, such bonds are an excellent protection against inflation for anyone living in Australia or wanting to settle there. Otherwise, Australian fixed-income securities are of limited interest to the United States resident since rates are generally somewhat lower than in several other countries.

Regulations and Taxes

A non-resident of the Sterling area must have approval from the Australian Exchange Control Authority before he can buy an Australian security. This is, in most cases, a formality which takes about 24 hours, and is generally handled by the broker or bank serving the investor. The permit number is usually endorsed on the stock certificate. All Australian stock certificates are registered in the name of the owner and sent by the registrar directly to the owner, not the broker.

Thus, there can be no "street name" accounts as in the United States, where an investor can leave his certificate in the hands of his broker and borrow money on it for purchases "on margin." An investor in Australian stocks can, however, appoint a nominee—a bank or a custodial service—for safekeeping of his securities. For a non-resident investor this is, no doubt, the most practical thing to do. A custodian will take care of all necessary formalities in buying, selling, and registering the shares; and he will collect dividends and interest due and exercise or sell rights in accordance with standing instructions from the investor. When a non-resident of Australia wants to repatriate the proceeds from the sale of Australian securities, a permit from the Exchange Control Authority is needed; but again, this is, in most cases, a formality, attended to by the broker or the custodian.

There is a withholding tax on both dividends and interest on Australian securities held by non-residents. The tax on dividends is 15% for residents of countries with which Australia has a double taxation agreement—the United States, Canada, New Zealand, the United Kingdom, Singapore, and Japan. For residents of all other countries the withholding tax on dividends is 30%. On interest received from Australian securities the tax is 10% for all non-residents. Certain government bonds are exempt from withholding tax.

Sources of Information

Disclosure by Australian companies is a good deal more limited than that by American companies, but improvements are in progress. Both the Sydney and the Melbourne Stock Exchanges publish information sheets on many listed companies. Other worthwhile publications, available from the publications departments of the Melbourne and Sydney Stock Exchanges, include *Australian Shareholders Guide, Jobson's Yearbook of Public Companies, Jobson's Mining Digest Yearbook,* and *Australian Securities Markets.* Most brokers and some of the trading banks publish information on specific Australian securities and the market in general.

The leading financial publications are the *Australian Financial Review* (daily), and the weeklies the *Bulletin* and the *National Times.* Other publications of interest to investors include the *Australian Stock Exchange Journal* (monthly), *Rydges Digest* (monthly), and the *Australian Miner* (weekly).

Several Australian daily newspapers have good business coverage, including *The Australian,* the *Daily Telegraph* in Sydney, the *Sydney Morning Herald,* and *The Age,* Melbourne.

Some of the Larger Member Firms of the Melbourne Stock Exchange

Clarke & Co. / 365 Little Collins Street / Melbourne
Davies & Dalziel / 408 Collins Street / Melbourne
A.C. Goode & Co. / 395 Collins Street / Melbourne
Guest & Bell / 446 Collins Street / Melbourne
McCaughan Dyson & Co. / 412 Collins Street / Melbourne
Wm. Noall & Son / 461 Bourke Street / Melbourne
Ian Potter & Co. / 325 Collins Street / Melbourne
Wallace H. Smith & Co. / 351 Collins Street / Melbourne
Vinton Smith, Dougall, Grant Reed & Co. / 351 Collins Street / Melbourne
J. B. Were & Son / 379 Collins Street / Melbourne

Some of the Larger Members of the Sydney Stock Exchange

Constable & Bain / 6-10 O'Connell Street / Sydney
Clarence Degenhardt & Co. / 117 Pitt Street / Sydney
Hattersley & Maxwell / 105 Pitt Street (2nd Floor) Sydney
Jackson, Graham Moore & Partners / 56 Pitt Street / Sydney
Ralph W. King & Yuill / 33 Bligh Street / Sydney
Lionel A. McFadyen & Co. / 20 O'Connell Street / Sydney
A.D. Meares & Bishop / 33 Bligh Street / Sydney
Ord Minnett, T.J. Thompson & Partners / 34 Tower Building, Australia Square / Sydney
Patrick Partners / Patrick House, 5 Gresham Street / Sydney
Pring Dean & Co. / 20 O'Connell Street / Sydney
William Tilley, Hudson, Evans & Co. / 15-19 Bent Street / Sydney
A.B.S. White & Co. / 82 Pitt Street / Sydney

Four Leading Banks Handling Investment Business

Australia and New Zealand Banking Group Ltd. / 351 Collins Street / Melbourne
(New York Office: 63 Wall Street / New York, New York 10005)
The Bank of New South Wales / 60 Martin Place / Sydney
(New York Office: 270 Park Avenue / New York, New York 10022)
Commercial Banking Company of Sydney Ltd. / 343 George Street / Sydney
(New York Office: 450 Park Avenue / New York, New York 10022)
The National Bank of Australasia Ltd. / 271-285 Collins Street / Melbourne
(New York Office: 375 Park Avenue / New York, New York 10022)

Most Actively Traded Australian Industrial Stocks

A.V. Jennings Industries (Australia) Ltd. (builders, property developers)
Australian Consolidated Industries Ltd. (glass, plastics, engineering)
Carlton and United Breweries Ltd. (brewery)
Dunlop Rubber Australia Ltd. (tires and rubber)
F & T Industries Ltd. (floor coverings, fibers)
*G.J. Coles & Co. Ltd.** (retailing)

Hooker Corporation Ltd. (real estate, building, mutual funds, hotels)

I.A.C. (Holdings) Ltd. (installment loan company)

Mayne Nickless Ltd. (security transport and equipment)

Pioneer Concrete Services Ltd. (concrete)

Repco Ltd. (automotive parts, machine tools)

The Bank of New South Wales (banking)

The Broken Hill Proprietary Co. Ltd.* (steel, oil, heavy manufacturing)

Thomas Nationwide Transport Ltd. (freight transport)

The Herald & Weekly Times Ltd. (newspaper publishing)

The Myer Emporium Ltd.* (retailing)

The National Bank of Australasia Ltd. (banking)

Swan Brewery Company Ltd. (brewery)

The Colonial Sugar Refining Company Ltd. (sugar)

Most Actively Traded Australian Mining Stocks

Broken Hill South Ltd.
Bougainville Mining Ltd.
Conzinc Riotinto of Australia Ltd.
Hamersley Holdings Ltd.
MIM (Holdings) Ltd.
NBHC Holdings Ltd.

Peko Wallsend Ltd.
Poseidon Ltd.
Utah Mining Australia Ltd.
Western Mining Corporation Ltd.
Woodside-Burmah Oil N.L.*
Woodside Oil N.L.

* Traded in the United States over-the-counter in the form of American Depositary Receipts.

Partial List of Australian Unit Trusts

Australian Capital Fund Inc. / 411 Collins Street / Melbourne 3000, Victoria

Australian Fund of Funds / 19 London Circuit, 4th Floor / Canberra 2600, A.C.T.

Australian Income Fund / 411 Collins Street / Melbourne 3000, Victoria

Australis Investment Co. Ltd. / 50 Young Street / Sydney 2000, New South Wales

Capel National Fund Inc. / 6th Floor, 379 Collins Street / Melbourne 3000, Victoria

CNF Income Trust / *CNF Investors Trust* / *CNF Midway Trust* / Capel Court, 379 Collins Street / Melbourne 3000, Victoria

Cowan Capital Fund Inc. / *Cowan High Income Fund Inc.* / *Cowan Mutual Fund Inc.* / *Cowan Natural Resources Fund Inc.* / 457 Little Collins Street / Melbourne 3000, Victoria

Darling Dual Fund Ltd. / *Darling Fund* / 50 Young Street / Sydney 2000, New South Wales

Delfin Australian Fund, Inc. / 16 O'Connell Street / Sydney 2000, New South Wales

Enterprise Growth Fund / 1st Floor, 121 London Circuit / Canberra 2601, A.C.T.

Fifth Universal Flexible Trust / Universal House, 25 Elizabeth Street / Melbourne 3000, Victoria

First Australian Growth and Income Fund / 84 Pitt Street, 9th Floor Sydney 2000, New South Wales

Fourth Federal Flexible Trust / 4th Floor, 351 Collins Street / Melbourne 3000, Victoria

Intra-Pacific Unit Trust Fund / Stock Exchange House, 351 Collins Street / Melbourne 3000, Victoria

Investors Income and Growth Fund / *Investors Maximum Income Fund* / 411 Collins Street / Melbourne 3000, Victoria

London Australia Investment Co., Ltd. / Victoria House, 44 Hunter Street / Sydney 2000, New South Wales

Scottie Balanced Fund / *Scottie Capital Growth Fund* / *Scottie Income Fund* / 4th Floor, 351 Collins Street / Melbourne 3000, Victoria

Second Australian Growth and Income Fund / 84 Pitt Street, 9th Floor / Sydney 2000, New South Wales

Second CNF Income Trust / Capel Court, 379 Collins Street / Melbourne 3000, Victoria

Second Federal Flexible Trust / 4th Floor, 351 Collins Street / Melbourne 3000, Victoria

Share Australia Fund / 40th Level, Australia Square / Sydney 2000, New South Wales

Third CNF Income Trust / Capel Court, 379 Collins Street / Melbourne 3000, Victoria

Third Federal Flexible Trust / 4th Floor, 351 Collins Street / Melbourne 3000, Victoria

Third Universal Flexible Trust / Universal House, 25 Elizabeth Street / Melbourne 3000, Victoria

Universal Flexible Trust-Balanced Fund No. 1 / *Universal Flexible Trust-Capital Growth Fund No. 1* / *Universal Flexible Trust-Earnings Fund No. 1* / Universal House, 25 Elizabeth Street / Melbourne 3000, Victoria

Wales Unit Investment Limited Group / The Wales House, 66 Pitt Street / Sydney 2000, New South Wales

Sources of Information

Investment reviews of individual companies are available from The Stock Exchange of Melbourne Ltd. / Stock Exchange House, 351 Collins Street / Melbourne 3000

Publication Department, The Sydney Stock Exchange Ltd. / 13-15 O'Connell Street / Sydney

Also available from the Sydney and Melbourne Stock Exchanges: *Australian Shareholders Guide, Jobson's Yearbook of Public Companies, Jobson's Mining Digest Yearbook,* and *Australian Securities Markets.*

Financial Publications

The Australian Financial Review (daily) / Broadway / Sydney (New York Address: 1501 Broadway, New York, New York) *The Australian Miner* (weekly) / 36 Carrington Street / Sydney

Australian Stock Exchange Journal (monthly) / P.O. Box 3186, GPO / Sydney

The Bulletin (weekly) / P.O. Box 4088 / Sydney

The National Times (weekly) / Jones Street / Broadway / Sydney

Rydges Digest (monthly) / 74 Clarence Street / Sydney

Newspapers with Good Business Coverage

The Age / 250 Spencer Street / Melbourne 3000, Victoria

The Australian / 2 Holt Street / Sydney

The Daily Telegraph / 168 Castlereigh / Sydney 2000, New South Wales

The Sydney Morning Herald / 235 Jones Street / Broadway / Sydney

9

HONG KONG AND SINGAPORE
TWO TREASURE ISLANDS

The Hong Kong and Singapore markets, in 1971 and 1972, shot up like Roman candles and came down just as fast in 1973. It was strictly a game for local crap shooters.

Hong Kong

The index of the leading exchange, the Hong Kong Stock Exchange, started out at 329 in January 1972, reached 1700 by March 1973, and was down again to below 600 by the end of September 1973. Some days, more than 30 million shares changed hands. Stock prices as high as 300 times reported earnings were common.

This sudden outburst was caused by a number of factors: a sudden influx of overseas Chinese money on the run from the crumbling American dollar; a prospering export business in garments, textiles, electronics, toys, and other light industrial products; soaring real estate prices on a tight little island; and the inveterate gambling spirit of the Chinese. A Chinese coolie carrying rice bags on his back 12 hours a day thinks nothing of gambling one-month's earnings away in a few hours in a game of dice, bingo, or poker. When the stock market took off, practically everybody threw in his chips, from the panhandler who was arrested while listening to the latest stock reports on his transistor radio to the head of a large Chinese trading house.

On October 3, 1973 the Singapore dollar (S$) was valued at U.S. 42.9¢ and the Hong Kong dollar (HK$) was valued at U.S. 20¢.

Yet with the rapprochement between Mainland China on one hand and the United States and Japan on the other, Hong Kong may very well have become a place for serious long-range investments rather than a gambling casino. The one Damoclean threat that had hung over the British Crown Colony for the past 25 years—that of a take over or throttling by the Chinese Communists—seems to have been removed almost indefinitely; and thanks to its strategic position at what is at present the main entry point to Mainland China, it should greatly benefit from the increasing traffic in people, goods, and money. Hong Kong has traditionally played an important role as regional warehouse, transshipment, and distribution center.

Former White Man's Burden

Hong Kong is an anachronistic leftover from the colonial days when the British carried the "white man's burden" to all corners of the earth and returned with a sackful of £s to retire in Bath or Bournemouth. The 32-square-mile island of Victoria, on which downtown Hong Kong is located, was ceded by a weak, isolation-minded China, not entirely voluntarily, to the British at the end of the Opium War in 1842. A much larger, 360-square-mile area on the mainland was leased by the British in 1898 for 99 years. For reasons of their own, the Chinese Communists left both the island and the mainland portion of Kowloon unmolested when they drove the Nationalist Chinese into the sea in 1949. Hong Kong is still a Crown Colony ruled, in theory, by the Queen of England, through a Governor. Hong Kong became a key refugee haven and transient point for Chinese who escaped the communist regime. Its population increased from about 3 million in 1961 to over 4 million in 1972. Hong Kong also became a focal banking and trading point for overseas Chinese and others doing business in the Far East. For all practical purposes, it became the only point of entry to, and exit from, Mainland China for members of non-communist countries. It became a major producer of light industrial products made with low-cost labor, as well as an important traffic hub for air and shipping lines. Foreign visitors— tourists and businessmen—exceeded 1 million in 1972, an increase of about 20% over the previous year. One of the best indicators of economic growth are exports, which increased by 432% between 1960 and 1972, from HK$ 2.867 billion (U.S. $572 million) to HK$ 15.245 billion (U.S. $3.05 billion).

Because of the complete impracticability of controlling the beehive-like economic and financial activities of some 4 million people, many of them operating only with an abacus and a few brush strokes, if they keep any records at all, Hong Kong is probably also the freest of all economies in the world (but also one with some big gaps in economic statistics). There is nothing one cannot do with money—receive it from anywhere, send it anywhere, exchange it into any other money or value, and buy anything one wants from anywhere in the world, without having to report any transaction to anybody. Nobody knows how much money is there. Hong Kong's licensed banks, at the end of 1972, had about U.S. $1.4 billion in demand and time deposits, after an increase of the money supply in 1972 of about 40%. In addition, the Hong Kong government and the banks had about U.S. $2.5 billion in reserves in England. How much more there was in the hands of merchants, unlicensed bankers, and the general public is impossible to say.

Stock Exchange Frenzy

Even though the Hong Kong Stock Exchange has been around since 1891, it did not really come alive until the end of the 1960s to start a freewheeling life that was almost unequalled in recent stock market history (Singapore and Brazil being other contenders). The trading boom got so much out of hand that the Hong Kong Stock Exchange could no longer handle it all, and three competitive exchanges sprang up—the Far East, Kam Ngan, and Kowloon exchanges. (But a fifth one was stopped from opening by the government.) These exchanges traded many of the same issues that were traded on the Hong Kong Stock Exchange, as well as new, unseasoned issues that could not find a place on the Hong Kong Exchange, which has rationed the admission of new issues.

The situation became so chaotic, with many malpractices being reported, that the Legislative Council of Hong Kong, in 1973, prepared the Securities Bill and Protection of Investors Bill that would require the compulsory registration of brokers and investment advisors, and establish a securities commission with statutory powers to police the market.

Almost 200 issues are listed on the Hong Kong Stock Exchange. The most actively traded stock is that of the venerable *Hong Kong and Shanghai Banking Corporation,* which for all practical purposes has acted as Hong Kong's central bank and printed most of Hong Kong's bank notes. It also does about 60% of all Hong Kong's com-

mercial and private banking business, and it could not help but benefit from the financial boom. Its earnings more than doubled between
1969 and 1972, and its stock price more than quadrupled between
1970 and 1972.

Another prestigious Hong Kong enterprise that has its roots in the
pre-World War I old-China-hand days is *Jardine, Matheson & Co.,
Ltd.,* an export and import trading company involved in banking and
finance and many other ventures, including distribution, transportation, and real estate. Its earnings and stock price also received a great
boost from the Hong Kong boom.

The most popular stocks in Hong Kong were those of real estate
developers and property managing firms. With space so obviously
limited, real estate prices, even after a temporary reaction from excess speculation, can only go up over the long pull. Nevertheless, in
1973 the choice of sound and seasoned stocks was limited, and all
others were really only suitable for investors on the scene.

Information Limited

Information published by Hong Kong-based firms is scanty. Many
of them do not even reveal sales figures. The Hong Kong Stock Exchange publishes a certain amount of information, including a
Monthly Gazette, a year book, and research bulletins on some of the
leading companies. Foreign brokerage houses operating in Hong
Kong are the most likely sources for a foreign investor, and they can
also handle his transactions. An investor wanting to take a shot at
the Hong Kong market may also want to consider a Hong Kong-
based investment fund, managed by one of the reputable local financial houses, such as *Jardine Securities Ltd.* At least they have a close-
up view of what is going on in the fast moving game.

Singapore More Sedate

In spite of the same roller-coaster stock market action, the investment scene appears somewhat more solid in Singapore than in Hong
Kong, based as it is on more diversified manufacturing and banking
activities.

For anyone but the romanticizing armchair traveller, Singapore, in
the pre-World War II colonial days, was known as by far the dullest
city in the Far East. Founded in 1819 as a British naval outpost on a
225-square-mile tropical island fringed by mudflats and mangrove
swamps, it had no history and local color to build on. It was popu-

lated by a small band of British bureaucrats, naval men, and merchants, and by a much larger contingent of hard-working Chinese coolies, shopkeepers, and traders. The spirit was clean, honest, and puritanical, at least on the surface—ladies of light virtue were kept under wraps—but the dullness of the place, according to the late British novelist W. Somerset Maugham, drove some colonials to such desperation that like some bored American suburbanites they resorted to wife swapping for kicks (after having had dinner in formal white dinner jackets, of course).

The spirit of hard work, honesty, and puritanism has carried into the modern island state of Singapore, making it one of the most reliable and rewarding places in all of South and East Asia to build up industry and deposit, borrow, and invest money. In 1972 and 1973, the gross national product in real terms was rising at a rate of better than 10%, the budget was balanced, and foreign currency reserves were building up at an annual rate of about 30% a year to over U.S. $2½ billion in mid-1973. The per capita income of the 2.2 million multiracial people—75% Chinese, 14% Malay, 8% Indian, plus 3% others—is the second highest in Asia, following Japan.

In a world that has lived with a thousands-of-years-old tradition that considered thriving cities desirable prizes to be conquered, Singapore has the unique distinction of having been expelled from the country to which it belonged. After the departure of the British Raj, Singapore, in 1963, became part of the Federation of Malaysia, which occupies the Malay peninsula south of Thailand and part of the island of Borneo. The Federation was to be peacefully multiracial, but friction soon built up between the Singapore Chinese and the Malays, who made up the majority of the other parts of the Federation. Views on economics also diverged widely. The hard-working Singaporeans objected to the Federal government's policy of handouts to the poorest in the Federation, clinging to the old-fashioned Chinese notion that it is better to teach a man to fish than to give him a fish. To avoid bloody clashes, Singapore was asked to leave the Federation in 1965.

Booming Economy

Under the very energetic prime minister, Lee Kuan Yew, who had been in power since 1959, Singapore quickly built up its economy and ability to defend itself. Foreign direct investments were encouraged, and by the end of 1972, they had reached an estimated

S$ 2 billion (U.S. $860 million), about one-third of it from United States firms, followed by the British, Dutch, and Japanese. Much of it was in the petroleum industry—refining, exploration, and manufacture of drilling, production, and offshore equipment. But many other industries were also developed, including electronics, photographic, pharmaceuticals, chemicals, shipbuilding, construction, etc. In addition, Singapore built up its traditional role as an international trading, shipping, and ship repair center.

Thriving Banking

One of the greatest boosts to the economy was the decision to make Singapore the banking capital of Southeast Asia. Banking deposits were encouraged by guaranteeing bank secrecy and abolishing the withholding tax earned on deposits and other interest producing investments made by non-residents. This brought in a flood of money from Chinese and others in neighboring states. Singapore banks also "invented" Asia dollar financing. Asia dollars are the same thing as Eurodollars (see Chapter 20), namely American dollars owned by non-residents of the United States. By amending tax and exchange control regulations, the Singapore government made it possible for Singapore and foreign banks setting up business in Singapore to conduct international financing operations from Singapore, thereby attracting to the city state about U.S. $2 to $3 billion of the $100 billion Eurodollars floating around the world.

Fly-Away Stock Market

This booming economy also reflected itself in the Singapore Stock Market, which, like the Hong Kong market, in 1972, ran away in a speculative fever. In 1973 it came down again to more realistic levels. In 1972 Singapore dropped all restrictions against foreign portfolio investments, thereby putting it on the map of international investment markets. Income from portfolio investments can freely be taken out of the country, and the original capital can be repatriated if the securities are sold.

Under a government act of December 1970, the Singapore market became self-regulatory, following the examples of the United Kingdom and Australia. It is government policy to develop the market into a good source for new capital and to encourage listings on the exchange, both by foreign and domestic firms. In 1973, less than 100 of the about 300 listings were of domestic companies. A good many of the

Singapore companies are partly owned by foreign parent companies, mostly British. Trading volume in most of them was relatively modest, so that caution is necessary in buying and selling shares.

Common Stock

Like in many other fast developing countries, the banks in Singapore offer one of the simplest and soundest opportunities to invest in the growing economy as a whole. All leading Singapore banks showed rapidly rising earnings in the years 1971 to 1973, including the *Development Bank of Singapore Ltd., Malayan Banking Bhd., Oversea-Chinese Banking Corporation, Ltd., Singapore International Merchant Bankers Ltd.,* and *United Overseas Bank Ltd.*

Another way to participate in the Singapore economy on a broad scale is through *Sime Darby Holdings Ltd. Sime Darby* is one of the old-time British trading and commodity firms, and while still very active in trading, the holding company today has a stake in the manufacture of tractors and other heavy equipment. Another widely diversified trading, shipping, and manufacturing organization is *Inchcape Bhd.*

Natural rubber and tin represented the main wealth of Malaya in colonial days, and with natural resources becoming scarce in the 1970s, they may again play an important role. The British *Dunlop Holdings Ltd.* has two subsidiaries listed on the Singapore Stock Exchange—*Dunlop Estates Bhd.,* a rubber plantation company, and *Dunlop Malaysian Industries, Bhd.,* a tire manufacturer. Other rubber plantation companies listed in Singapore include *Batu Kawan Bhd.* and *Kempas (Malaya) Bhd.* Tin mines include *Aokam Tin Bhd.* and *Berjuntai Tin Dredging Bhd.* while *Straits Trading Co. Ltd.* is a tin smelter.

Real estate development and construction companies thrived greatly in the economic boom, but there may be a slow-down, especially in the hotel field. Some of the leading listed companies include *Bukit Sembawang Estates Ltd., Central Properties Ltd., Faber Union Ltd., Overseas Union Enterprise Ltd.,* and *Singapore Land and Investment Co. Ltd.*

Where to Buy Singapore Stock

All investment business in Singapore is handled by brokers who trade on the exchange and deal directly with the public. In 1973 there were no Singapore brokers or banks represented in the United States.

An American investor must go either to one of the American brokers handling foreign business (see listings at the end of Chapter 1), or communicate directly with a Singapore broker (see listings at the end of this chapter). Some London brokers, as well as some Japanese brokers, also have expertise in Singapore stocks.

Dividend Tax

Singapore companies pay a 40% tax against current and future dividends. The investor receives a tax credit with his dividend check, and this credit can be offset against his Singapore income tax. A United States resident can offset the tax against his taxable income reported on his Federal income tax return. There is no withholding tax on interest earned by a foreign investor from Singapore fixed-income securities.

Limits to Growth?

Being but an island, Singapore's industrial growth has its natural limits. In 1973, it was already experiencing a labor shortage. It is almost entirely dependent on imports for its raw material, and their supply may one day become a problem with a world-wide shortage of some natural resources. Singapore must even import most of its water from the mainland. On the other hand, there are few limits to Singapore's growth as an international banking, trading, and shipping center. With its strategic geographical location, Singapore is a natural stop-over point for the tourist and business traveller.

As in economics, too much success in politics may also have some drawbacks. Prime Minister Lee Kuan Yew, in 1972, won another five-year term in office, and his party garnered all 65 parliamentary seats, even though the opposition got 25% of the votes. This absolute power, according to an article in *Newsweek International,* induced the prime minister to jail a political opponent, close down two newspapers critical of him, ban movies showing "excessive" violence, and refuse passports to youths with hair hanging below the collar line. Of course, Puritans in New England and elsewhere in the world have also been known to lean towards intolerance, and most of them had a good business sense too.

Foreign Brokerage Houses Members of the Hong Kong Stock Exchange

Astaire & Co., Far East / Prince's Building, 20th floor / Hong Kong
Daiwa Securities International (HK) Ltd. / Solar House, 6th floor / Hong Kong
Hoare & Co. Govett (Far East) Ltd. / Connaught Center, 14th floor / Hong Kong
James Capel & Co. / Room 608, Hong Kong Hilton / Hong Kong
Joseph Sebag & Co. (Far East) Ltd. / Union House, Room 1232 / Hong Kong
Myers (Hong Kong) / Lane Crawford House, 4th floor / Hong Kong
The Nikko Securities (Asia) Ltd. / St. George's Building, 19th floor / Hong Kong
Nomura International (Hong Kong) Ltd. / Connaught Center, 14th floor / Hong Kong
Richardson Securities of Canada (Pacific) Ltd. / Bank of Canton Building / Hong Kong
Vickers, Da Costa & Co., Hong Kong, Ltd. / Connaught Center, 12th floor / Hong Kong
W.I. Carr, Sons & Co. (Overseas) / St. George's Building / Hong Kong

Partial List of Actively Traded Hong Kong Securities

Cathay Securities Ltd. (investment holding company)
China Light & Power Co., Ltd. (electric utility)
China Engineers (Holdings) Ltd. (contractors)
Eastern Asia Navigation Co., Ltd. (shipping)
Hang Seng Bank, Ltd. (banking [51% owned by *Hong Kong and Shanghai Banking Corp.*])
Hong Kong Electric Co., Ltd. (electric utility)
Hong Kong and Kowloon Wharf and Godown Co., Ltd. (dock warehousing)
Hong Kong Land Investment and Agency Co., Ltd. (real estate, hotel operation)
Hong Kong and Shanghai Banking Corp. (banking)
Hong Kong Telephone Co., Ltd. (telephone)
Hong Kong and Whampoa Dock Co., Ltd. (shipbuilding)
Hutchison International Ltd. (industrial and real estate holding company)
Jardine, Matheson & Co., Ltd. (trading, banking, transportation, real estate)
Sime Darby (trading, commodities)
Taikoo Swire (shipbuilding, steel fabrication, real estate)
Wheelock Marden & Co., Ltd. (holding company, shipping, real estate, trading, finance)
Wheelock Maritime International Ltd. (shipping)
Winsor Industrial Corporation Ltd. (textiles, apparel, shoes)

Hong Kong Investment Companies

Jardine Securities Ltd. / *Jardine Industries Ltd.* / *International Pacific Securities Co. Ltd.* / *Pedder American Investment Co. Ltd.* / *Pedder Australia Securities Ltd.* / Jardine House / Hong Kong

Shipping and General Investments Co. Ltd. / Prince's Building / Hong Kong
Slater Walker Overseas Investments Ltd. / Melbourne Plaza, 17th floor / Hong Kong
Hong Kong and Pacific Investments Ltd. / St. George's Building / Hong Kong

Sources of Information

Year Book, Monthly Gazette, Research Booklets on Leading Hong Kong Companies available from The Hong Kong Stock Exchange / Edinburgh House, Ice House Street / Hong Kong

Newspapers With Financial Coverage

Hong Kong Standard / 635 King's Road / Hong Kong
South China Morning Post / Tong Chong Street / Hong Kong

Financial Publications

Economic Reporter / 342 Hennesy Road / Hong Kong
Far Eastern Economic Review / Marina House / Hong Kong

Member Brokers of the Singapore Stock Exchange

Associated Asian Securities (Pte) / 7th floor, Overseas Union Shopping Center, Collyer Quay / Singapore 1
J. Ballas & Co. (Pte) / 5th floor, Straits Trading Building, 9 Battery Road / Singapore 1
Chan Lim Securities (Pte) / 17-A, Phillip Street / Singapore 1
Chia & Co. / 96B Robinson Road / Singapore 1
Fraser & Co. (Pte) / Maritime Building, Collyer Quay / Singapore 1
Kay Hian & Co. (Pte) / 100 Market Street / Singapore 1
Kim Eng Securities (Pte) / 5th floor, Clifford Center, Raffles Place / Singapore 1
Lee & Co. (Stock & Sharebrokers) (Pte) / 3rd floor, Interocean House, 1 Finlayson Green / Singapore 1
George Lim & Co. (Pte) / 3B Malacca Street / Singapore 1
Lim & Tan (Pte) / 96-C, Robinson Road / Singapore 1
Lyall & Evatt (Pte) / 12th floor, Robina House, Shenton Way / Singapore 1
Ong & Co. / 45-B Robinson Road / Singapore 1
Pacific Union Co. (Pte) / 41 Market Street / Singapore 1
J. M. Sassoon & Co. (Pte) / 33-36, 4th floor, Mercantile Bank Building / Singapore 1
E. G. Tan & Co. (Pte) / 1st floor, Malayan Bank Chambers / Singapore 1
Tsang & Ong (Pte) / 86 Market Street / Singapore 1
Vincent & Lam Co. (Pte) / 35/36 Phillip Street, 2nd floor / Singapore 1

Stocks of Some Singapore Based Companies Actively Traded on the Singapore Stock Exchange

Aokam Tin Bhd. (tin mining)

Batu Kawan Bhd. (natural rubber plantation and palm oil)

Berjuntai Tin Dredging Bhd. (tin mining)

Bukit Sembawang Estates Ltd. (real estate)

Central Properties Ltd. (real estate)

Chemical Company of Malaysia Bhd. (fertilizer and agricultural chemicals)

Cold Storage Holdings Ltd. (refrigerated foods, dairy products, soft drinks)

Development Bank of Singapore Ltd. (banking)

Dunlop Estates Bhd. (natural rubber plantation)

Dunlop Malaysian Industries Bhd. (tire and rubber manufacturing)

Faber Union Ltd. (real estate)

Fraser & Neave Ltd. (food)

Goodwood Park Hotel Ltd. (hotel)

Great Eastern Life Assurance Co. Ltd. (insurance)

Haw Par Brothers International Ltd. (investment banking)

Inchcape Bhd. (trading, shipping, manufacturing, distribution)

Island & Peninsular Development Bhd. (real estate)

Kempas (Malaya) Bhd. (natural rubber)

Malaya Borneo Building Society Ltd. (real estate)

Malayan Banking Bhd. (banking)

Malayan Breweries Ltd. (brewery)

Malayan Tobacco Co. Bhd. (cigarettes)

National Iron & Steel Mills Ltd. (steel)

North Borneo Timbers Bhd. (forest products)

Oversea-Chinese Banking Corporation Ltd. (banking)

Overseas Union Enterprise Ltd. (real estate)

Petaling Tin Bhd. (tin mining)

Robinson & Co. Ltd. (retailing)

Shangri-La Hotel Ltd. (hotel)

Shell Refining Co. (Fed. of Malaysia) Bhd. (petroleum refining)

Sime Darby Holdings Ltd. (trading, distribution, manufacturing)

Singapore International Merchants Bankers Ltd. (banking)

Singapore Land and Investment Co. Ltd. (real estate)

Straits Times Press (M) Bhd. (newspaper publishing)

Straits Trading Co. Ltd. (tin smelting)

Tasek Cement Bhd. (cement)

Tractors Malaysia Bhd. (tractor manufacturing)

United Engineers Ltd. (machinery and engineering)

United Overseas Bank Ltd. (banking)

United Plantations Bhd. (palm oil)

Wearne Brothers Ltd. (automobile assembly)

Sources of Information

Singapore Stock Exchange Journal (monthly) and *Financial News* (daily) available from the Stock Exchange of Singapore Limited / 601 Clifford Center, Raffles Place, P.O. Box 2306 / Singapore

Chief Newspaper with Financial Coverage

Straits Times / Singapore

10

UNITED KINGDOM
NEW "CITY" LIFE

From the downfall of Napoleon to the rise of Hitler, London had been the leading financial center of the world. The role was then taken over by Wall Street, but London has been making a strong comeback. The fiscal follies of the United States government and the dubauchery of the American investment community in the 1960s, combined with Britain's entry into the European Economic Community, have shifted the weight back towards London.

The turning point came in 1963 when the United States government, in an apparent misunderstanding of what was creating the dollar drain, imposed the Interest Equalization Tax on the purchase price of foreign securities by United States residents (explained in greater detail in Chapter 1). The tax not only discouraged most Americans from investing in foreign securities, but it also stopped completely the substantial borrowings of foreign governments and of other foreign organizations through Wall Street.

London Invents Eurodollar Bonds

The dollar drain continued in spite of the Interest Equalization Tax. Dollars began accumulating in the hands of foreigners at an increasingly rapid rate (from about $20 billion in 1962 to about $100 billion in 1973). Here the British merchant banks saw a new

On October 3, 1973 the pound Sterling was valued at U.S. $2.416.

business opportunity. They invented the "Eurodollar" bond issue. Eurodollars, discussed in greater detail in Chapter 20, are dollars owned by individuals, organizations, or governments outside the United States, not necessarily in Europe, but anywhere in the world. The British took over the financing business that American underwriters had lost when the Interest Equalization Tax was introduced, tapping the dollars that were accumulating in the hands of United States non-residents. They expanded the business as the pool of Eurodollars grew year by year. United States corporations needing money for their overseas expansion, and limited by the United States government in the amount of capital they could take out of the United States, joined foreign borrowers in tapping this huge supply of Eurodollars—not only in the form of bond issues, but also through regular commercial bank loans.

American bankers and brokers, as well as banks from many other parts of the world, joined the British merchant banks in selling Eurodollar bonds and making commercial loans in Eurodollars. The business was so attractive that scores of American and other foreign banks opened branch offices in London. Of the 243 foreign banks that had offices in London in mid-1973, 130 had come to London since 1962, and the Eurodollar boom was partly responsible for this influx. But it also reflects the renewed strength of London as an international financial center.

Stimulus from the EEC

Britain's entry into the European Common Market on January 1, 1973, further revived the financial business in London, and it is likely to do so to a much greater extent in the future. Continental European companies have suddenly become attractive merger candidates for British companies, and this means new business for the British merchant bankers who help negotiate and finance these deals. British investors and brokers began to look at Continental European stocks and found many of them undervalued in relation to British and American stocks. So they went on a buying spree in Europe in 1971 and 1972. British jobbers (market makers) on "The Stock Exchange," London, began to make a market in Continental stocks, and because the London exchange is a more sophisticated and larger market than most European stock exchanges, it is likely to get an increasing amount of trading volume in Continental stocks.

London has had a long tradition of making markets in foreign stocks, notably South African, Australian, and Canadian mining stocks. London brokers were among the first to promote gold stocks to investors throughout the world when the dollar debacle appeared imminent, and at an early stage they developed a good business in stocks of companies involved in North Sea offshore oil exploration. While American brokers and institutional investors remained hypnotized by the hothouse jungle of the American stock markets, British brokers turned to Japan, Hong Kong, Singapore, South Africa, and Europe, much to the benefit of their customers, and those that were particularly active on the international scene made good money while the American brokerage business went into a tailspin.

Old City Tradition

This success is based on international expertise, sophistication, and business ethics that have been built up in "the City" of London over centuries. (An Act of 1697 established regulations for stock brokers that to some extent still apply today.) A tradition of personal trust among the "in" members of the City was built up, and the opinion of a member was as important in making investment decisions as the analysis of a balance sheet. "Research" on American stocks, in the past decades, consisted often of regular visits to respected regional brokers in Cleveland, Chicago, Dallas, or Atlanta, who were intimately familiar with the local publicly owned companies. Today, the leading British brokerage houses, while not neglecting the old contacts, are also publishing highly informative research reports. But the City community has grown to such an extent that the personal contacts have necessarily become somewhat diluted.

Great investment sophistication is also prevalent among the British merchant bankers, who have a long tradition of financing international trade and industry and managing investment portfolios (they do not handle checking or savings accounts). Two of the largest ones in portfolio management, *Robert Fleming & Co.* and *Kleinwort, Benson, Londsdale Ltd.,* took a leading role in financing the construction of American railroads in the 19th century. British merchant banks today are still a leading force in international finance and investment—they are among the leading underwriters of international issues, they arrange for private placements and loans, they negotiate and finance international mergers, they manage investment trusts and unit trusts (British open-end mutual funds), and most of them will also manage large private portfolios. Their business is likely to increase with the involvement of Britain in the European Economic Community. As a

first step in this direction *S. G. Warburg & Co., Ltd.,* one of the leading British merchant banks, has exchanged some of its stock with that
of *Paribas,* the largest French financial house on the international
scene.

Some House Cleaning

Not everything is roses and fragrance in the City of London. There
have been a few financial scandals. Several highly promotional minded
merchant banks and financial conglomerates have appeared on the
scene that seem out of character with the City's tradition. A report
commissioned by the British Cabinet Office on "The Future of London as an International Financial Center" has been critical of many
practices and omissions. Among other points, it said: " . . . many
people in the country doubt if the City is making a good enough
contribution to the economy as a whole. The City is not generally
well-regarded by industry, by educated and professional people, or
by the populace at large. Even in the City itself, sober people say
privately that some of our financial institutions are sluggish and
complacent and, in certain cases, over-paid."

It is true that many businessmen travelling in Europe find that
they can make only about half the number of appointments in a
single business day in the City of London as they can make in Zurich,
and that many non-City people still believe, rightly or wrongly, that
the son of a well-connected family who has failed to learn any profession in particular is sent to the City.

Yet "sluggishness" and "complacency" are not doubt also found
in other sectors of the British economy and the family tradition of
finding a safe place for an underachieving son is worldwide. More
serious is the public concern about trading by City people on inside
information not available to the general public and about excessive
profits on deals open to only a happy few.

Nevertheless, the report commissioned by the Cabinet Office and
other public discussions show that soul-searching is underway, and
as a result of it, hopefully, the necessary steps will be taken to uphold
and strengthen what was good in the old traditions and to develop
new rules and methods that would help the City to reassume leader-
ship on the international scene.

The Stock Exchange, London

The regional British exchanges were combined with the London
exchange in March 1973, and the combined exchange became the

United Stock Exchange. Nevertheless, the London exchange, which moved into a spanking new skyscraper in 1972, continues to be called The Stock Exchange, as though there is only one in all the world that counts. In fact, London is the largest stock exchange in the world in terms of the number of securities listed, and second only to New York in terms of the value of transactions (though the Tokyo Stock Exchange also claims the latter right). The London exchange does not publish the number of shares traded every day, but there is an approximate score of the "bargains marked" every day. A "bargain" is one transaction, and "marking" it means that it is recorded on a slip of paper that is toted up with other slips at the end of the day. But there is no guarantee that all bargains are marked on a really busy day. Nevertheless, based on informal brokers' reports, during the twelve-month period ending September 30, 1972, total trading volume on The Stock Exchange was £63 billion ($150 billion). About £43.3 billion ($120 billion) was in fixed-income securities, the balance in common stocks. Since both sales and purchases are recorded, these figures must be halved to make them comparable to those of other exchanges. On the average, the value of traded stock on the New York Stock Exchange in 1972 was about twice as high as on the London exchange, but in New York 87% of the trades was in common stock.

Trading volume diminished in New York in 1972 and 1973, and the market became less and less liquid; the opposite was true in London. More than 9500 securities are listed on the London exchange. About 3000 are common shares of British companies. More than 400 are foreign securities, with the number increasing ripidly. Most others are fixed-income securities, a large percentage of them British government securities (gilt edged). There is practically no over-the-counter market in London outside the exchange. However, because of the relatively high commission fees, merchant banks in 1973 were trying to develop a "third market" outside the exchange to trade larger blocks of stock among themselves with the help of a computer that matches buy and sell orders.

The small British investor does not seem to have abandoned the stock market as many small United States investors had in 1971 and 1972 probably because he is not as disillusioned with his broker as Americans are. According to figures published by the London exchange, small investors account for about 45% of the trades. Another 20% of the trades is made on behalf of individual investors by the "clearing banks" (the commercial checking account banks) through which small investors can also place investment orders.

In addition to the securities listed on the London exchange, members of the exchange can trade on the floor of the exchange securities listed on any other recognized stock exchange of the world. This, combined with the fact that an increasing number of foreign stocks are being listed on the London exchange, is contributing greatly to the revival of London as the leading international investment center.

New Issues

Another healthy sign for the London exchange is the increasing number of new issues sold there. There were almost 300 in 1972, and the rate is comparable in 1973. New issues are sold directly to the public through advertisements and a prospectus, and an investor can subscribe by sending in his check directly to a member of the selling syndicate, bypassing a broker. When a new issue is popular it may be greatly over-subscribed, and a subscriber may receive only a small percentage of the number of shares he requested. As soon as the shares are traded on the Exchange, they command a premium over the subscription price. Anyone who received shares at the subscription price can make a handsome profit on the first trading day. Some investors borrow large sums of money to request the largest possible number of shares of a popular new issue (the more they request, the more they get if the distribution is on a percentage basis for each subscriber and the more money they can make selling them on one of the first trading days).

A publicly owned company listed on The Stock Exchange wanting to sell additional shares must offer these first to its existing stockholders on a pro-rated basis, and only if stockholders approve can the company sell new shares to outsiders. This protects stockholders from the dilution of their stock without their consent. If, for instance, a company with 1 million shares outstanding and earnings of $1 per share sells 100,000 new shares to outsiders, old stockholders will suddenly find their per-share earnings reduced to about 91 cents.

Trading Practices

Tradition and trading practices on The Stock Exchange are highly colorful and complex, and could in themselves make a subject for an entire book. Only jobbers and brokers can be members of the exchange; not banks. Jobbers make markets for individual stocks, and they trade for their own accounts. They do not deal with the public, but only among themselves and with brokers. Only brokers deal with the public, including banks and other institutional investors. Several jobbers may make a market for the same stock; and many jobbers make markets for several hundred stocks. The largest jobber reportedly makes markets for about 80% of the securities listed on The Stock Exchange. Different jobbers may quote different prices for the same stock. There is no central reporting system for prices; so a broker wanting to buy or sell a certain stock on behalf of a customer sends a "blue button" around—a clerk whose job it is to obtain the price quotations and collect other information. Thus, to make a trade, a broker must shop around and bargain as a shopper would do in a bazaar where merchants of the same type of merchandise have established their stalls in the same vicinity. Since jobbers usually do not know whether an inquiring broker wants to buy or sell, they always quote two prices, comparable to the "bid" and "ask" prices of over-the-counter dealers in the United States. Like bazaar merchants, competing jobbers often shout their prices at the top of their voices to be heard above the din of the trading floor. The "blue button" information service may soon be replaced by closed-circuit radio and TV.

There are three types of orders under which a broker may operate—"discretion," giving him unspecified leeway; "best," instructing him to execute the order immediately at the best possible terms; and "limit," defining the price within which he may execute the order.

Options deals are comparable to those in the United States, including "call options," under which an investor can buy or not buy a certain security at an agreed price within an agreed period of time; "put options," permitting the investor to sell or not to sell a certain security at an agreed price within an agreed period of time, and "double options," which are "put" and "call" options. Options are bought in the same way as ordinary securities and usually run for three months.

Settlement in common stock is normally about two or three weeks after the transaction, making it possible to "reverse" a deal and avoid stock transfer.

Investing in the United Kingdom

The expertise of the London financial community and the versatility of the stock market may persuade a foreign investor to place his business with a London firm, but it is not necessarily an inducement to invest in British securities. After a nice spurt upwards in 1967 and 1968, and again in 1971, the London market averages have been going sideways with a strong downwards trend late in 1973. In spite of a bear market, British stock prices in early 1973 were still considered somewhat high relative to most European Continental stocks and certainly in most United States stocks. The British economy has a number of built-in problems, not the least of them unhappy labor relations. In 1973, there was again a serious balance of payment problem, and the pound Sterling weakened.

This does not mean, of course, that individual stocks, judiciously picked, could not outperform the London market, or any other market of the world.

Many British banks have reflected the booming international financial business in rising earning curves over the last few years, including the four leading clearing banks (retail banks), *Barclays Bank Ltd., Lloyds Bank Ltd., Midland Bank Ltd.,* and *National Westminster Bank* and two of the leading merchant banks, *Kleinwort, Benson, Lonsdale Ltd.* and *Hambros Bank Ltd.*

Several of the insurance companies have done well, including *General Accident Fire and Life Assurance Corp. Ltd., Eagle Star Insurance Co. Ltd.,* and *Phoenix Assurance Co. Ltd.*

In the retail field, *Marks & Spencer Ltd.,* a food and clothing chain store, has been a favorite of British investors for many years because of its steady earnings improvements year after year. Some other retail operations have done at least equally well, including *British Home Stores Ltd.,* a variety chain store; *Freemans (London SW9) Ltd.,* a mail-order house; and *Curry's Ltd.,* an appliances, TV, and radio retail chain. *United Drapery Stores Ltd.* and *Great Universal Stores Ltd.* are two of the largest department store operations, with steady growth records.

Fisons Ltd., a very profitable producer of agrochemicals, pharmaceuticals, and foods has not only appealed to British investors but also found favor among United States investors who bought American Depositary Receipts of the stock.

In the publishing field, *The Thomson Organisation Ltd.,* which includes in its stable *The Times* and *The Sunday Times* as well as scores of newspapers in Canada and the United States, has been particularly successful. So has *W. H. Smith & Son Holdings Ltd.,* the ubiquitous newspaper retailer and wholesaler that peddles the British Thomson products and every other British publication.

The Rank Organisation Ltd., closely affiliated with *Xerox* through the *Rank-Xerox* subsidiary, in which it has a 49% interest, has shown strong stock action since 1969 in spite of a temporary earnings plateau in 1971. *Rank-Xerox* markets *Xerox* products outside the United States and Southeast Asia. *The Rank Organisation* itself is heavily involved in the leisure industry, producing films, operating movie theaters, and involved in hotel operations. It also manufactures consumer electronics products and instruments. *Rank* American Depositary Receipts are probably the most actively traded in the United States.

Audio fans high on *EMI,* the producer of *London* and *Capitol* records, as well as the appliances, radios, and TV sets, may have been disappointed with the company's flat stock action. On the other hand, they would have done very well with *BSR Limited,* another maker of hi-fi equipment.

This is, of course, only a small sampling from among the 3000 British companies whose stocks are traded on the London exchange, and as no seasoned investor needs to be reminded, records of past earnings are no guarantee for the future.

Fixed-Income Securities

Fixed-income securities, including government securities, have always played an important role on the British investment scene; and yields have usually been relatively high. In 1973, an investor could find sound bonds yielding about 10%. Nevertheless, for a non-resident investor, the appeal is limited because of a 30% withholding tax on many of the bonds and the fact that the British pound does not compare favorably with some other currencies as a hedge against devaluation of his own currency. In addition, a United States resident must pay the Interest Equalization Tax. A number of British government bonds, including the British War Loan, are, on application, exempt from withholding tax if purchased by a non-resident. With a coupon of $3\frac{1}{2}$% (on £ 100), the War Loan sold in June 1973, at $34\frac{1}{2}$, produces an effective interest income of 10.173%. The War Loan is probably the most actively traded and most widely held security in the United Kingdom.

Investment Funds

Because of their "image" of thrift, the Scots are often identified with the development of the investment fund—a portfolio of many different securities of which the individual investor can buy a share, managed by a professional fund manager. The investor thereby achieves a diversification of his investment, which he cannot get himself with limited funds (and diversification generally means greater safety than putting all one's eggs in one basket). He also gets professional investment management.

Today there are more than 500 British investment funds—some 300 investment trusts (closed-end funds) with total assets of more than £ 5 billion ($12 billion) and 200 unit trusts (open-end funds) with total assets of more than £ 1.5 billion ($3.6 billion).

Shares of the investment trusts are listed on The Stock Exchange, and the number of outstanding shares usually remains the same. Theoretically, the price is determined by the asset value of the fund, which is the total market value of all securities in the fund at any given time. But investment trust shares often sell considerably below asset value, which is not always readily available because many trusts do not publish their portfolios.

This is not true of unit trusts, which are not traded on the London exchange. An investor can always redeem his unit trust share at net asset value with the management company or a bank.

Unit trusts are comparable to open-end mutual funds in the United States. They are sold directly to the public by the management company or through the retail banks. As with all open-end funds, additional shares are sold to new subscribers. Most unit trusts are managed by banks; some by insurance companies.

Through an investment trust or a unit trust, a small investor can accomplish any kind of specialized investment objective—diversification nationally or internationally; specific industries, including gold and other mining; specific countries or world regions; government securities or other fixed income; combined income and growth, etc. There are unit trusts that offer a fixed income, plus appreciation potential, plus life insurance.

Among the larger unit trust management companies are the *Save and Prosper Group, London Wall Groups,* and *Jessel Britannia Group.* All five clearing banks have unit trusts.

A non-resident investor who wants to put part of his money in the British economy without himself trying to analyze British stocks may find that the easiest solution is to buy a few shares of a British investment trust or unit trust with a purely British portfolio. (As a United States resident he would have to pay the Interest Equalization Tax of 11.25%.)

Where to Buy British Stocks

In England, an investor can buy securities either from a broker or from one of the many offices of a clearing bank (retail bank). (The name "clearing" bank, incidentally, is derived from the fact that these banks "clear" checks. This is a service that the merchant banks do not perform although in most other financial matters clearing banks and merchant banks are increasingly competing with each other.) Brokers prefer to let the clearing banks deal with small investors because of the problem of credit risk and the unprofitability of handling small accounts. They split the commission with the clearing bank; thus the investor does not pay more when he buys his shares from the clearing bank.

Brokers are willing to handle the small-investor business from the clearing banks because of other investment business they receive, notably that from the unit trusts which clearing banks manage. With a minimum amount equivalent to perhaps $50,000 to $75,000 some leading London brokers will accept discretionary or consulting accounts from individuals. In the case of discretionary accounts, the broker makes his investment decisions without consulting the customer. Under normal circumstances, a portfolio managed by a London broker for growth would be international in nature rather than purely British. In 1973, four British brokers had offices in the United States (see the listing at the end of this chapter); and one or two others were planning to establish offices. However, they were set up to accept business only from institutions, not from individual investors.

British brokers, incidentally, do not advertise or otherwise promote their services. An investor wanting to select a broker must rely on the recommendation of a friend, banker, or other knowledgeable person, or go shopping among a number of them to find one that suits his specific investment requirements.

An investor with $250,000 and more would also be welcomed as a customer by one of the leading merchant banks which manage portfolios of many hundreds of millions of dollars.

Regulations

A non-resident can buy British securities provided he pays for them in a foreign currency or Sterling converted from a foreign currency or from a Sterling account held outside the United Kingdom. A few British companies have company articles forbidding foreign ownership of their shares. There were primarily instituted to prevent Gernans and other enemy aliens from buying into British industry in imes of war.

For an investor wanting to become a British resident it is important to know that a British investor can buy non-British securities only by paying for them in so-called "investment currency." The xchange rate for such investment currency is usually considerably bove the rate for normal commercial transactions, and varies with he demand for such currency. When a British investor sells a foreign ecurity, he must surrender 25% of the proceeds to the Bank of England for conversion into £ Sterling at the regular rate of exhange. He may re-invest the remaining 75% in foreign securities, but if he wants to invest the full 100%, he must buy back the 25% n investment currency at the investment currency rate.

Thus, if the investment currency sells at 20% above the commercial rate, a "switch" from one foreign security to another of the ame price costs the British investor an additional 5%. The foreign ecurities bought by a British resident must be placed in custody of an "Authorized Depository."

In the past, securities from former Sterling-area countries such as Australia, New Zealand, British West Indies, South Africa, and others, were exempt from the investment currency requirements. As of June 26, 1972, the definition of "foreign" securities to be paid in nvestment currency was extended to include all parts of the Sterling area, except the Isle of Man, the Channel Islands, and the Republic of Ireland. On the other hand, it is expected that with the entry of he United Kingdom into the European Economic Community securities of the EEC countries will eventually be exempt from the investment currency requirements.

British institutional investors can avoid paying the premium for nvestment currency for the purchase of foreign securities by taking up so-called back-to-backloans. With special permission of the Bank of England, institutional investors can borrow a specific amount of foreign currency from British or foreign banks for an indefinite period of time to buy foreign securities. They are expected to repay the loans from the sale of these foreign securities. If the securities have declined and the proceeds are less than the original purchase price, the difference has to be paid in investment currency bought at the prevailing premium. When the institutional investor "switches" from one foreign security to another, he does not have to surrender the 25% from the sales proceeds as the individual investor must do.

Thus, a British individual investor who wants to invest in foreign securities without having to pay the premium for the investment currency can do so by buying the shares of a British investment fund with a portfolio of foreign securities.

A British investor who buys a foreign stock traded on the London exchange does not pay the investment currency premium directly, but the price he pays may be somewhat higher than on the home exchange of the stock to reflect the investment currency premium the jobber has paid. A foreign investor who buys a non-British stock through a London broker does not have to pay the investment currency premium as long as he pays for the stock in a recognized foreign currency, or Sterling converted from such currency.

Transfer of ownership of stock and bonds is not quite as simple in London as it is in some other European countries that have a central clearing agency for stock transfer or deal primarily in bearer shares (which are not registered in the name of the owner and can be handled like cash).

In the United Kingdom practically all shares are registered in the name of the owner. When the stock is sold the seller must sign a stock transfer form. For an investor living outside the United Kingdom or travelling much, the only practical way is to have his shares registered in the name of a nominee, often a legal entity especially created for this purpose by the bank or brokerage house through which the investor deals. A stockholder can instruct his nominee how to vote at the annual shareholders meeting.

Taxes

A new tax law which became effective in April 1973, changed the system of withholding tax on dividends and interest. Formerly, companies withheld 38¾ % of the dividends paid to residents and non-residents alike.

Under the new law, tax on dividends is no longer withheld at the source. A company pays a higher corporation tax than before—usually 50% instead of 40%—on all profits whether distributed or undistributed. When dividends are paid, the company pays an "advance corporation tax" of 30 pence on the £ to the Inland Revenue, which will be offset against the campany's corporation tax bill on its total profits for the year. The recipient will be entitled to a corresponding tax credit on his own income tax return.

A non-resident receiving 70% of the dividend due to him from a British corporation can claim part or all of the 30% back from the

British tax authorities depending on the terms of the double taxation agreement that his country has with Great Britain.

At the time of writing it appeared that a United States resident could claim 15% of the 30% from the British government under the double taxation agreement between the United States and the United Kingdom, but reportedly it is a complicated procedure. An investor whose home country has no double taxation agreement with the British government cannot reclaim any part of the 30% from the British (but depending on the tax laws in his own country, an investor may offset taxes paid in England against his own taxable income)

Investment trusts pay no income tax on dividends but let the dividend and tax credit flow through to their shareholders. They do pay a corporate tax, however, on interest received from government securities on which there is no withholding tax.

There is a withholding tax of 30% on interest that foreign shareholders receive from many British fixed-income securities except most government bonds (gilt edged).

United Kingdom residents pay a capital gains tax of 30% on all profitable transactions irrespective of the length of time the securities are held. Non-residents pay capital gains tax, if applicable, in their own countries. Investment trusts pay 15% capital gains tax and the shareholder pays 15%. It is impossible for a non-resident to reclaim this capital gains tax from the British tax authorities (and probably often not from his own tax authorities).

Sources of Information

Under the most recent Companies Act of 1967, standards of company accounting and disclosure were improved in England, but they still fall a good deal short of the practices in the United States. Most companies have at least a semi-annual interim report in addition to the annual report and they pay two dividends per year. Year-end results may be published anytime between one and four months after the end of the fiscal year.

Two organizations provide extensive investment information services with detailed reports on several thousand British companies as well as on several hundred Continental European companies— *Extel Statistical Services Ltd.* and *Moodies Services Ltd. Moodies* also publishes a quarterly *Investment Handbook,* providing company information by industry groupings, and *Moodies Review,* a weekly London stock market letter. It also provides information on Australian, South African, Canadian, and United States stocks. *Investment Research* provides chart services as well as individual stock recommendations.

Most of the brokerage houses and merchant banks with institutional or private customers publish investment information for their customers, often on a world-wide basis, rather than limited strictly to British securities. Many of the houses are quite secretive about these reports, limiting them strictly to customers, but a few brokerage houses now offer such research services on a subscription basis, which customers may set off against commissions, including *Hoare & Co., Govett Ltd., Vickers, Da Costa & Co. Limited,* and *James Capel and Co. Hoare & Co., Govett* also offers on a subscription basis or against commission fees a computerized information retrieval system on a time-sharing basis which makes it possible for subscribers to have up-to-date information at their finger tips on several thousand companies.

Reuters provides an instant stock quotation service from about a dozen stock markets all over the world. This is widely used by brokers and portfolio managers.

The leading financial newspaper is the *Financial Times,* comparable in stock market coverage to the *Wall Street Journal,* but with far more extensive international coverage.

The *Financial Times,* through its Investment Bureau, also provides at relatively low cost a personal investment advice service that includes portfolio reviews and a weekly *Investment Review* with individual stock recommendations.

The *Investors Chronicle and Stock Exchange Gazette* is a widely read weekly investment publication which, in addition to regular news, feature articles, and editorials, includes stock analyses and recommendations. The publication also has an investment advisory department which publishes a separate weekly *News Letter.* The *Economist* is a weekly business and financial publication of high repute. Some of the national daily newspapers have extensive busines and stock market coverage, notably the *Times,* the *Daily Telegraph,* and the *Guardian.* So do the three leading Sunday papers, the *Sunday Times,* the *Observer,* and the *Sunday Telegraph.* The *Evening Standard* and the *Evening News* find a good readership among investment professionals on their homeward commute.

London Brokers With Offices in the United States

James Capel and Co. / Winchester House, 100 Old Broad Street / London EC2
(James Capel Inc. / 209 South LaSalle Street / Chicago, Illinois 60604 and 310 Sansome Street / San Francisco, California 94104)
Cazenove & Co. / 12 Tokenhouse Yard / London EC2
*(67 Wall Street / New York, New York 10005 and 405 Montgomery Street / San Francisco, California 94104)
Rowe & Pitman / Woolgate House, Coleman Street / London EC2
*(111 Pine Street / San Francisco, California 94111)
Joseph Sebag & Co. / P.O. Box 511, Bucklersbury House, 3 Queen Victoria Street / London EC4
*(523 West 6th Street / Los Angeles, California 90014)

Partial List of Other London Brokers Doing International Business

Astaire and Co., Limited / 119 Bishopsgate / London EC2
W. I. Carr, Sons and Co. / Ocean House, 10/12 Little Trinity Lane / London EC4
Colegrave and Co. / Hamilton House, 1 Temple Avenue / London EC4
Hoare & Co., Govett Limited / Atlas House, 1 King Street / London EC2
Kitcat and Aitken / 9 Bishopsgate / London EC2
L. Messel and Co. / Winchester House, 100 Old Broad Street / London EC4
J. and A. Scrimgeour Limited / Mansion House Place / London EC4
Vickers, Da Costa and Co. Limited / Regis House, King William Street / London EC4

Clearing Banks (Commercial and Retail)

Barclays Bank Ltd. / 54 Lombard Street / London EC3
Lloyd's Bank Ltd. / 71 Lombard Street / London EC3
Midland Bank Ltd. / Poultry / London EC2
National Westminster Bank / 326-333 High Holborn / London WC1
Williams & Glyn's / 20 Merchant Lane / London

Merchant Banks (Investment Banking; Fund and Portfolio Management)

Arbuthnot, Latham & Co., Ltd. / 37 Queen Street / London EC4
Baring Brothers & Co. Ltd. / 8 Bishopsgate / London EC2
William Brandt's Sons & Co., Ltd. / 36 Fenchurch Street / London EC3
Brown Shipley & Co., Ltd. / 20 Moorgate / London EC2
Charterhouse, Japhet & Thomasson Ltd. / 1 Paternoster Row / London EC4
Dawney, Day & Co. Ltd. / 31 Gresham Street / London EC2
Robert Fleming & Co. / 8 Crosby Square / London EC3
(New York Office: 100 Wall Street / New York, New York 10005)
Antony Gibbs & Sons Ltd. / 22 Bishopsgate / London EC2

Guinness, Mahon & Co. Ltd. / 3 Gracechurch Street / London EC3
Hambros Bank Ltd. / 41 Bishopsgate / London EC2
Hill, Samuel & Co., Ltd. / 100 Wood Street / London EC2
(New York Office: *Hill, Samuel Securities Corp.* / 375 Park Avenue / New York, New York 10022)
Keyser Ullman Ltd. / 31 Throgmorton Street / London EC2
Kleinwort, Benson, Lonsdale Ltd. / 20 Fenchurch Street / London EC3
(New York Office: 100 Wall Street / New York, New York 10005)
Lazard Brothers & Co., Ltd. / 11 Old Broad Street / London EC2
Samuel Montagu and Co., Ltd. / 114 Old Broad Street / London EC2
Morgan Grenfell & Co., Ltd. / 23 Great Winchester Street / London EC2
N.M. Rothschild & Sons / New Court, St. Swithin's Lane / London EC4
(New York Office: *New Court Securities Corp.* / 1 Rockefeller Plaza / New York, New York 10020)
Singer & Friedlander / 20 Cannon Street / London EC4
J. Henry Schroeder Wagg & Co., Ltd. / 120 Cheapside / London EC2
S. G. Warburg & Co., Ltd. / 30 Gresham Street / London EC2
(New York Office: *S. G. Warburg Securities Corp.* / 640 Fifth Avenue / New York, New York 10019)

Partial List of Actively Traded British Stocks

Albright & Wilson Ltd. (chemicals)
Allied Breweries Ltd. (breweries)
Associated British Foods Ltd. (food products)
Barclays Bank Ltd. (banking)
Bass Charrington Ltd. (alcoholic beverages)
Beecham Group Ltd. (pharmaceuticals)
The Boots Company, Ltd. (pharmaceuticals)
The Bowater Corp. Ltd.[3] (paper, packaging)
C. T. Bowring & Co. Ltd. (banking, finance)
British American Tobacco Co. Ltd.[2] (tobacco, paper products)
British Home Stores Ltd. (retailing)
British Insulated Callender's Cables Ltd. (engineering, cables)
British Leyland Motor Corp. Ltd. (automotive)
British Oxygen Co. Ltd. (gases, chemicals)
British Petroleum Co. Ltd.[1] (integrated petroleum)
BSR Limited (electronics)
The Burmah Oil Co. Ltd.[3] (petroleum products)
Cadbury Schweppes (food, beverages)
Carrington Viyella Ltd. (textiles)
Coats, Patons Ltd. (textiles)
Courtaulds Ltd.[2] (synthetic fibers)
Curry's Ltd. (retailing)
The Delta Metal Co. Ltd. (non-ferrous metals)
Dickinson Robinson Group Ltd. (paper products)
Distillers Co. Ltd. (alcoholic beverages)
Dunlop Holdings Ltd.[2] (tire and rubber goods)
Eagle Star Insurance Co. Ltd. (insurance)
EMI Ltd.[1] (records, electronics)

Fisons Ltd.[3] (food, pharmaceuticals)
Freemans (London SW9) Ltd. (mail order)
General Accident Fire and Life Assurance Corp. Ltd. (insurance)
General Electric Co. Ltd. (electric equipment)
Glaxo Holdings Ltd.[3] (drugs, food products)
Grand Metropolitan Ltd. (hotels, catering)
Great Universal Stores Ltd. (retailing)
Guest, Keen & Nettlefolds Ltd. (automotive, industrial equipment)
Arthur Guinness Son & Co. Ltd. (breweries)
Hambros Bank Ltd. (banking)
Hawker Siddeley Group Ltd. (aerospace engineering)
Imperial Chemical Industries Ltd.[2] (chemicals)
Imperial Tobacco Group[2] (tobacco, food, paper)
Kleinwort, Benson, Lonsdale Ltd. (banking)
Lloyd's Bank Ltd. (banking)
Lucas Joseph Industries Ltd. (automotive, aircraft equipment)
Marks & Spencer Ltd. (retailing, apparel)
Midland Bank Ltd. (banking)
National Westminster Bank Ltd. (banking)
Peninsular and Oriental Steam Navigation Co. (shipping)
Phoenix Assurance Co. Ltd. (insurance)
Pilkington Brothers Ltd. (glass)
Plessey Co. Ltd.[1] (telecommunications)
The Rank Organisation Ltd.[3] (leisure time)
Ranks Hovis McDougall Ltd. (food products)
Reckitt & Colman Holdings Ltd. (food, household products)
Reed International Ltd. (paper products)
The Rio Tinto-Zinc Corp. Ltd. (mining, chemicals)
Sears Holding Ltd. (textiles, apparel, shows)
Shell Transport and Trading Co. Ltd.[1] (petroleum products)
W. H. Smith & Son Holdings Ltd. (news dealers)
Standard and Chartered Banking Group Ltd. (banking)
Tarmac Ltd. (building materials)
Tate & Lyle Ltd. (food, shipping)
The Thomson Organisation Ltd. (publishing)
Thorn Electrical Industries Ltd. (radio, TV, appliances)
Trust Houses Forte Ltd. (hotels, catering)
Tube Investments Ltd. (tubes, bicycles, engineering)
Turner & Newall Ltd. (automotive parts, building materials)
Unilever Ltd.[1] (foods, soaps, cosmetics)
United Drapery Stores Ltd. (retailing)
F. W. Woolworth & Co. Ltd.[2] (retailing)

[1] Also traded on the New York Stock Exchange.
[2] Also traded on the American Stock Exchange.
[3] Also traded over-the-counter in the United States.

Investment Trusts Organizations

The Association of Investment Trust Companies (closed-end funds) /
7 Angel Court, Throgmorton Street / London EC2

Association of Unit Trust Managers (open-end funds) / 306-308 Salisbury House, Finsbury Circus / London EC2
Both provide lists of their member funds.

Investment Information Services

Extel Statistical Services Ltd./ 37/45 Paul Street / London EC2
Investment Research / 36 Regent Street / Cambridge, CB 2, 1DH
Moodies Services Ltd. / Moodies House, 6/8 Bonhill Street / London EC2

Leading Financial Publications With Financial Advisory Service

Financial Times (daily) / Bracken House, 10 Cannon Street / London EC4
Investors Chronicle & Exchange Gazette (weekly) / 30 Finsbury Square / London EC2

Other Business and Financial Publications

Business and Finance / Botanic Road / Dublin 9
City Press / 4 Moorfields / London EC2
The Economist / 25 St. James Street / London SW1
Euromoney / 14 Finsbury Circus / London EC2
Financial World /79 Temple Chambers, Temple Avenue / London EC4
Investors Guardian /13-14 Charterhouse Square / London EC1
Investors Guide /'The Outer Temple, 222-225 Strand / London WC2
Investors Review / 79 Temple Chambers, Temple Avenue / London EC4
Journal of Business Finance / Mercury House, Waterloo Road / London SE1
Money Management (published by *Institutional Investor*) / 30 St. James Square / London SW1
Money Management and Unit Holder / 3-4 St. Andrew's Hill / London EC4
Planned Savings (unit trust publication) / 15 Lincoln's Inn Fields / London WC2
Shareholder and New Investor / 4th Floor, 11-17 Harrington Street / Liverpool 2

National Daily Newspapers With Extensive Financial Coverage

Daily Telegraph—Investment Business / 135 Fleet Street / London EC4
Evening News / Northcliffe House / London EC4
Evening Standard / 47 Shoe Lane /London EC4
The Guardian—Business Guardian / 21 John Street / London WC1
The Times—Business News Section/Printing House Square/London EC4

National Sunday Newspapers With Extensive Financial Coverage

The Observer—Business Observer / 160 Queen Victoria Street / London EC4
Sunday Telegraph—City Pages /Fleet Street / London EC4
Sunday Times—Business News /200 Grays Inn Road / London WC1

11

SWITZERLAND
LIMITS OF GROWTH

Switzerland is probably the first country in the world that has reached its limit to growth and is consciously doing something about it.

Limits of Growth is the title of a study prepared in 1971 by a team of experts at the Massachusetts Institute of Technology at the behest of a group of international businessmen and professionals, calling themselves "The Club of Rome," who were concerned about the runaway industrial expansion, population growth, and pollution of our planet. The study, projecting consumption rates of various raw materials, population growth and rate of pollution, came to the conclusion that at our present rate of expansion we would exhaust most of our raw materials by the year 2000, that we would run out of space in most of the densely populated countries, and pollute almost everything in sight.

The study was pooh-poohed in the United Statets by many experts in different fields of raw material production and industrial endeavor, and it was ignored by the population at large, including their elected officials.

Yet, two years later we have an energy crisis, including shortages of oil and natural gas, chemicals, and a host of other materials, as well as soaring prices (which to some extent reflect shortages in addition to other inflationary pressures); we have a mounting opposition to

---

On October 3, 1973 the Swiss franc (SFr.) was valued at U.S. 33.53¢.

nuclear power plants, oil pipelines and mining, lumbering, and other ventures that would further ruin nature. Even while some of this opposition may be emotional rather than factual, its simple underlying principle is undoubtedly correct: at some point in time we will reach our limits to growth on this planet, and unless we find an equilibrium in consumption and production and in the population level, our descendants will find themselves in the state of permanent undernourishment, lingering sickness, and poverty in which the fellaheen of Egypt and the peasants of the subcontinent of India have found themselves for centuries after their civilizations had passed their peaks.

Switzerland is the first country that has taken steps to cope with its limits of growth. It is a small country of about 16,000 square miles, about 1/10 the size of Montana, to which it can be compared in topography and scenery, with a population of about 6 million, including about 1 million foreigners. This is about seven times as many people as Montana has, giving Switzerland a population density of almost 400 people per square mile as compared with Montana's 7. Only about 60% of Switzerland's area is fit for living, working, and farming, with the living and working area constantly encroaching on the farmland (most of it used for grazing). About 17% of the area is occupied by forests. Inhospitable but dramatic mountains and glaciers take up 23% of the country's area.

Freedom Tradition

Switzerland's growth dilemma is partly the result of its attraction as a financial and retirement haven. It has become such a haven because of its long tradition of fiercely defended freedom and democracy. The first three cantons (comparable in constitutional rights to the States of the Union) formed a defense alliance against the autocratic and arbitrary rule of the Hapsburg Empire in 1291. (The Wilhelm Tell legend has its origin in that time.) In the course of the centuries, 19 other cantons joined the original three, including French- and Italian-speaking areas. Switzerland received its status of neutrality after the Napoleonic Wars during which it had been occupied by both parties. The neutrality was preserved in both World Wars I and II. (The fact that every adult Swiss carried arms and every Swiss mountain was spiked with fortifications and modern weaponry probably helped during World War II.)

Democracy is practiced to such an extent that most matters affecting the pocketbook, life style, and principles of the citizens are decided by plebiscite rather than by the decisions of the elected officials at the municipal, cantonal, or federal levels.

Nest Egg Haven

Neutrality, bank secrecy, stable government, and the rule of law have made Switzerland for many years the haven for the nest eggs of the rich, and often their retirement haven or second home as well. But until World War II, these rich were only a happy few, and Switzerland could easly cope with their number and their money. While the Swiss did not make it easy for foreigners to reside in their country and become citizens (after a minimum stay of ten years), anyone with enough money, perseverance, and a clean past could usually settle there.

After World War II, the situation changed radically. Switzerland had again proven that its neutrality worked. It emerged as one of the few countries where savings had been preserved without serious devaluation. As Europe recovered from the devastations of the war and became prosperous again, and as other nations came into money, notably those that had oil or other treasures in the ground, the happy few taking their nest eggs into Switzerland became a stampeding crowd. The influx swelled to a veritable flood late in the 1960s when the dollar became increasingly unstable. Bank deposits of the leading Swiss banks increased about 2½ times from 1967 to 1972.

The influx of money and people created an industrial and construction boom in Switzerland. In addition to retirement and second homes for foreigners, the Swiss built second homes for themselves in the choicest scenery. There were not enough Swiss workers to cope with the increasing manufacturing and construction output. So the Swiss, like several other European countries, admitted foreign workers, many of them from nearby Italy, until foreigners represented about 20% of the total Swiss population. These foreign workers needed places to live, too, further fanning the construction boom. Soon it became obvious that Switzerland was running out of space, its beautiful streams and lakes were being polluted, its services and resources became strained, and the financial institutions were being drowned in money.

So the Swiss took drastic steps. They restricted further immigration of foreign workers and in 1973 actually reduced their number. They have made it almost impossible for even the wealthiest to settle there. Foreign companies operating in Switzerland have trouble getting work permits for their own nationals in Switzerland even on a temporary basis. The Swiss discourage new money from abroad being deposited in their banks in Swiss francs by paying very little or no interest and from June 1972 to September 1973 they even charged a negative interest rate of 2% per quarter. They no longer allow non-residents to buy real estate. They no longer permit non-residents to buy Swiss securities unless this is done with the proceeds from the sale of Swiss securities by another non-resident. In practice, such "proceeds" or quotas from the sale of Swiss securities by non-residents are generally available at Swiss banks because Swiss common stocks have become unpopular as a result of the economic restrictions. Fixed-income securities, except as a hedge against currency devaluation, are not attractive for non-residents because yields are much lower than in most other European countries.

Common Stock

By limiting the size of the labor force, the Swiss have put a ceiling on their industrial growth. This means that, theoretically, there are no more "growth stocks" to be found in Switzerland. To some extent this has reflected itself in the Swiss stock prices, which were in a general decline during 1973. In practice, there may always be smaller companies that offer a growth potential because of special products or market developments. More importantly, many of the larger Swiss companies derive a good deal of their sales and earnings from abroad and are, therefore, not so dependent on the Swiss economy.

Foremost among international money earners are the Swiss banks, notably the "Big 3"—*Schweizerische Bankgesellschaft, Schweizerischer Bankverein,* and *Schweizerische Kreditanstalt.* All three, over the past ten years, have shown a steady increase in earnings and dividends, and their stock prices appreciated since the low point in the Swiss market in 1966. Most industrial stocks did less well.

Switzerland claims two of the largest pharmaceutical manufacturers in the world—*F. Hoffmann-La Roche & Co. A.G.* with about $1.8 billion estimated sales (the company does not publish sales and earnings figures) and *Ciba-Geigy A.G.* with a sales volume of about SFr. (Swiss francs) 2.5 billion ($760 million). A considerable portion of their earnings comes from abroad but this was not necessarily a blessing in the years from 1971 to 1973 since dollar income represented a major setback in earnings in terms of Swiss francs.

In addition, *Hoffmann-La Roche,* makers of the comforters to millions of tense people all over the world—Librium and Valium—is in serious trouble with the British National Health Service, which has asked the company to slash prices by some 60% and refund about $30 million in excess charges. The two tranquilizers were also put under strict control by the Food and Drug Administration in the United States.

Ciba-Geigy represents a 1970 merger of *Ciba* and *Geigy*—a merger that may not have been fully digested. Because of lack of labor and pressures from ecological groups, the company has shut down some of its Swiss operations and is planning no new expansion there.

An exceedingly efficient Swiss operation, heavily dependent on foreign income, and known to many travellers, is *Swissair.* In contrast to most other international airlines, *Swissair* has consistently made money but the stock price has remained relatively unchanged.

Another giant Swiss company well known outside Switzerland is *Nestlé,* with a total sales volume of about SFr. 15 billion ($4.95 billion). Much of its earnings are derived from its far-flung international operations. Earnings during the years 1969 to 1971 have been relatively flat.

For believers in the future of the electronic equipment manufacturing industry as a result of the energy crisis, *Brown Boveri & Cie A.G.* may represent a potential recovery situation. With a sales volume of SFr. 1.2 billion ($396 million), a substantial stake in a German manufacturing operation, and other international income, the company has had a relatively undistinguished earnings record during the years 1969 to 1972.

Gebrüder Sulzer A.G., with a sales volume of about SFr. 3 billion ($990 million), derives about two-thirds of its income from exports. It is one of the world's largest manufacturers of marine diesel engines and also makes textile machinery, heating and air conditioning equipment, and a range of other machinery.

Aluminium Suisse S.A., whose stock is one of the most actively traded Swiss stocks, is a major producer of aluminum, and one of the very few Swiss firms that can be considered a "natural resource" supplier.

Types of Shares

In Switzerland three types of shares are traded, and it is important to know the difference: *Inhaberaktie*—bearer certificate; *Namens-aktie*—registered certificate; and *Partizipationsschein*—participation certificate. Few companies have issued all three, but many have issued at least two. The "Big 3" banks are among the exceptions that have issued only one type of shares —bearer certificates.

Bearer certificates show no name. They are as good as cash. They carry dividend coupons which must be detached when due (usually only once a year) to collect the dividend. The shares can be voted and the owner can take advantage of any rights offering if he claims his rights.

Registered certificates are registered in the owner's name, and the dividends are usually paid directly to the owner or his custodian bank. Some companies restrict the sale of registered shares to non-residents so as to prevent control of the company from passing into foreign hands. Swiss nationals and bona fide Swiss residents usually can buy most registered shares and vote them.

To further limit outside control, some companies have also issued participation certificates, which have no voting rights, but usually carry all other benefits of the other types of shares, including dividends and rights offerings.

With a company that has issued two or three types of shares, dividend rates may be the same for all, or they may differ with each type. Where the dividend rate is the same, the bearer certificate usually sells at a premium—often a substantial one. Thus, when the *Ciba-Geigy* registered certificate sold at about SFr. 1400 in 1973, the bearer certificate was selling at SFr. 2300. Both paid dividends of SFr. 22 per share. The differential reflects the anonymity value and cash nature of the bearer certificate. The yield, on the other hand, is better on registered shares.

There is a withholding tax of 30% on dividends and interest from Swiss securities held by non-residents. A United States taxpayer can offset this against his taxable income.

Stock Trading

Switzerland has seven stock exchanges. By far the largest is Zurich, followed by Geneva and Basel. Regional exchanges are in Bern, Lausanne, Neuchatel, and St. Gall.

Trading volume on the Zurich exchange in 1972 was about SFr. 74 billion ($24.5 billion), making it probably the second most important stock exchange in Europe after London. However, a good deal of trading is carried on outside the exchange over the telephone among the banks that are members of the exchange, as well as among non-member banks and brokerage houses that have been licensed to deal in securities. (Licenses for banking and brokerage business are issued by the cantonal authorities and are valid only in the canton in which they are issued.)

All trading on the Swiss stock exchanges is in the hands of the member banks, but licensed non-member banks and brokers can deal outside the exchange "over-the-counter." Membership on the leading three exchanges is somewhat exclusive. In addition to the "Big 3" banks, only a limited number of other banks are members of the Zurich exchange. Total membership in 1973 was 25. Only one foreign bank is a member—*American Express International Banking Corporation* and this membership goes back many years. Today it would probably be very difficult for a foreign bank to become a member of the Zurich exchange.

Total membership of the Basel stock exchange is 22, and of the Geneva exchange, 16. The "Big 3" banks are members of all three exchanges.

Of the more than 1400 securities listed in Zurich in 1973, about 130 were Swiss shares and about 100 foreign securities. The balance was fixed-income securities. Most of the important Swiss corporations are also listed in Geneva and Basel. Except for the largest Swiss corporations, the market for corporate securities is thin, making it difficult to buy or sell larger quantities of shares. Thus, caution or expert advice is essential in such deals.

Switzerland, as most other European countries, has a central agency for the transfer of stock, called *Schweizerische Effekten Giro A.G. (SEGA),* which makes it possible to register change of share ownership without physical exchange of stock certificates. *SEGA* cooperates with *SICOVAM* in France and the *Kassenverein* in Germany, its equivalents in those countries, in the international transfer of ownership on the basis of bookkeeping records.

A non-resident investor is well advised not to take physical possession of a Swiss stock certificate but leave it in the custodial hands of the Swiss bank through which he deals. There are a number of good reasons: ownership is more promptly established through bookkeeping record rather than physical possession of the certificates, and it is safer; the bank will maintain the confidential nature of the account; and the bank will collect the dividends and take care of rights offerings or other actions connected with the stock ownership.

Swiss Investment Funds

A non-resident can buy shares of Swiss investment funds without needing a quota if the portfolio contains 80% or more of foreign securities. All others can be bought only with a quota accrued from sales of Swiss securities by non-residents.

At the end of 1972, there were 139 Swiss investment funds. Many of them included substantial holdings of foreign securities. Many others were real estate funds, or mixed securities and real estate funds, most of them with Swiss real estate in their portfolios, but some with foreign real estate holdings. Only a few funds confine themselves to Swiss securities exclusively. A number of closed-end funds are traded on one or the other of the Swiss stock exchanges. A complete list of both Swiss and foreign funds traded in Switzerland is published at the end of the year by *Eidgenössiche Bankenkommission, Kammer für Anlagefonds,* Bern. The list includes the address and sponsoring bank of each fund, the total asset value, and the nature of its portfolio.

Where to Buy Swiss Securities

Because of the special nature of the Swiss investment market, the most practical way of buying Swiss securities is by opening an account with a Swiss bank. Several of them are represented in the United States. There will be a management fee and a custodial fee, depending on the size of the account, but commissions will generally be lower if a Swiss security is bought through a member of a Swiss stock exchange rather than through a non-member.

International Portfolio Management

In any case, in an international portfolio, Swiss securities at this stage are likely to play a minor role. The real benefit that an international investor can reap in Switzerland is the expertise in international portfolio management that the Swiss have built up over many years of money management for the rich from all over the world.

The number of both Swiss and foreign banks, brokerage houses, and investment advisory services offering international portfolio management in Switzerland is legion, and in spite of the relatively small country there are distinct regional characteristics.

Zurich, the largest financial center, has the reputation of taking a conservative approach. Together with Basel, it has primarily appealed to the Germanic countries to the North. Hot money from Eastern Europe reportedly also tends to flow to Zurich.

Two of the "Big 3" are headquartered in Zurich—*Schweizerische Bankgesellschaft* and *Schweizerische Kreditanstalt.* The third—*Schweizerischer Bankverein*—is headquartered in Basel.

Geneva and Lausanne have the reputation of a more aggressive and imaginative investment approach. They have appealed primarily to investors from the French-speaking countries, the Middle East, and Latin America.

Lugano and the border town of Chiasso have blossomed out as relatively new investment centers, catering primarily to Italians who want to invest their savings abroad.

The best procedure to select a Swiss portfolio manager is probably by questioning a number of non-interested authorities, such as other investors or commercial bankers or brokers who are not themselves involved in international portfolio management.

Sources of Information

All Swiss banks listed at the end of this chapter provide investment information, but mostly with a world-wide viewpoint rather than strictly focused on Swiss securities.

The "Big 3" banks publish yearly statistical guides to Swiss stocks in French and German. An independent guide to Swiss securities, without investment recommendations, is *Handbuch der Schweizerischen Anlagewerte (Guide des Valeurs Suisse de Placement)*, published by *Editions Cosmos, S.A.,* Bern. A number of specialized Swiss financial publications report in detail about the Swiss stock markets and Swiss companies, leading among them *Finanz und Wirtschaft* and *Finanz-Revue/Schweizerisches Wirtschaftsblatt.*

The leading newspapers in Zurich, Basel, and Geneva provide good financial coverage—the *Neue Züricher Zeitung,* the *Basler Nachrichten,* and the *Journal de Genève.*

Capital Research and Management, a leading American investment advisory fund management operation, has its international research affiliate, *Capital International S.A.,* headquartered in Geneva. It publishes research information and charts on some 1000 companies in 17 countries.

Instant television transmission from Swiss stock exchanges as well as world-wide instant stock quotation systems are well developed in Switzerland. Thanks to *Reuters,* a Swiss portfolio manager can get immediate quotations from New York, London, Paris, Milan, Amsterdam, Brussels, Tokyo, Sydney, and the Swiss stock exchanges, as well as quotes on Eurodollar bonds, European commodity prices, and United States bonds.

Information from many Swiss companies themselves is still very scanty by American or British standards, but the Swiss association of financial analysts is making major efforts to induce companies to improve their financial disclosure methods, and some progress in this direction is being made.

Partial List of Swiss Banks Handling Investment Accounts

The "Big 3"

Schweizerische Bankgesellschaft / Bahnhofstrasse 45 / Zurich
(New York Securities Affiliate: *UBS-DB Corp.* / 40 Wall Street / New York, New York 10005)
Schweizerische Kreditanstalt / Paradeplatz 8 / Zurich
(New York Securities Affiliate: *Swiss American Corp.* / 100 Wall Street / New York, New York 10005)
Schweizerischer Bankverein / Aeschenvorstadt 1 / Basel
(New York Securities Affiliate: *Basel Securities Corp.* / 120 Broadway / New York, New York 10005)

Other Banks—Zurich

Bank für Handel und Effekten / Talacker 50 / Zurich
Bank Leu & Co. A.G. / Bahnhofstrasse 32 / Zurich
Julius Bär & Co. / Bahnhofstrasse 36 / Zurich
(New York Securities Affiliate: *Baer Securities Corp.* / 67 Wall Street / New York, New York 10005)
Guyerzeller Zurmont Bank A.G. / Genferstrasse 8/Zurich
Handelsbank in Zürich / Talstrasse 59 / Zurich
Schweizerische Volksbank / Bahnhofstrasse 53 / Zurich
J. Vontobel & Co. / Bahnhofstrasse 3 / Zurich

Other Banks—Geneva

Bordier & Cie / rue Hollande 16 / Geneva
Darier & Cie / rue Saussure 4 / Geneva
De L'Harpe, Leclerc & Cie / boulevard Théâtre 2 / Geneva
Ferrier Lullin & Cie / rue Petitot 15 / Geneva
Hentsch & Cie / rue Corraterie 15 / Geneva
Lombard, Odier & Cie / rue Corraterie 11 / Geneva
Pictet & Cie / rue Diday 6 / Geneva

Other Banks—Basel

Dreyfus Söhne & Cie A.G. / Aeschenvorstadt 16 / Basel
E. Gutzwiller & Cie / Kaufhausgasse 7 / Basel
La Roche & Co. / Rittergasse 25 / Basel
A. Sarasin & Cie / Freie Strasse 107 / Basel

Partial List of Actively Traded Swiss Stocks

Aluminium Suisse S.A. (aluminum)
C.F. Bally S.A. (shoe manufacturing and retail
Bank Leu & Co. A.G. (banking)
Brown Boveri & Cie A.G. (electric and electronic equipment)
Ciba-Geigy A.G. (pharmaceuticals)
Elektro-Watt (electric utility and industrial holding company)
General Shopping S.A. (retail holding company)
Helvetia Schweizerische Feurversicherungsgesellschaft (insurance)
F. Hoffmann-LaRoche & Co. A.G. (pharmaceuticals)
Interfood S.A. (food and household products)

Jelmoli S.A. (retailing)
Landis & Gyr A.G. (electrical and electronic equipment)
Lonza Elektrizitätswerke und Chemische Fabrik A.G. (chemicals)
Motor-Columbus (electric utility)
Nestlé Alimentana S.A. (food and household products)
Sandoz, S.A. (pharmaceuticals)
Adolph Saurer S.A. (machinery and engineering)
Schweizerische Bankgesellschaft (banking)
Schweizerische Kreditanstalt (banking)
Schweizerische Rückversicherungsgesellschaft (insurance)
Schweizerische Volksbank (banking)
Schweizerischer Bankverein (banking)
Gebrüder Sulzer A.G. (machinery and engineering)
Swissair (airline)
Winterthur (insurance)
Zürich Versicherungsgesellschaft (insurance)
Zyma S.A. (pharmaceuticals)

Leading Swiss Fund Management Companies

	Sponsoring Banks
Intrag A.G. / Bahnhofstrasse 45 / Zurich	*Schweizerische Bankgesellschaft*
Société International de Placement/ Elisabethenstrasse 43 / Basel	*Schweizerische Kreditanstalt* and *Schweizerischer Bankverein*
A.G. für Fondsverwaltung / Poststrasse 9 / Zug	*Handelsbank in Zürich*
Kafag A.G. / Bahnhofstrasse 53 / Zurich	*Schweizerische Volksbank*

Each management company manages several different funds.
A complete list of Swiss-based funds, as well as of foreign funds admitted for sale in Switzerland, is available from *Eidgenössische Bankenkomission, Kammer für Anlagefonds* / Bern

Sources of Information

Investment information in Switzerland comes almost exclusively from the banks. All banks listed in this appendix provide investment information in greater or lesser detail, some of it in English.
Particularly useful are *Schweizer Aktienführer,* published by *Schweizerische Bankgesellschaft,* and *Kleines Handbuch der Schweizer Aktien,* published by *Schweizerischer Bankverein.*
An independent guide to Swiss securities is *Handbuch der Schweizerischen Anlagewerte (Guide des Valeurs Suisse de Placement)* published by *Editions Cosmos S.A.* / Aarbergergasse 46, Case postale 2637 / Bern

Leading Swiss Newspapers With Financial Coverage

Basler Nachrichten / Basel
Journal de Genève / Geneva
Neue Züricher Zeitung /Falkenstrasse 11 / Zurich

Specialized Financial Publications

Agence Economique et Financière / 4 rue Montblanc / Geneva
Finanz   Revue / *Schweizerisches   Wirtschaftsblatt* / Lowenstrasse   11 /
  Zurich
Finanz und Wirtschaft / Werdstrasse 11 / Zurich
Schweizerische Finanzzeitung / St. Alban Anlage 14 / Basel
Schweizerische Handelszeitung / Postfach 434 / Zurich

12

FRANCE
THE CHARMED CIRCLE

To many Americans who try to do business in France, the French seem to be an exasperating lot—uncooperative, unbending in their ways, and outrightly discourteous. The feelings are generally reciprocated. To many Frenchmen most Americans appear dull witted, insensitive to the true values of life, and singularly untalented to learn the only language worth speaking.

The obvious recommendation is: leave the French alone in their charmed circle if they like it the way it is, and their feelings will not be hurt. It may also save money. *General Electric* lost an estimated $50 million in an aborted liaison with a French company, *Machines Bull.*

American tourists also have become somewhat disillusioned with France—with the staggering prices in Paris and the rather unloving way in which they are treated by some of the natives. Nevertheless, for the connoisseur, Paris isn't France. He seeks out the provinces for travel, and an increasing number of foreigners consider the French countryside the most pleasing in the world for retirement.

Apart from the overcrowded French Riviera and some parts of the industrial Northeast, France is the most unspoiled and the least crowded of all the industrial nations of Europe. The French seem to have recognized long ago that overcrowding reduces the quality of life, and they have exercized population control for over a hundred years

---

On October 3, 1973 the French franc (FFr.) was valued at U.S. 23.65¢.

—much to the exasperation of the politician who needed cannon fodder to keep the Prussians at bay. (There has been a slight increase in the birth rate since World War II.)

Much of the French countryside has maintained its pristine rural character. It is dotted with architectural gems. And the French tolerate no compromise with the quality of their wine and food—no matter how much this costs—in contrast to many other countries where suppliers often counterbalance rising costs by lowering quality when the customers don't know the difference. There has probably been no scandal more upsetting to Frenchmen in many years than the one in 1973 exposing the adulteration of large quantities of Bordeaux wine.

Thus, the purchase of a small farm for retirement purposes, preferably with a vineyard attached, is probably one of the most gratifying investments one can make these days in France. Even better is income producing property in France, according to a banker who asked to remain nameless because his job is selling securities. Unlike dividend income, rents collected are not subject to the withholding tax, and there is an almost guaranteed appreciation of the capital.

Revival of the Stock Market

Until recently, the French stock market may have seemed as inhospitable to the foreign investor as some Frenchmen appear to the tourist. Many French themselves despised and distrusted the market, made cautious by financial scandals in the course of several countries. Repeated spurts of inflation of the French franc have also made fixed-income securities of questionable value to some French investors. Many of them developed the practice of hoarding their savings in socks and under mattresses, preferably in the form of gold. It is estimated that even today they still have the equivalent of about $5 billion in gold stashed away at home. Compared to anyone who invested in a typical American glamor stock such as *Memorex,* which declined from $200 in 1970 to $4 in 1973, a Frenchman hoarding gold is way ahead of the game. Some Frenchmen, for tax or other reasons, have invested their money in foreign securities via Switzerland, but those who were strongly committed in the United States market in 1969 and thereafter may have become distrustful of all stock markets.

Nevertheless, there are major efforts underway to revitalize the French stock market. All restrictions against purchases of French securities by non-residents were lifted in 1971, and the French market, which had been mostly in a declining trend since 1962, took decided upward turns in 1972, and again in 1973, partly as a result of foreign buying, led by the British, and followed by German, Swiss, and Japanese investors. Trading volume increased by about 50% in 1972.

A special commission was appointed in the late 1960s—the Baumgartner Commission—which, in 1971, published a comprehensive report on what ails the market, including recommendations on how to make the Paris Bourse more attractive to the investor and build it up as a truly international investment center that could rival London. While so far only a few of the recommendations have been implemented, it clearly remains official government policy to develop a healthy capital and investment market in France.

One of the more important steps forward has been the strengthening of the role of the official brokers who are the only agents who can trade on the floor of the exchange. They have been allowed to merge to reduce their number and strengthen the remaining firms. They can now advertise and open branch offices to compete with the banks for the investment business of the public. They are organized in an association, *Compagnie des Agents de Change,* which has embarked on an active public relations campaign to educate the public on the operations of the stock market and investment procedures. Together with government bodies, the association has also started a program aimed at encouraging French companies to provide more meaningful information to shareholders and potential investors.

Strong Economy

The best inducement to invest in France is the healthy economy and the relatively strong currency. No matter what one thinks about de Gaulle and his attitude toward the United States, he provided France with a long period of stable government under which business could flourish and make long-range plans. France can look back on ten years of steady economic growth, and it has become the second largest trading nation in Europe, following Germany, but ahead of the United Kingdom. The re-election of a conservative government in March 1973, has maintained confidence in the French economy among French businessmen and foreign investors. Long range, the economic forecasts are even brighter. Both a capitalist study by the Hudson Institute in the United States and a communist study by the Economic Science Research Institute of Moscow have predicted that by 1980 France will be the fourth largest economic nation in the world, following the United States, Japan, and the Soviet Union. Of course, one has to take such predictions with a grain of salt—a mere little thing such as an energy shortage can trip up even the best economic forecasters. Nevertheless, the real growth rate of the gross national product in 1972 was close to 6%, and the government plans to maintain this rate through the 1970s. The stock market has not yet fully reflected this strength of the French economy, and professional investors consider many French stocks still undervalued by standards applied in other countries, and one of the best vehicles for long-term steady growth investments anywhere in the world.

Cash and Forward Market

There are about 800 companies listed on the Paris Stock Exchange, but only some 200 are actively traded. There are two types of markets on the Paris Bourse—"cash" and "forward." All officially admitted securities can be traded on the cash market, which requires immediate settlement. It is primarily used for purchases of odd (small) lots of stocks and for the trading of most bonds.

Only actively traded common stocks and the most actively traded government bond issue, *Rente Pinay,* were admitted to the forward market in 1973. *Rente Pinay,* which was tied to the price of gold, was by far the most popular issue with the French public, and it accounted for about 10% of all forward transactions. However, it was redeemed in 1973.

Settlement of all transactions of the forward market take place once a month, usually between the 20th and 24th day. Forward market transactions can be "margined," which means that the buyer puts up only a part of the total purchase price until he decides to take delivery of the shares. The percentage of the required margin is determined by the bank or broker executing the order, and may range from 30% to as low as 10%. Such a low margin represents considerable speculative risk.

There are two types of forward trades—the "firm trade" under which the buyer commits himself to take delivery at a firm price, and the "conditional trade." The firm trade provides for three options:

1. the buyer pays the full price of the securities on the settlement day and takes delivery;

2.   the deal is cancelled by a reverse trade in which the buyer sells the securities before the settlement day and collects the net profit from the operation or pays for the loss;

3.   the deal is extended to the next settlement day, either by the buyer or the seller. If the buyer extends the deal, he borrows the necessary money to carry the stock until the settlement day, and he will usually have no trouble doing this since the interest the lender receives on this loan is tax free. On each settlement day the price at which the deal is renewed is fixed by the Stock Exchange. If the price is above the price at which the deal was previously made, the buyer collects the difference, less the carrying costs. If the price at renewal is lower, the buyer pays the difference plus the carrying charge. If the seller renews the deal, he must find someone who is willing to lend him securities to make delivery. This is equivalent to carrying a short position. The cost in this case is the cost of borrowing the securities, plus the stock exchange commission. In both cases, the renewal can be made from month to month and is only done by investors working on margin.

The "conditional" forward market is comparable to option trading in the United States. Two types of options are offered to the investor:

1.   *option,* a put-and-call option, which gives the buyer the right to either buy or sell a certain number of securities for the duration of the contract (up to 12 months) at the last price paid in the forward market, on the day the option was purchased, and

2.   *prime,* which is a call only on any one of the three account days following the contract, and the buyer pays the price of the option only if he does not take delivery of the securities at the price which was agreed upon when the deal was made (a price substantially above the current price on the forward market).

Common Stock

Many French stocks have a thin float (a small number of shares actually available for trading), and this can lead to erratic price movements. The thin float, even with some large companies, may be the result of several factors—close family control, part ownership by the government, by holding companies or by banks; or interlocking ownership with other companies. This interlocking ownership is widespread throughout France and occurs even within the same industry—unthinkable in the United States under the antitrust laws.

Thus, for instance, the well-known French tire maker, *Michelin,* has a major holding in *Kléber-Colombes,* a smaller French tire maker. *Michelin* pioneered the steel-belted radial tire, which in 1973 was beginning to make its entry into the United States. To participate in this business, *Michelin* built plants in Canada and the United States in 1973. *Kléber* is competing with *Michelin* only in a limited way since it makes only rayon-belted radial tires.

Michelin, still closely held by the family, is as uncommunicative with its stockholders as it is communicative with tourists in its famous red and green guide books about tourist sites, hotels, and good eating places. It does not even publish sales figures. Nevertheless, the stock of *Michelin B* (the publicly traded holding company) is the third most actively traded stock on the Paris exchange, and it outperformed the rising market average in 1971 and 1972.

The two most actively traded stocks are those of two oil companies —*Compagnie Française des Pétroles,* 35% government owned, and *Société Nationale des Pétroles d'Aquitaine SNPA,* 51% government owned. Like many government enterprises, their performance has been undistinguished and stock prices have remained relatively flat over the past few years.

Three other companies on top of the active list are better known outside France—*Rhône-Poulenc S.A., Saint-Gobain-Pont-à-Mousson,* and *Péchiney-Ugine Kuhlmann. Rhône-Poulenc,* of which Mr. Baumgartner, who headed up the Baumgartner Commission, was a director, is a large producer of chemicals, synthetic fibers, pharmaceuticals, and photographic films. Its earnings and stock price were on the skids during the early 1970s.

Saint-Gobain-Pont-à-Mousson, which is about 20% owned by a leading financial holding company, *Compagnie Financière de Suez,* has a 35% interest in *Certain-Teed Products Corporation,* a United States building materials manufacturer listed on the New York Stock Exchange. *Saint-Gobain* has shown a modest upward trend in its earnings and stock price during 1970 to 1972.

Also with a stake in the United States, through a 70% ownership of *Howmet Corp.,* is *Péchiney-Ugine Kuhlmann,* a major producer of aluminum and other non-ferrous metals and chemicals. Its earnings and stock price have been on the decline.

Dear to the hearts of both its consumers and stockholders has been *Moët-Hennessy,* makers of excellent champagne, cognac, and perfumes. Earnings have been on a strong upward trend, and the stock price increased from about FFr. 350 in 1969 to FFr. 950 in mid-

1973. In 1973 *Moët-Hennessy* bought some vineyards in California to make "French" California champagne.

Peugeot S.A., whose products are also well known outside France, has also shown a strong performance, with its stock price doubling between early 1972 and mid-1973.

France, a land of small shopkeepers, has bypassed the supermarket era and gone straight from the small corner grocery store to what is described as a "hypermarket"—an oversized supermarket combined under one roof with an oversized Sears-Roebuck type of store, set in the middle of an empty countryside at a comfortable driving distance from several population centers. The company which took this step under dire predictions of failure from all merchandising experts is *Carrefour,* whose stock increased from FFr. 640 in 1970 to FFr. 5200 in mid-1973.

Other stocks popular with French investors include *L'Air Liquide,* a producer of industrial gases which has established itself in the United States through *Liquid Air Corporation of America; Bic,* a maker of ball point pens and pencils which went public in 1972; and *Club Méditerranée,* which has so successfully combined recreation with dating opportunities.

Fixed-Income Securities

France has an extremely active market for fixed-income securities, which account for perhaps 40% of all transactions on the Paris Bourse. The French government itself is a substantial borrower in the capital market, and early in 1973 floated what is probably the largest issue in the history of the Paris Bourse—FFr. 6.5 billion ($1.5 billion) of 7% bonds, to be redeemed by 1988. Other borrowers include government agencies, such as the mail and telecommunications office, government broadcasting corporation, utilities, and roads, as well as municipalities, overseas territories, credit institutions, and state-owned banks and corporations. Sometimes a number of smaller municipalities jointly sell a bond issue.

Some bond issues are sweetened by a lottery. There are regular drawings and the winner either gets cash or other value. The railroads, for instance, give a pass for a certain amount of free miles of travel. These lottery drawings have nothing to do with the drawing for redemption. Most bond issues are redeemed over a specified period of time and the numbers of the certificates to be redeemed at a given time are picked by lot. An investor in a 15-year bond issue, whose "number is up" after a year, may thus find his bond redeemed 14 years before the final redemption.

Increasing money rates usually decrease the current market prices of bonds that were sold earlier at lower rates. But since the bonds are eventually redeemed at the issue price, the investor buying a bond at a depressed price, in addition to collecting his interest, also gets a capital gain on bonds. This capital gain can be substantial in a short span of time if the investor holds a long-term bond certificate with a number that is drawn for early redemption.

As the rate for first-rate bonds crept up to 9% in the second half of 1973, many older bonds with rates ranging from 3% to 7% sold at a discount.

Investment Funds

Until 1964, French law did not permit open-end mutual funds—funds that continually sell additional shares to new investors and redeem outstanding shares. It had about 20 closed-end funds (*Sociétés d'Investissements fermées*) but these did not have much appeal to the general public and remained primarily the domain of the financial holding and portfolio management companies. All closed-end funds are traded on the Paris Stock Exchange. Their total assets are estimated at more than $500 million.

Most of the open-end funds (*SICAVs—Sociétés d'Investissment à Capital Variable*) are managed and sold by banks. Some are sold by insurance companies in conjunction with life insurance. With a particularly strong push from the retail banks through their branch offices, their assets rapidly increased to more than $4 billion by the end of 1972. In 1973 there were more than 70 *SICAVs*. Many of them have an international portfolio and all of them include a certain percentage of French fixed-income securities—originally a government requirement. Financial reports of *SICAVs* performance records and composition of portfolios can be picked up at the various bank offices that sell them, but each bank, naturally, promotes only its own funds. An investor who wants a choice from among the full range of funds should consult a stock broker, or obtain the yearbook of the French investment companies association, *L'Association des Sociétés et Fonds Français d'Investissement,* 1 rue d'Astorg, Paris 8.

Sources of Information

Many formerly close-mouthed French companies have in the last two years or so suddenly opened the floodgates of financial communications, with detailed, colorful annual reports, press releases, conferences, public relations campaigns, and meetings with security analysts. They may have done this for two good reasons: one, to be a step ahead of anticipated government legislation requiring more detailed financial disclosure, and two, to improve the price earnings ratio of their stock. This would make them less vulnerable to take-over bids by British and other foreign companies on the prowl and make it easier for themselves to acquire other companies. While most French companies formerly did not release their yearly results until publication of the annual report sometime in May or June, some companies now release their figures a few weeks after the end of the year, including *Peugeot* and *Saint Gobain-Pont-à-Mousson*. Several companies have begun to translate their annual reports into English.

Two official bodies have established reference libraries where investors can get comprehensive information on all publicly traded companies. One is the information center of the stock brokers association, *Centre de Documentation et d'Information du Chambre Syndicale des Agents de Change*, which has information files on over 2000 French and foreign companies, and the other is the *Centre d'Information* of the *Commission des Opérations de Bourse*, a government watchdog operation, comparable to the SEC, which has complete information files on all listed French companies.

The most widely used investment information sources are the *fiches* (sheets) on French companies prepared regularly by *SEF— Société d'Editions Economiques et Financières*. These can be bought individually at most French book stores; or if not in stock, most bookstores will oblige by ordering them. *SEF* also publishes weekly bulletins with company information and general stock market news.

All the leading French banks active in investments have created a joint securities research organization, *DAFSA—Société de Documentation et d'Analyses Financières,* which publishes a great amount of investment information that is made available to the member banks as well as to outsiders at subscription fees. The material includes information sheets, comparable to *Standard & Poor's* cards, on about 500 French companies and about 500 foreign companies, as well as quarterly information on the *SICAVs* French mutual funds. It also provides detailed analyses on all leading French companies as well as on a number of foreign companies and it prepares studies on specific industries. Together with similar organizations in other European countries, it is developing a unified "European method" of security analysis that is aimed at making it possible for investors to compare performances of different companies in different countries.

The French financial press is rather numerous, maintained to a large extent by financial and corporate advertisers who pay not only for their advertisements but also for the editorial coverage of their news. This is not quite as nefarious as it sounds, since the better publications separate the "company news" from the copy prepared by the editorial staff. Nevertheless, it is possible for a company to get its news releases printed as written if the space is paid for.

Some of the weekly publications present stock recommendations and analyses, in addition to regular financial news, including *La Vie Française, L'Opinion Économique et Financière,* and *Le Journal des Finances.* The leading daily financial papers are *AGEFI, Cote Desfossés, Les Échos,* and *Le Nouveau Journal.* They publish extensive company news in addition to general financial and economic news and detailed stock market reports. The two leading general Paris dailies, *Le Figaro* and *Le Monde,* also have good stock market coverage, in addition to general business and economic news. *Le Monde* publishes an extensive economic supplement once a week.

Leading French banks and French brokers publish a certain amount of investment information for their customers. British brokers have become quite active in French stock analysis, notably *Vickers, Da Costa & Co. Limited,* and research services in most other European countries include a certain amount of French stock reviews.

Where to Buy French Stocks

In France, both banks and stock brokers can sell securities directly to the public. The retail banks have the edge with small investors because of their wide-ranging branch office network. They also offer portfolio management and sell investment fund shares. Sophisticated portfolio management is provided by some of the leading brokers and private banks in Paris.

The three largest French banks are government owned—*Société Générale, Crédit Lyonnais,* and *Banque Nationale de Paris.* All three have offices plus an investment affiliate in New York for investment banking and portfolio investments.

Some of the leading French private banks have for a long time played a major role on the international investment scene. The largest, and strictly speaking a financial holding company, is *Compagnie Financière de Paris et des Pays-Bas (Paribas).*

Paribas has major operations in the United States, Belgium, Switzerland, and the Netherlands, and it is in a joint venture in Luxembourg with the Bank of America. It has arranged an exchange of stock with the leading British merchant bank, *S. G. Warburg & Co., Ltd.*, thus establishing strong ties with the United Kingdom at a time when that country joined the European Common Market in 1973.

Another large French financial holding company is *Campagnie Financière de Suez* which came into existence in its present form in 1956 when the Suez Canal was nationalized. Formerly less involved in banking than in money management, it has since acquired a more than 50% interest in two French banks—*Crédit Industriel et Commercial* and *Banque de l'Indochine*. Assets of the holding company and the two banks combined exceed those of *Paribas Corporation*. *Suez* is represented in the United States through *Suez American Corporation*.

Among other leading French banks on the international investment scene are *de Neuflize, Schlumberger, Mallet; Banque Rothschild;* and *Banque Worms*. A complete list of French banks is available from *Association Professionelle des Banques,* Paris.

Individual orders are accepted by most French banks and brokers in France, but a regular custodial account would be almost essential. Even though most French shares are bearer shares (they do not carry the owner's name and can be cashed by anyone who holds them), in practice most French shareholders, through their banks or brokers, have their shares on deposit with the French central clearing agency for stocks, *SICOVAM*. The custodian bank or broker will collect the owner's dividends and watch over other benefits, such as rights offerings, that may accrue to him. French banks represented in the United States will handle orders for French stocks from institutional investors, but only to a limited extent, if at all, from private investors. French securities can be bought through United States brokers specializing in foreign trading (listed in Chapter 1).

Taxes

French companies pay a 50% corporate tax. In order to avoid double taxation, the French tax authorities permit investors to use 50% of their dividends as a tax credit (*avoir fiscal*) against their income tax. For a non-resident investor there is a 10% withholding tax on dividends. A United States citizen or resident filing a Federal income tax return can apply the 10% withholding tax as well as the 50% *avoir fiscal* against his taxable income.

The first FFr. 1000 interest from French fixed-income securities is tax free. Beyond that amount, the French taxpayer has the choice of either adding the interest income to his other taxable income or paying tax on the interest at a flat rate of 25%.

There is no capital gains tax for French residents, but a United States resident has to pay capital gains tax at United States rates.

All French securities are subject to the Interest Equalization Tax.

Partial List of French Bank Representatives in New York
Involved in Security Transactions

Anjou Securities, Inc. / 1 State Street Plaza / New York, New York 10004 (represents *Banque de l'Indochine*)

EuroPartners Securities Corp. / 1 World Trade Center / New York, New York 10048 (represents *Crédit Lyonnais*)

European American Banking Corporation / 10 Hanover Square / New York, New York 10004 (represents *Société Générale*)

French American Capital Corporation / 40 Wall Street / New York, New York 10005 (represents *Banque Nationale de Paris*)

New Court Securities Corporation / 1 Rockefeller Plaza / New York, New York 10020 (represents *Banque Rothschild*)

Parisbas Corporation / 40 Wall Street / New York, New York 10005 (represents *Banque de Paris et des Pays-Bas*)

Suez American Corporation / 77 Water Street / New York, New York (represents *Compagnie Financière de Suez* and *Crédit Industriel et Commercial*)

French Nationalized Banks

Banque Nationale de Paris / 16 boulevard des Italiens / Paris
Crédit Lyonnais / 19 boulevard des Italiens / Paris
Société Générale pour favoriser le développement du Commerce et de l'Industrie en France / 29 boulevard Haussmann / Paris

Leading French Publicly Owned and Private Banks

Banque Commerciale Privée / 9 rue Scribe / Paris
Banque Française / 32 rue Notre-Dame-des-Victoires / Paris
Banque Française du Commerce Extérieur / 21 boulevard Haussmann / Paris
Banque Française Commerciale / 74 rue Saint-Lazare / Paris
Banque de Gestion Privée / 20 rue de la Baume / Paris
Banque de l'Indochine / 96 boulevard Haussmann / Paris
Banque de Paris et des Pays-Bas / 3 rue d'Antin / Paris
Banque Rothschild / 19-21 rue Laffitte / Paris
Banque de Suez et de l'Union des Mines / 9 rue Louis-Murat / Paris
Banque de l'Union Parisienne / 6 and 8 boulevard Haussmann / Paris
Banque Worms / 45 boulevard Haussmann / Paris
Compagnie Bancaire / 23-25 avenue Kléber / Paris
Crédit Commercial de France / 103 avenue des Champs-Élysées / Paris
Crédit Français / 37 rue des Mathurins / Paris
Crédit Industriel et Commercial / 66 rue de la Victoire / Paris
Crédit Parisien / 33 rue Cambon / Paris
Hottinguer et Cie / 38 rue de Provence / Paris
Lazard Frères & Cie / 5 rue Pillet-Will / Paris
Louis-Dreyfus / 6 rue Rabelais / Paris
de Neuflize, Schlumberger, Mallet / 12 place de la Bourse / Paris

Pommier & Cie (Banque Commerciale d'Escompte de Paris) / 57 rue de
   Faubourg-Poissonnière / Paris
Rivaud & Cie / 13 rue Notre-Dame-des-Victoires / Paris
Société Anonyme de Crédit a l'Industrie Française / 93 rue de Provence /
   Paris
Société Française de Banque / 119 boulevard Haussmann / Paris
Union Bancaire du Nord / 10-12 rue du Colonel-Driant / Paris
A complete list of banks in France is available from *Association Profes-*
   sionelle des Banques / 18 rue La Fayette / Paris

Partial List of Paris Brokerage Houses

Bacot, Allain, Farra & Cie / 13 rue La Fayette / Paris 9
Bonnet, Roquet & Cie / 4 rue de Choiseul / Paris 2
Boscher & Cie / 18 rue du Croissant / Paris 2
P. Bottmer, J. François-Dufour & Cie / 116 rue Réaumur / Paris 2
Bourdel, Delahaye & Cie / 178 rue Montmartre / Paris 2
J. Cappeliez, Y. Michelez, J. Tricart & Cie / 99 rue de Richelieu / Paris 2
R. Cheuvreux, R. de Virieu & Cie / 12 place Vendôme / Paris 1
Desaché, Goirand & Cie / 21 rue d'Antin / Paris 2
X. L. Dupont, F. Denant, R. Dubois & Cie / 42 rue Notre-Dame-des-
   Victoires / Paris 2
Emery, Sitri & Cie / 107 rue Réaumur / Paris 2
Pierre Ferri, Georges Ferri, Marc Pujos & Cie / 53 rue Vivienne / Paris 2
X. de la Fournière, H. Le Febvre & Cie / 25 rue Joubert / Paris 9
Goy, Hauvette & Cie / 142 rue Montmartre / Paris 2
Guiard, Tuffier & Cie / 10 rue du 4-Septembre / Paris 2
Hamant, La Fortelle & Cie / 19 rue Le Peletier / Paris 9
Bernard Jac, Perreau-Saussine & Cie / 8 rue Sainte-Anne / Paris 1
Jullien, Ducatel & Cie / 4 rue de la Bourse / Paris 2
Lacarrière, Koller & Cie / 16 rue Halevy / Paris 9
Lambert, Etienne & Cie / 13 rue du 4-Septembre / Paris 2
Lebel, Laborne, Wolff & Cie / 10 rue d'Uzès / Paris 2
Le Guay, Massonaud & Cie / 25 rue de Choiseul / Paris 2
F. Mayer, L. Vialettes & Cie / 10 rue du 4-Septembre / Paris 2
Meeschaert & Cie / 16 boulevard Montmartre / Paris 9
Yves Meunier, Jean Benoit & Cie / 40 rue Notre-Dame-des-Victoires /
   Paris 2
B. Michel, Y. Perlès & Cie / 34 rue Lafitte / Paris 9
Nivard, Flornoy & Cie / 20 boulevard Montmartre / Paris 9
J.-J. Perquel, A. Krucker & Cie / 17 rue de la Banque / Paris 2
Bérnard Pierre, Jean Girardet & Cie / 7 rue Drouot / Paris 9
Rondeleux, Oudart & Cie / 20 rue Drouot / Paris 9
Ch.-Max Roth le Gentil, Jean Varangot & Cie / 10 cité Rougemont /
   Paris 9
Jacques Sargenton, Jean Saintoin & Cie / 3 rue des Mathurins / Paris 9
Jean Schelcher, Michel Dumont & Cie / 1 rue Taitbout / Paris 9
Sellier, Labbé et Cie / 12 rue d'Uzès / Paris 2
Soulié, Tellier & Cie / 3 rue Rossini / Paris 9
Hayaux du Tilly, Lanquest & Cie / 19 rue de Provence / Paris 9

Partial List of Most Actively Traded French Stocks

L'Air Liquide (industrial gasses)
Aquitaine (Société Nationale des Pétroles d') (petroleum)
Banque de l'Indochine (banking)
BSN (Boussois-Souchon-Neuvesel S.A.) (glass, beverages, food)
Carrefour (retailing)
Casino, Guichard, Perrachon & Cie (retailing)
Ciments Lafarge (cement)
CIT-Alcatel (electrical products and electronics)
Compagnie Bancaire (credit, financing)
Compagnie Française des Pétroles (petroleum)
Compagnie Générale d'Électricité (electrical manufacturing)
Crédit Foncier de France (mortgage banking)
Denain Nord-Est Longwy (steel)
Eaux (Compagnie Générale des) (utility)
Financière de Paris et des Pays-Bas (Compagnie) (banking)
Librairie Hachette (publishing)
Kléber-Colombes (tires)
Locafrance (equipment leasing)
Machines Bull (Compagnie des) (electrical products and electronics)
Le Matériel Téléphonique (electrical products and electronics; ITT owns
    68%)
Michelin (tires)
Moët-Hennessy (champagne, cognac, perfumes)
Le Nickel (nickel, uranium)
L'Oréal (consumer products)
Paris-France (retailing)
Péchiney-Ugine Kuhlmann (aluminum, electrometallurgy)
Pernod (liquors)
Peugeot S.A. (automotive)
Printemps (retailing)
Rhône-Poulenc S. A. (chemicals, synthetic fibers, pharmaceuticals, film)
Roussel-Uclaf (pharmaceuticals)
Saint-Gobain-Pont-à-Mousson (glass)
Source Perrier (flour milling, bakery, animal feed)
Suez et de l'Union Parisienne (Compagnie Financière de) (financial hold-
    ing company)
La Télémécanique Électrique (electrical products and electronics)
Thomson-Brandt (radio, TV, appliances)
Usinor (steel)

Partial List of French Investment Funds

Acier-Investissement
Actanea
Actions Selectionnées
Aedificandi (Union-Sequanaise- Ur-
    baine)
America Valor
Assurances Placements

Ceninve
CIP-Compagnie d'Investissement et
    de Placement
C.I.P.E.C.
Compagnie Générale d'Investisse-
    ment (C.G.I.)
Credinter

Drouot-Investissements
Elysées Valeurs
Epargne Assurance
Epargne Croissance
Epargne Institutions
Epargne Obligations
Epargne Revenu
Epargne Unie
Epargne Valeur
Euro-Croissance
Fortune 1
France-Croissance
France-Epargne
France-Garantie
France-Investissement
France-Placement
Fructidor
Gestion Rendement
Gestion Sélective
IMSI
Indo-Valeurs
Intercroissance
Intersélection
Laffitte-Rendement
Livret-Portefeuille, Le
L'U.A.P.-Investissements
Oblisem
Optima
Paribas Gestion
Pierre Investissement
Placements Institutionnels
Première Catégorie
Risques-Investissements
Rothschild-Expansion
Sécurité Mobilière, La
Sélection-Croissance

Sélection Etrangère
Sélection Mondiale
Sélection-Rendement
S.I. Est
Sicavimmo
Slivafrance
Slivam
Slivarente
Slivinter
S.M.I.
Société d'Epargne Mobilière
Société d'Investissement et de Gestion
Société de Gestion Mobilière
Société de Placements Internationaux
Société de Placements Sélectionnés en France et a l'Etranger
Société Nationale d'Investissement
Société Nouvelle France-Obligations
Société Parisienne de Placement et de Gestion
Sofragi
Sogepargne
Sogevar
Soginco
Soginter
Soleil-Investissement
Solpi
Ufinord
Unigestion
Univalor
Valorem
Vivax

A complete list with addresses and sponsoring banks is available from *L'Association des Sociétés et Fonds Français d'Investissement* / 1 rue d'Astorg / Paris 8

Main French Sources of Investment Information

SEF—Société d'Editions Economiques et Financières / 31 rue de Rome / Paris 8

DAFSA—Société de Documentation et d'Analyses Financières / 125 rue Montmartre / Paris 2

Centre de Documentation et d'Information, Chambre Syndicale des Agents de Change / 4 place de la Bourse / Paris 2

Centre d'Information, Commission des Opérations de Bourse, Tour Nobel / 3 avenue du Général de Gaulle / 92-Puteaux

Main Daily Newspapers with Extensive Financial Coverage

Le Figaro / 14 Rond-Point des Champs-Élysées / Paris 8
International Herald Tribune / 21 rue de Berri / Paris 8 (English language)
Le Monde / 5 rue des Italiens / Paris 9

Specialized Daily Financial Publications

L'Agence Economique et Financière / 108 rue de Richelieu / Paris 2
L'Agence Quotidiene d'Informations Economiques et Financières / 36 rue Vivienne / Paris 2
Le Capital / 1 rue Saint-Georges / Paris 9
Cote Desfossés / 42 rue Notre-Dame-des-Victoires / Paris 2
Les Echos / 37 Champs-Élysées / Paris 8
Le Nouveau Journal / 108 rue de Richelieu / Paris 2
La Presse Française / 17 rue Cadet / Paris 9

Principal Economic and Financial Weeklies

La Cote Bleue / 17 rue Saint-Joseph / Paris 2
L'Echo de la Finance / 9 boulevard des Italiens / Paris 2
L'Economiste de Paris / 17 rue Saint-Joseph / Paris 2
Entreprise / 13 rue Saint-Georges / Paris 9
Fortune Française / 17 rue d'Anjou / Paris 8
Les Informations Industrielles et Commerciales / 142 rue Montmartre / Paris 2
Le Journal des Finances / 122 rue Réaumur / Paris 2
L'Opinion Economique et Financière / 1 rue Saint-Georges / Paris 9
Perspectives / 55 rue de Châteaudun / Paris 9
Valeurs Actuelles / 14 rue d'Uzès / Paris 2
La Vie Française / 67 avenue Franklin-Roosevelt / Paris 8

Other Periodical Business and Financial Publications

L'Actionnaire / 21 boulevard Montmartre / Paris 2
La Conjoncture Economique et Financière / 17 avenue La Bourdonnais / Paris 7
L'Economie / 118 rue de Turenne / Paris 3
Etudes et Conjoncture, édité par les Presses Universitaires de France / 108 boulevard Saint-Germain / Paris 8
L'Expansion / 25 rue de Berri / Paris 8
Le Hors-Cote / 1 rue Saint-Georges / Paris 9
Le Moniteur Economique et Financier / 29 boulevard Poissonière / Paris 9
Revue Banque / 49 avenue de l'Opéra / Paris 1
S.E.D.E.I.S., Bulletin de la Société d'Études et de Documentations Economiques Industrielles et Sociales / 205 boulevard Saint-Germain / Paris 7
Le Journal des Tirages Financiers / 6 rue du Faubourg-Montmartre / Paris 9

13

GERMANY
MIDAS' PLIGHT

After having been the *Wirtschaftswunder* (economic miracle) in
the 1950s and 1960s, Germany became a *Geldwunder* (money miracle) in the early 1970s. A veritable flood of foreign exchange poured
into Germany until foreign currency reserves reached the staggering
amount of about DM 85 billion ($34 billion) in mid-1973. The
German mark was revalued three times in relation to the United
States dollar between 1971 and 1973, for a total of almost 40%.
Yet, this monetary affluence did very little for the German stock
market. Its performance remained undistinguished in 1973, and investment opportunities appeared to be fewer and more hazardous than
in several other countries. Yet, Germany is one of the strongest industrial countries in the world, with a gross national product second
only to the United States and on a par with Japan—two countries
that have far more liquid and active stock markets than Germany.

Bank Power

There seem to be a number of varied and complex reasons why the
German stock market should be so much weaker than the economy.

One still frequently mentioned by investors, both inside and outside Germany, is that "the banks control everything, including the
stock markets." German bankers are very sensitive about this repu-

On October 3, 1973 the Deutsches mark (DM) was valued at U.S. 41.39¢.

tation, and it may no longer be justified. Nevertheless, this sentiment exists, and in the stock market what people believe often counts as much as what is fact.

But here are some facts: German banks control a good many of the larger publicly owned companies. They are both commercial and investment bankers (functions that are separated in the United States). They also lend money to the retail customer, they provide him with mortgages, and they take in his deposits and savings. They are the only stockbrokers dealing with the public; they are major investors themselves, as well as investment advisors; they are stock traders; and they own the management companies of most of the German investment funds.

Of course, in other Continental European countries banks also play a dominant role, but in Germany this "bank power" seems particularly pronounced, and even though it exists without obvious abuse, it nevertheless seems to have had a retarding effect on the development of active investment markets.

A Limited Market

German industry is still largely financed by bank loan rather than equity (common shares, or bonds convertible into common shares). Only a few new issues have come to the market in recent years.

The best known among them is the *Volkswagen* issue sold by the Federal government to the public, with unhappy results to the investor who bought the stock at the issue price. The stock price declined precipitously because of declining earnings, poor management decisions, and very bad handling of the bad news. Other new issues included *VEBA A.G.* (utility and chemicals), *Deutsche Lufthansa A.G.* (airline), *Neckermann Versand K.G.a.A.* (a mail-order firm), and *Horton A.G.* (department store). Nevertheless, the number of German companies listed on the German stock exchanges has actually decreased from 643 in 1962 to 505 at the end of 1972.

Of these 505 shares, not many more than 20 are traded in such volume that fairly large orders can be executed without excessive disturbance of the price. Another 40 to 50 stocks have enough trading volume for smooth execution of retail orders or small block orders. Most of the others are issues of small capitalization or stocks of regional companies. A large number of German companies are controlled by family groups, banks, holding companies, or investment companies to such an extent that only a relatively small percentage of the outstanding shares is available for public trading. However, there is no secret about this ownership. *Commerzbank A.G.,* one of the three largest German banks, regularly publishes a directory, *Wer gehört zu wem* (Who Belongs to Whom), which gives very precise information about holdings in German companies.

Much of the trading volume of the smaller German stock exchanges seems to be arbitrage business among the banks—they buy a stock on one stock exchange and at the same time sell it on another for fractional *pfennigs* of profit. This keeps the prices of stocks listed on several stock exchanges about the same, but it does not really add anything to genuine portfolio investments.

Political and Economic Factors

There are also a number of political, economic, and social factors that have a dampening effect on the German stock markets. Under a socialist government that looked firmly ensconced in the fall of 1973, the banks themselves face some clouds. There was talk in 1973 of nationalization of the "Big 3"—*Deutsche Bank A.G., Dresdner Bank A.G.,* and *Commerzbank A.G.*—or at least a separation of the banking business from the investment business and from some of the industrial holdings. Even though this was a remote possibility in 1973, it is not exactly a bullish factor for bank stocks, nor perhaps for the stocks of some of the companies banks control.

Some government intervention is expected in other areas—the most immediate one in the fiscal area to curb inflation, which in 1973 progressed at an annual rate of 8%. Interest rates in 1973 were pushed up to 10% and more, and common stock prices, as they usually do in times of rising interest rates, declined. Tax measures, both for corporations and individuals, were planned to siphon off funds, and a number of Federal government expenditures were to be suspended. These measures might depress stock prices.

The attitude of many Germans toward the stock market in the past has been erratic and unsophisticated. After a long history of apathy and ignorance during which the average German put his money into savings accounts or fixed-income securities, the Germans in the 1960s broke out into an investment frenzy, partly sparked by the high-pressure sales methods of "Bernie" Cornfeld's *IOS* locust swarm of mutual fund salesmen.[1] After the collapse of *IOS* and *Gramco* (another questionable investment fund operation that appealed to many gullible Germans), the sobering awakening swung the pendulum in the opposite direction, and even dead-honest and successful mutual funds had some trouble selling their shares in Germany. New stringent regulations governing the sale of foreign mutual fund shares were introduced in 1969, which radically reduced the number of foreign funds offered in Germany. This gave a boost to the German investment trusts, which after a lull in 1970 and 1971 found new money coming in 1972 and 1973, even though a good number of them did not have very persuasive performance records.

There seem to be an unusually large number of "hot tip sheets" in Germany, and as long as they find readers one must assume that many German investors still prefer to act on the basis of "hot tips." On the other hand, the banks are making every effort to disseminate sound investment information, and this should help to develop more sober, long-term investment practices among German investors.

Foreign Buying Restricted

Probably also working as a depressant on the German stock market in 1973 were the restrictions on the sales of German securities to non-residents, which were imposed in February 1973, following the second dollar devaluation, and tightened in August 1973. According to the August 1973 regulations of the German *Bundesbank,* a non-resident can buy a German security from a German bank only if he has sold or redeemed German securities of at least the same value as those he wants to buy, thereby establishing a "quota" for himself at the bank. There are two non-resident quotas—"A," covering German common stocks, warrants, convertible bonds, investment fund shares, and a few others; and "B," primarily covering German straight bonds. A credit under the "A" quota can no longer be used for the purchase of "B" quota securities, and vice versa, as was possible before August 1973.

German shares are, of course, also actively traded outside Germany on the leading European stock exchanges, and these can be bought by non-residents of Germany without restrictions. When the restrictions in Germany were imposed in February 1973, German shares abroad began to sell at a premium ranging up to 8% above the prices on the German exchanges (down to about 2% late in 1973). This led to brisk *Koffergeschäfte* (suitcase deals) across the border by German residents who bought German securities in Germany, put them in their suitcases, transported them across the borders and sold them at premiums abroad. This business was particularly easy since most German shares, excluding many insurance company shares, are not registered in the owner's name, but are made out to "bearer." Whoever holds them can sell them or collect the dividend due. Such "exports" of German securities now require a permit from the German *Bundesbank,* but permitless exports are obviously difficult to control and to prosecute because of the anonymous nature of bearer certificates and the ease with which paper can be carried or shipped. To stop the *Koffergeschäfte,* German banks agreed to stop selling bearer certificates over the bank counters against cash. Nevertheless, the efforts of the *Bundesbank* are just another illustration of how government interference in normal economic processes creates distortions and circumventions, without necessarily achieving their original intention.

Fixed-Income Securities

Koffergeschäfte for a time also developed in the opposite direction. Non-residents bought German shares outside Germany and sold them inside Germany to build up a quota with a bank to buy fixed-income securities with a higher yield than those obtainable outside Germany. This business came to an end in August 1973, when the quota for common stock was separated from that for bonds.

Nevertheless, German fixed-income securities in 1973 remained highly attractive because of a yield of 10% and more and the protection that the German mark had offered against the devaluation of the dollar in the past.

A German-speaking widow, who in 1970 decided to retire from the music world of New York to the shores of a Bavarian lake, converted most of her American stock and mutual fund shares into German fixed-income securities on her arrival. At that time interest rates in Germany also were at a peak, and her average income from securities was close to 10%. If she had left her savings in American securities, her income would have been much lower; and she would have lost about 40% *vis-à-vis* the German mark and would not have been able to maintain her living standard.

Between the peaks of 1970 and 1973, German interest rates were considerably lower, and these great swings offer an interesting appreciation possibility in older bonds that are bought at the peak of the interest curve. It works in theory like this: As yields from new bonds increase, the prices of older bonds sold at lower yields decrease, so that their current yield approximates the yield of the new bonds. But when bonds mature, they are redeemed by the issuer at the original issue price. The number of years remaining to maturity reflect in the price of the bond. A bond close to maturity will sell at a higher price (and lower yields) than one that still has many years to go.

In Germany, in mid-1973, an investor could buy a safe corporate bond originally sold at DM 100 for about DM 75 with an annual coupon of DM 6 (an effective yield of 8%), with 15 years to go to maturity. This means that in addition to his 8% income, he would have a capital appreciation of DM 25, or 33%, over 15 years until maturity when the bond is redeemed at its issue price of DM 100. This is an average gain of 2% a year. Short-range—over, say, a year or two—the appreciation may be much higher if interest rates would suddenly come down. And this is a distinct possibility in Germany where interest rates have fluctuated widely because of government policy rather than as a result of the supply of money. Thus, a bond selling at DM 75 in 1973 may well go up to 85 in a year or two if interest rates come down by 2% or more.

Common Stock

For anyone venturing into German common stock, it would be prudent to stay with a few, well recognized values, unless he has a discretionary account with a sophisticated portfolio manager who relieves him of all investment decisions. Among the most active shares on the German stock exchanges are the three largest banks—*Deutsche Bank A.G., Dresdner Bank A.G.,* and *Commerzbank A.G.* —and the three chemical giants, successor companies of *IG Farben* —*Bayer A.G., Farbwerke Hoechst A.G.,* and *BASF.* All of them are traded over-the-counter in the United States in the form of American Depositary Receipts. The banks were not widely recommended in 1973 because of the uncertainties concerning their future. The *IG Farben* successor companies were considered long-term recovery situations. More popular was *Schering A.G.,* a successful pharmaceutical company, with a total sales volume of about DM 1.2 billion annually and a stock price appreciation from about DM 160 in 1966 to DM 550 in 1973. Other good stock market records were established by the German automobile manufacturers *Daimler-Benz A.G.,* maker of the Mercedes, and *BMW A.G.,* whose new sports cars have become popular in the United States and other parts of the world. *Daimler-Benz* stock increased from about DM 100 in 1966 to DM

400 in 1973; *BMW* increased from about DM 60 in 1967 to DM 250 in 1973. *Volkswagen,* whose price collapsed after going public, was considered a good recovery situation in 1973.

Another recovery situation is *Neckermann Versand K.G.a.A.,* a giant mail-order firm, with an annual sales volume of more than DM 2 billion. The firm has gone heavily into the travel business. After having stubbed its toes badly in the investment management and advisory business, *Neckermann* has recovered from a bad earnings decline in 1969. The stock price also recovered from a low of about DM 60 in 1970 to about DM 150 in 1973.

Germany, like the United States, has two electrical equipment manufacturing giants—*Siemens A.G.* and *AEG*—which may benefit from the increasing world-wide energy demand. Of the two, *Siemens* in 1973 was considered the much sounder investment while *AEG* still had to solve some internal problems.

Interest rates are likely to remain a major factor in German stock prices. When interest rates peak out—and they may go as high as 12%, according to some German bankers—it may be the time to go back into German common stock. As interest rates decline to more normal levels, German stock prices are likely to stage a comeback.

As one seasoned investment professional said, timing is of particular importance in the German stock market. He buys German stocks when few people want them and sells them when everybody wants them. Because of the relatively thin market of many German stocks, it is difficult to buy at reasonable prices in a bull market and sell easily in a bear market. Under this formula, 1973 was a good year to buy German stocks. Nevertheless, sophisticated professional advice would seem to be particularly needed in Germany.

Information

The German accounting profession has the reputation of employing first-class, above-board auditing methods. However, by American standards, the presentation of German financial statements leaves something to be desired, and they cannot be easily interpreted by anyone but the initiated. German firms have the tendency to set aside large reserves and understate their earnings. The purpose is to report smooth earnings progress year after year and to maintain the dividend rate even in poorer years. Efforts are underway, including efforts by the German Financial Analysts Association, to encourage companies to report earnings more accurately and present financial figures more in accordance with internationally accepted accounting principles.

Inside information not available to the public has been a problem in the past, but a special commission set up by the Federal government submitted a report and recommendations in 1973, which were accepted by the investment community and are expected to solve this problem.

In general, there is a large amount of investment information available in Germany, a good deal of it in English.

Deutsche Bank A.G., Dresdner Bank A.G., and *Commerzbank A.G.*—as well as other German banks listed at the end of this chapter —provide ample information on German stocks, some of it in English. *Deutsche Bank* has established a completely independent investment service—*Deutsche Gesellschaft für Anlageberatung m.b.H.,* in Frankfurt, whose services are sold not only to customers of *Deutsche Bank* but also to competitor banks and industrial clients. The service includes reports on industrial companies, German as well as non-German, industry reports, and statistical material. Reportedly, the bank has established this independent advisory service as a safeguard against the potential separation of the investment business from the banking business.

Among the private banks, *Georg Hauck & Sohn, Bankiers,* Frankfurt/Main, and *BerlinerHandels-Gesellschaft-Frankfurter Bank,* Frankfurt/Main, publish comprehensive investment reports in English.

By far the largest publisher of investment information, as well as of other business and financial reference books, information services and directories, is *Verlag Hoppenstedt & Co.,* Darmstadt. Investment information services include company fact sheets, comparable to those published by *Standard & Poor's* in the United States, a fixed-income guide, chart service, a *Vademecum* (guide) on German and foreign investment funds sold in Germany, and statistical stock market data. In conjunction with the French investment information firm of *DAFSA, Hoppenstedt* is developing a unified European system of security analysis that is intended to make it possible to compare results of companies in different countries and evaluate their comparative stock market values.

Institut für Bilanzanalysen, Frankfurt/Main, sells in-depth studies of German companies, comparable in detail and approach to American institutional reports.

Outside Germany, the London brokerage house of *Vickers, Da*

Costa & Co. Limited publishes reports on German stock markets as well as recommendations of individual German stocks.

The *Handelsblatt,* the German *Wall Street Journal,* and the *Börsen Zeitung* include in their pages reports on individual German companies and stock market opinions. The *Frankfurter Allgemeine Zeitung* and *Die Welt,* two leading general newspapers, also have excellent stock market coverage. In addition, there are a number of specialized investment publications and "tip sheets."

Investment Funds

The *Bundesverband Deutscher Investment Gesellschaften* provides information on German investment funds, including the names of the sponsoring banks through which they are sold. Practically all mutual funds in Germany are owned and sold by banks. Only open-end funds are permitted in Germany. The total asset value of all German securities funds, in July 1973, was about DM 15 billion ($6.15 billion). About 40% of the total was in German common stock, 40% in German fixed-income securities, 8% in foreign securities (an unusually low percentage), and the balance in cash (an unusually high percentage). Thus, German funds offered the small investor the opportunity to invest in the German economy on a diversified basis. There are also a number of real estate funds in Germany.

Where to Buy German Securities

Only banks can trade on the German stock exchanges on behalf of investors. (There are some floor brokers, but they cannot trade with the public.) Practically all member banks on the stock exchanges are German, but a few foreign banks have lately penetrated the formerly closed circle, notably *Chase Manhattan Bank* and *Chemical Bank.* The two are members of the Frankfurt Stock Exchange and can buy and sell German securities directly, without having to go through a German bank. The *Bank of America* is a member of the Düsseldorf Stock Exchange.

Frankfurt claims to be the largest of the eight German stock exchanges, with an unofficially estimated 45% of all trades in German common stocks and 75% of all trades in bonds. But Düsseldorf might dispute this claim, and is certainly a close second. Hamburg and Munich are numbers three and four, and much smaller exchanges are in Berlin, Bremen, Hannover, and Stuttgart. Most of the large

German companies are traded on several or all of the exchanges, and for an investor it is of little interest where his order is executed. The larger banks are members of several or all of the exchanges.

Nevertheless, Frankfurt has emerged as the main financial center of Germany, while Düsseldorf is more important as an industrial center, and Hamburg the place for international oil companies and for commodity trading. Recently, *Commerzbank* transferred its head office from Düsseldorf to Frankfurt, so that all three of the "Big 3" are now headquartered in Frankfurt. An increasing number of foreign banks have established themselves in Frankfurt, and the Frankfurt exchange also leads in the number of foreign stocks listed on German exchanges.

Formerly much of the common stock was traded among the banks outside the exchanges, but according to a recent agreement among the banks, all common stock should be traded on the exchanges, unless a customer specifically requests otherwise. Such an agreement is, of course, difficult to police, but it may be assumed that reported trading volume today reflects a fair picture of actual activities. Most of the bonds are still traded among the banks outside the stock exchange over the telephone.

The "Big 3" have branch offices throughout Germany, and most of these offices have a securities counter where a bona fide German resident with an account, or cash, can buy German securities. Verification of the legal residence is usually not required. Investment advice at the branch office is, of course, limited, but on the other hand, there is also no effort made to steer a customer into any particular investment since the banks sell everything—German and foreign common stock, German and foreign bonds, investment fund shares, and gold. For fully professional investment advice, an investor would have to open a discretionary account with one of the main offices of the banks. The minimum portfolio for such an account at the Big 3 ranges from DM 350,000 ($144,000) to DM 500,000 ($200,000).

All three banks are represented in the United States, and their American offices will accept orders for German stocks from institutional investors, brokerage houses, and larger individual investors. Smaller individual investors would have to work with one of the American brokers accepting retail orders for foreign securities (listed at the end of Chapter 1).

Some German private banks may be able to give somewhat more personalized management and counseling services than the big banks. Most of them also have a minimum for managed accounts—somewhat lower than that of the big banks.

Taxes

Non-residents pay a withholding tax of 28.25% on dividends and interest received from German securities they own. If their country of residence has a double taxation agreement with Germany (which the United States does), they can apply for a refund of 10% from the German tax authorities so that their effective withholding tax is 18.25%. There is no withholding tax on interest from DM bonds issued by a non-German organization, a foreign government agency, or a United States corporation.

German residents pay a capital gains tax (*Spekulationssteuer*— speculation tax) on any gains above DM 1000 made on the sale of securities held less than six months. The gain is simply added to the regular taxable income. There is talk of extending the capital gains tax on values held for longer than six months.

For a non-resident it is most practical to leave his German securities in custody with a bank. The Germans have an excellent system of stock ownership transfer by simply bookkeeping entry through a central office, the *Kassenverein*. The custodian bank will collect dividends and interest and be alert to rights issues. German companies issuing additional shares offer these to existing stockholders through rights, often under a somewhat complicated formula that requires familiarity before a reasonable evaluation can be made. Rights not taken up are sold on the last trading day of the new rights issue, and the proceeds are paid to the owner of the original shares.

Leading German Banks
The Big 3

Commerzbank A.G. / Grosse Gallusstrasse 17-19 / Frankfurt
(New York Securities Affiliate: *EuroPartners Securities Corporation* /
    1 World Trade Center / New York, New York 10048)
Deutsche Bank A.G. / Grosse Gallusstrasse 10-14 / Frankfurt
(New York Securities Affiliate: *UBS-DB Corporation* / 40 Wall Street /
    New York, New York 10005)
Dresdner Bank A.G. / Gallusanlage 7 / Frankfurt
(New York and Boston Securities Affiliate: *ABD Securities Corporation* /
    53 State Street / Boston, Massachusetts 02109 / and 84 William Street /
    New York, New York 10038)
These are headquarters addresses. The banks have branch offices in most
parts of the Federal Republic of Germany.

Major Regional Banks

(roughly in the order of the size of their assets)

Bayerische Hypotheken und Wechsel-Bank / Theatinerstrasse 8-17 /
    Munich
(New York and Boston Securities Affiliate: *ABD Securities Corporation* /
    53 State Street / Boston, Massachusetts 02109 / and 84 William Street /
    New York, New York 10038)
Bayerische Vereinsbank / Kardinal-Faulhaber-Strasse 14 / Munich
Bank für Gemeinwirtschaft A.G. / Mainzer Landstrasse 16-24 / Frank-
    furt
Berliner Handels-Gesellschaft-Frankfurter Bank / Bockenheimer Land-
    strasse 10 / Frankfurt
Investitions- und Handels-Bank A.G. / Bethmannstrasse 45-56 / Frank-
    furt
Berliner Bank A.G. / Hardenbergstrasse 32 / Berlin
Westfalenbank A.G. / Huestrasse 21-25 / Bochum
Vereinsbank in Hamburg / Alter Wall 20-30 / Hamburg
Westbank A.G. / Neue Grosse Bergstrasse 1 / Hamburg
Westdeutsche Landesbank Girozentrale / Friedrichstrasse 56-60 /   Düs-
    seldorf
Bankhaus I. D. Herstatt K. G. a. A. / Unter Sachsenhausen 6 / Cologne

Major Private Banks

Delbrück & Co. / Gereonstrasse 15-23 / Cologne
Gebrüder Bethmann / Mainzer Landstrasse 16 / Frankfurt
Georg Hauck & Sohn, Bankiers / Kaiserstrasse 24 / Frankfurt
Merck, Finck & Co. / Pacellistrasse 4 / Munich
Sal. Oppenheim Jr. & Cie / Unter Sachsenhausen 4 / Cologne
Schröder, Münchmeyer, Hengst & Co. / Ballindamm 33 / Hamburg
C. G. Trinkaus & Burkhardt / Königsallee 17 / Düsseldorf
M. M. Warburg-Brinckmann, Wirtz & Co. / Ferdinandstrasse 75 / Ham-
    burg

American Members of German Stock Exchanges

Bank of America N.T. & S.A. / Königsallee 33 / Düsseldorf
(Düsseldorf Stock Exchange)
Chase Manhattan Bank, N.A. / Taunusanlage 11 / Frankfurt
(Frankfurt Stock Exchange)
Chemical Bank / Bockenheimer Landstrasse 2-8 / Frankfurt
(Frankfurt Stock Exchange)

Selected List of Actively Traded German Stocks

Automotive
Bayerische Motorenwerke A.G. (BMW)
Continental Gummiwerke A.G.
Daimler-Benz A.G.
Volkswagenwerk A.G.

Banking
Aachener & Münchener Versicherungs-Gesellschaft
Allianz Versicherungs A.G.
Bayerische Hypotheken- und Wechsel-Bank
Bayerische Vereinsbank
Commerzbank A.G.
Deutsche Bank A.G.
Dresdner Bank A.G.
Frankfurter Hypothekenbank

Building Materials
DLW A.G.
Dyckerhoff Zementwerke A.G.
A.G. der Gerresheimer Glashüttenwerke
Grün & Bilfinger
Heidelberger Zement A.G.
Philipp Holzmann A.G.

Chemical Manufacturing
BASF
Bayer A.G.
Deutsche Gold- und Silber-Scheideanstalt
Farbwerke Hoechst A.G.
Schering A.G.

Electrical Manufacturing
Allgemeine Elektrizitäts-Gesellschaft-AEG-Telefunken
Brown Boveri Mannheim
Siemens A.G.
Varta A.G.

Machinery
DEMAG A.G.
Deutsche Babcock & Wilcox A.G.
Gutehoffnungshütte Aktienverein
Klöckner-Humboldt-Deutz A.G.
Linde A.G.
Maschinenfabrik Augsburg-Nürnberg A.G.

Retailing
Horten A.G.
Karstadt A.G.
Kaufhof A.G.
Neckermann Versand K.G.a.A.

Steel
Hoesch A.G.
Mannesmann A.G.
Rheinstahl
August Thyssen-Hütte A.G.

Utilities
Nordwestdeutsche Kraftwerke A.G.
Rheinische-Westfälisches-Elektrizitätswerk A.G.
VEBA A.G.
Vereinigte Elektrizitätswerke Westfalen

Miscellaneous
Deutsche Lufthansa A.G. (airline)
Dortmunder Union-Schultheiss Brauerei (brewery)
Gelsenberg A.G. (oil, gas, electricity, chemicals)
Girmes-Werke A.G. (textiles, shoes, apparel)
Harpener A.G. (holding company)
Metallgesellschaft A.G. (non-ferrous metals)
Preussag A.G. (diversified metals and other raw materials)

German Investment Funds and Fund Management Companies

ADIG Allg. Deutsche Investment-
Ges. mbH.
Adifonds
Adirenta
Adiropa
Adiverba
Fondak
Fondis
Fondra
Plusfonds
Tresora

Deutsche Investment-Trust,
Gesellschaft für
Wertpapieranlagen
Concentra
Deutscher Rentenfonds
DIT-Fonds für Vermögensbildung
Industria
Interglobal
Internationaler Rentenfonds
Thesaurus
Transatlanta

Deutsche Gesellschaft für
Wertpapiersparen mbH.
Akkumula
Inrenta
Inter-Renta
Intervest
Investa
Re-Inrenta
Ring-Aktienfonds DWS
Ring-Rentenfonds DWS

Deutsche Kapitalanlagegesellschaft
mbH.
Accudeca
Arideka
Dekafonds

Dekarent International
Geodeka
Renditdeka
Commerzbank-Fonds-Verw.
GmbH.
Cofonds
Allfonds-Gesellschaft für
Investment Anlagen mbH.
Allfonds
Allrenta
Allmerika
Allvestor
Union Investment GmbH.
Atlanticfonds
Europafonds 1
Unifonds
Unirenta
Unispecial 1
Kapitalfonds-Kapitalanlageges.
mbH.
Gerling Dynamik Fonds
Gerling Rendite Fonds
ivera fonds
Kapitalfonds 1
Miscellaneous
Analytik-Fonds
Dt. Vermögensbildungsfonds A
Dt. Vermögensbildungsfonds R
Dt. Vermögensbildungsfonds I
Hansaprofit
Hansarenta
Hansasecur
Inka-Global
Interkapital
Interspezial
Interzins
Medico-Invest
Oppenheim Privat
VAF—Vermögensaufbau-Fonds

Detailed information on investment policy and results of most funds is
available from *Bundesverband Deutscher Investment-Gesellschaften* /
Eschenheimer Anlage 26 / Frankfurt

Sources of Information on German Securities

Bundesverband für Anlageberatung und Vermögensplanung / Oberlindau
3 / Frankfurt

Deutsche Gesellschaft für Anlageberatung m.b.H. / Postfach 2643, Reuterweg 51 / 6000 Frankfurt
Institut für Bilanzanalysen / Corneliusstrasse 28 / 6000 Frankfurt
Verlag Hoppenstedt & Co. / Postfach 4006 / Havelstrasse 9 / D 6100 Darmstadt
In addition, all major German banks provide investment information on German securities.

Leading Financial Publications

Blick durch die Wirtschaft, Frankfurter Allgemeine Zeitung / Hellerhof-strasse 2-4 / Frankfurt
Börsen Zeitung / Düsseldorferstrasse 16 / Frankfurt
Handelsblatt / Kreuzstrasse 21 / Düsseldorf
Die Welt (National daily with financial coverage) / Kaiser Wilhelm Strasse 1 / Hamburg

Partial List of Other German Publications

Aktien Börse / Königsallee 6 / Düsseldorf
Der Aktionär / Pressehaus / Hamburg
Capital / Pressehaus / Hamburg
Frankfurter Börsenbriefe / Arndtstrasse 33 / Frankfurt
Fuchs-Briefe / Koblenzerstrasse 37-39 / Bonn-Bad Godesberg
IFA Investment Fonds Analyst / Charlottenstrasse 32 / Düsseldorf
Das Wertpapier / Lindemannstrasse 34 / Düsseldorf
Wirtschaftswoche / Oederweg 16-18 / Frankfurt
Wirtschaft und Investment / Hermann-Aust-Strasse 4, Postfach 245 / Bad Wörishofen

Notes

[1] Bernard Cornfeld, an American with highly developed promotional instincts and a taste for girls and other sybaritic trappings, invented the *Fund of Funds*, a mutual fund which included only shares of other mutual funds. The SEC did not allow him to sell the *Fund of Funds* in the United States, so he sold it in Europe and other areas of the world, building up one of the largest financial card houses in the world's history of financial scandals. It came crashing down in 1969 with millions of small investors holding bags of worthless IOS shares. Cornfeld was arrested by the Swiss in 1973.

14

THE NETHERLANDS
HIGH FLYING LOW LANDS

With the British, the Dutch share the reputation of being the best investment managers in the world. They have a long tradition of international trade and finance, and the Amsterdam exchange claims to be the oldest in the world where stocks were traded. The first shares admitted were those of the East India Company, founded in 1602, and reportedly shareholders received some of their first dividends in the form of spices rather than cash.

The Dutch have always taken a global view of investments—out of necessity, because their own small country does not offer enough investment outlets for the huge sums that the Dutch have always earned through international trade, shipping, and finance. Investments in the leading Dutch "international" companies—*Royal Dutch Petroleum, N.V., Philips Gloeilampenfabrieken N.V., Unilever N.V.*—represent an international investment rather than an investment in the Dutch economy since the majority of their earnings comes from outside the country.

A Model Investment Trust

The best illustration of Dutch investment skill and stock selection is probably the *Robeco* investment trust—*Rotterdamsch Beleggings-consortium N.V.* to give its full name.

On October 3, 1973 the Dutch guilder (fl.) was valued at U.S. 39.83¢.

Robeco is not a mutual fund in the American sense, but rather a publicly-held corporation whose business consists of investing money. It has no separate management company and no sales force; hence no sales commissions and "front-end loads."

An investor wanting to develop a truly international portfolio could benefit from studying the trust's investment policy—or much more simply buy *Robeco* shares. At this time they are not traded in the United States, and a United States resident would have to go to an American broker dealing in foreign shares or to a bank in Holland to buy the shares on the Amsterdam Stock Exchange. He would have to pay the Interest Equalization Tax of 11.25% of the purchase price of the stock. This tax has so far kept *Robeco* away from the American stock market. Residents of other countries can easily buy the shares on their local stock exchanges. *Robeco* shares are listed on the stock exchanges of Amsterdam, Antwerp, Berlin, Brussels, Dublin, Düsseldorf, Frankfurt, Hamburg, Hong Kong, London, Luxembourg, Munich, Paris, Vienna, and Stockholm.

At the end of 1972, total assets of *Robeco* were about Fl. 4.1 billion (close to $1.65 billion), and the composition of the portfolio by industries and by countries was:

Spread of Investments by Industries		Spread of Investments by Countries	
financial institutions	19.57%	United States	37.00%
public utilities	10.00%	Canada	2.84%
oil	9.70%	Dutch local stocks	7.98%
foods	8.41%	Dutch internationals	7.93%
electrical equipment	7.10%	Germany	6.79%
commercials & transportation	6.21%	France	5.20%
office equipment	6.13%	United Kingdom	2.74%
chemicals and glass	5.47%	Belgium	2.61%
pharmaceuticals	5.27%	Switzerland	1.85%
property shares	1.92%	Italy	1.10%
mines	1.03%	Sweden	0.71%
engineering	1.02%	Spain	0.20%
other industries	15.71%	Austria	0.07%
cash or equivalent	2.46%	Japan	17.50%
		Australia	1.69%
		South Africa	1.33%
		cash or equivalent	2.46%

Between 1963 and 1973 the value of *Robeco* shares in terms of dollars increased by an average of almost 10% a year. *Robeco* management keeps the share price closely linked to the net asset value by setting the price every day on the Amsterdam Stock Exchange, with a difference of about Fl. 1.50 (60 cents) between the bid price at which *Robeco* is prepared to redeem its shares and the ask price at which it issues new shares. Prices on other stock exchanges where *Robeco* shares are traded follow suit thanks to the activities of the arbitragers who will buy and sell these shares at the different stock exchanges if they can make a small profit from the price differentials that may exist. If the demand for *Robeco* shares drives prices up beyond net asset value, *Robeco* is prepared to sell additional shares at the fixed price. If selling pressure tends to drive the price below the net asset value, *Robeco* is prepared to buy back some shares. This is a unique feature of the fund, not offered by any other management fund in the world.

Another noteworthy feature of the *Robeco* fund is the fact that management expenses in 1972 were only about 0.17% of assets, far below those of practically any other fund in the world. (The average figure in the United States is about four to five times higher.)

Robeco offers certain attractive features to the small investor—in the Netherlands an automatic dividend re-investment plan under which a shareholder remains fully invested down to four decimals of a guilder, and outside the Netherlands a Geneva-based "shareholder account," based on the same re-investment principles, but geared especially to the foreign investor, and optionally offering a linked policy covering him against stock exchange risks.

Robeco management also operates two other funds—*Rolinco,* an international growth stock fund; and *Utilico,* an international fund with a portfolio of gas and electric utility company stocks. Since their introduction in 1965, *Rolinco* shares, including stock dividends, doubled in value. Composition of the portfolio by countries is comparable to that of *Robeco.*

Robeco has been so successful that in recent years it bought three major Dutch investment funds which were losing ground and were selling much below asset value. Together with *Rolinco* and *Utilico,* *Robeco* now accounts for about 75% of the Dutch investment fund assets. Two larger funds that remain are *ABN-Beleggingspool,* managed by *Algemene Bank Nederland N.V.,* and *Amro-Pierson Fund,* jointly managed by two other leading Dutch banks, *Amsterdam-Rotterdam Bank N.V.* and *Pierson, Heldring & Pierson.*

Investing in Management

Security analysts who evaluate a company for a recommendation of its stock usually try to assess one factor that is not spelled out in the financial statements—the effectiveness of management. *Robeco*'s management, which has produced such a good fund performance at such low management costs, seems typical of the way the entire country is run; and based on the management factor alone, the Dutch economy should be a good long-range investment. Many who have had the occasion to deal with the Dutch or work with them on a common project are impressed by the quiet efficiency with which they come to the point and achieve results—an efficiency that does not run rampant for its own sake and seems singularly free from status seeking, pretensions, and showmanship. It is an efficiency that was born in long, hard struggles against hostile men and elements in which no movement could be wasted and everyone had to pitch in, irrespective of rank, wherever he was needed.

The Dutch won their freedom from the then powerful Spanish during the second half of the 16th century. They have conducted a never-ending struggle against the sea. Disastrous floods in the Middle Ages, notably the one of 1421 which wiped out 72 villages and more than 100,000 lives, spurred the Dutch into developing their sophisticated dike building techniques and other methods of controlling the sea. Taking the offensive, they have reclaimed lost areas from the sea, the largest and most recent of these projects being the gigantic Delta Plan, under which many of the wide arms of the Rhine-Maas-Schelde estuaries are filled in and the islands connected to the mainland. Today the Dutch are also major participants in the exploration of the North Sea gas and oil fields.

Twice during their history the Dutch had their economic base completely wiped out by wars of others fought on their soil—first during the Napoleonic Wars when the French occupied the country and cut it off from all its international trade routes to spite the British; and the second time during World War II, when in the very last months of the war fierce battles were fought in Holland and the retreating Germans left nothing but destruction and bare cupboards behind. There was not a stitching needle to be found in a store.

Soon after World War II the Dutch lost their Indonesian possessions with a population of 70 million—10 times more than in the home country—and a source of great natural wealth.

The Dutch rebuilt Holland with amazing speed and the help of foreign capital. As soon as practical they returned to the principles of free trade and free flow of capital. Having, over the centuries, developed particular skills in shipping, finance, trading, insurance, and marketing, they earn almost as much money from these "service industries" as they do from manufacturing.

The Dutch also maintain an open-door policy to foreign investments in their own country and to foreign firms and individuals who want to do business in the Netherlands. In the course of the recent influx of Japanese into Europe, Holland—and in particular Amsterdam— seems to have become the most favored European place for Japanese to establish a home away from home. Possibly they feel an affinity with the calm, efficient working habits of the Dutch and with the neatness of the crowded Dutch habitations. Or they appreciate the fact that raw fish is available at its freshest in Holland. (A non-Japanese foreign visitor not accustomed to heavy food should be cautioned, however, that fresh herring, which the Dutch eat raw in season, may slip deceptively smoothly over the tongue and past the palate to settle in the stomach like a lump of clay.)

The Big Dutch Internationals

Mere efficiency is, of course, not the only criterion for investing in a company or a country. There are often other factors beyond management control that can affect earnings.

With a socialist government having been elected early in 1973, there is concern today in the Netherlands that some of the free economy features may be abandoned with detrimental effects on the earnings potential of Dutch companies.

Moreover, the Dutch, being so dependent on international trade and finance, are, of course, vulnerable to the economic problems of other parts of the world (and the inefficiencies that may prevail elsewhere). This is particularly true of the "Big Six" Dutch international companies which derive much of their income from abroad— *AKZO N.V.*, *Hoogovens N.V.*, *KLM N.V.*, *Royal Dutch Shell*, *Philips N.V.*, and *Unilever N.V.*

That the six largest Dutch companies should be international rather than national reflects two features in the Dutch economy—the smallness of the country itself which does not offer enough room for a company to grow beyond a certain size, and the international orientation of the Dutch businessman. However, possibly because of the international and conglomerate nature of their far-flung businesses, earnings and stock market performance of these six giants has ranged from fair to undistinguished.

KLM, even though efficiently managed, suffers from the same problems that all transatlantic airlines suffer from—overcapacity and chaotic, not to say questionable, pricing and marketing practices. It was operating at a loss in 1973.

Royal Dutch-Shell Group, the second largest integrated oil company in the world, and a large chemical producer, had declining earnings in 1972, but was strongly recovering in 1973. It is controlled by two holding companies—*Royal Dutch Petroleum N.V.* (Dutch), owning a 60% interest, and *Shell Transport & Trading Co. Ltd.* (British), owning a 40% interest. The stocks of both holding companies are traded on the New York Stock Exchange. The American *Shell Oil Company*, one of the largest U.S. integrated oil companies, is 69% controlled by the *Royal Dutch-Shell Group*, and is also traded on the New York Stock Exchange. An "integrated" oil company is one that does everything from exploring for oil to marketing it, including drilling and production, transportation, refining, and distribution.

The Dutch *Unilever N.V.* and the British *Unilever Ltd.* are operated as one company. They have identical boards of directors. In general, any operation located in what was the former British Commonwealth is held by *Unilever Ltd.,* and the other interests are held by *Unilever N.V.,* including the two United States subsidiaries, *Lever Brothers Co.* and *Thomas J. Lipton Inc.* In terms of sales, the *Unilever* group is the ninth largest industrial enterprise in the world, operating in about 70 countries and producing fats and oils, soap and detergents, processed food, animal feed, toilet preparations, and chemicals. It also operates plantations. Earnings over the past several years, as well as stock prices, have shown a steady upward trend. Both *Unilever* companies are traded on the New York Stock Exchange.

Philips Lamp, owned 99% by the Philips holding company, *Philips N.V.,* is the largest non-American manufacturer of light bulbs and electric and electronic equipment. The company recently recovered from a serious earnings slump. *Philips* shares are traded in the United States on the over-the-counter market.

AKZO N.V. is a European giant in the man-made fiber, plastics, and chemical business, and *Hoogovens* is an iron and steel holding company. Both had declining earnings in 1972. American Depositary Receipts of the shares of both companies are traded over-the-counter in the United States.

Dutch National Companies

An investor will find better performance among some of the Dutch "national" companies that derive most of their earnings from the Dutch economy (although there are few that are completely isolated from international trade). The best known, and perhaps the only one known to most Americans, is *Heineken N.V.*, the Dutch brewery, which exports about 20% of its output and has some financial interest in non-Dutch breweries. Even though the annual growth rate of Dutch beer consumption has slowed down from about 10% to 8%, earnings have been growing at a faster rate thanks to an outstanding marketing job abroad and entry into the soft drink and wine business. *Heineken's* stock price increased from about Fl. 45 ($18) in 1966 to Fl. 320 ($127) in mid-1973.

Other companies of uninterrupted stock market appreciation include *Elsevier N.V. Uitgeversmaatschappij,* an international publishing house; *IHC Holland N.V.*, a maritime construction company heavily involved in the North Sea offshore drilling operations; and *Bredero N.V.*, a real estate financier and developer. Anything to do with the exploration of North Sea gas and oil fields, in which the Dutch are heavily involved, is considered prime growth potential by European investors and so is anything to do with real estate in an overcrowded, prosperous country running out of space.

The *Robeco* portfolio of Dutch stocks includes *Heineken* (almost 1% of total assets) and *Elsevier*. Otherwise, it is weighted with Dutch bank and insurance stocks (2.3% of total net assets).

When looking at Dutch national stocks, it should be borne in mind that most of them have a small "float" (very few shares are available for trading). This makes it difficult to buy and sell shares at a given time and at a given place. Smaller Dutch companies are not yet very communicative toward their stockholders, although there is improvement under way. Management is often controlled by a family or a few insiders. In fact, management control of many Dutch companies, including some of the very big ones, is by a few, including the government, banks, family, and preferential shareholders, rather than the many shareholders at large. It is reported, for instance, that *Philips*, a company with a sales volume of more than $6 billion, is effectively controlled by only ten registered priority shareholders. This close control may shield some managements from investment community pressure to perform for the benefit of the shareholders.

Amsterdam Stock Market

Like several other European exchanges, the Amsterdam Stock Exchange has become more active again since 1972, offering better opportunities to trade. The exchange has had its ups and downs during its more than 300-year history. After a flourishing start, it was wrecked by the Napoleonic Wars and did not revive until the second half of the 19th century. At that time it became an important factor in the financing of American railroads, and by the turn of the 20th century Amsterdam had become the most important trading center for American securities outside the United States. After World War I, Amsterdam played a major role in financing the development of Dutch international companies. As these companies became listed on other stock exchanges throughout the world, and as an increasing number of foreign stocks was listed on the Amsterdam exchange, Dutch brokers and bankers developed the most active arbitrage business in the world, buying the stock of a company on one stock exchange and selling it on another to take advantage of the small price differentials that often exist between such multiple listings.

World War II again wrecked the business of the Amsterdam Stock Exchange which, like most other European stock exchanges, remained in the doldrums until about 1958. The more recent strong revival may well lead to reestablishing Amsterdam as one of the most important stock exchanges of the world. A new wave of listings of foreign stocks took place in 1972, including many Japanese issues.

Well over 500 foreign bonds and stocks are presently listed. Arbitrage business is again flourishing. But actual investment purchases of foreign stocks in Amsterdam is also on the increase, and with the increasing internationalization of investment portfolios all over the world, trading volume is likely to pick up considerably in the next few years. In 1972 it was about $20 billion.

The Amsterdam Stock Exchange is considered to have one of the best standards in trading practices of any exchange in the world, and it is also the only exchange in the world charged with the protection of the shareholders, a function normally performed by a government agency.

Both banks and brokers can trade on the Amsterdam exchange, but as far as investors are concerned the only practical relationship is with a Dutch bank. Because of the financial resources of the banks and their nation-wide and world-wide organizations, individual Dutch brokers cannot effectively compete with banks, except on the floor of the Amsterdam exchange.

Practically all Dutch stock certificates are made out to "bearer"— they do not show the name of the owner. The owner must claim his dividends and interest when due. Recently Amsterdam introduced a system of central custody of securities, with centralized collection of dividends and interests which are then distributed to the shareholders via the bank offices that use the central custody service. Change of ownership of securities can be accomplished by simple change of records.

Foreign Buying of Dutch Securities

Non-residents can freely buy all Dutch common shares listed on a Dutch stock exchange (in addition to Amsterdam, there is a relatively inactive exchange in Rotterdam). However, they need a special permit to buy unlisted stocks, which any bank can obtain for them. Unlisted stocks are usually those of smaller or closely-held companies, many of which do not want to conform to the reporting requirements of the stock exchange. Thus, they are not suitable investments, except for the initiated or someone advised by an initiate.

Since the dollar crisis of 1971, non-residents can buy Dutch fixed-income securities only with so-called "O" guilders. These are guilders that have become available from the sale of Dutch fixed-income securities by a non-resident. "O" guilders have sold at premiums ranging from 1% to 7% above the rate for the regular commercial guilder. With a yield of $7\frac{1}{2}\%$ to 8%, Dutch fixed-income securities that have to be paid with "O" guilders are not as attractive as fixed-income securities in some other countries, except as a hedge against devaluation of the dollar or other weak currencies.

There is a withholding tax of 25% for non-residents on dividends received from Dutch stocks, but not on interest from fixed-income securities. There was no capital gains tax in Holland in 1973, but there was talk of one.

Where to Buy Dutch Securities

The representative offices in the United States of some Dutch banks accept business from institutional investors but not from individual investors. Thus, the individual investor will have to go to a United States broker accepting business for foreign stocks or open an account with a Dutch bank in the Netherlands. The banks will handle discretionary accounts and charge a management and custodial fee, but the accounts must be of a certain minimum size, which varies with the banks. They will try to steer smaller investors into buying shares of an investment fund, such as *Robeco*.

Information

All banks listed at the end of this chapter provide stock market information, including stock reference booklets, general market letters, and individual stock recommendations. Some of the material is in English, including a very lively weekly newsletter, *Amro Stock Market News,* published by the *Amsterdam-Rotterdam Bank N.V.*, and *Dutch Market Review*, published by *Algemene Bank Nederland N.V.*

There is also a surprisingly large number of good independent stock information services in relation to the relatively small size of the country, reflecting the great professional investment interest in Holland. They include: *Van Oss' Effectenboek*, a loose-leaf binder with descriptions of some 1000 companies, updated at regular intervals; *Gids bij de Prijscourant van de Vereeniging voor de Effectenhandel te Amsterdam*, a reference book on about 2400 companies, grouped by industries; *Wegwijzer voor Nederlandse Effecten*, a publication appearing ten times a year providing information about the main companies traded in Amsterdam, classified by industry; *Tabel van Laagste en Hoogste Koersen*, price information on all Dutch and foreign companies listed on the Amsterdam Stock Exchange over a period of eight years.

Dutch Securities Traded on the New York Stock Exchange

KLM Royal Dutch Airlines N.V. (airline)
Royal Dutch Petroleum Company N.V. (petroleum)
Unilever N.V. (food products and toiletries)

Dutch Securities Traded Over-the-Counter in the United States

AKZO N.V. (synthetic fibers)
Hoogovens (steel)
Philips Lamps (lamps and electrical equipment)

Partial List of Dutch Securities Actively Traded on the Amsterdam Stock Exchange

Algemene Bank Nederland N.V. (banking)
Albert Heijn N.V. (supermarket and grocery chain)
Amsterdam-Rotterdam Bank (Amro) N.V. (banking)
Bols (liquors)
Bredero N.V. (real estate)
Bührmann-Tetterode N.V. (paper, machinery, office equipment wholesaler)
Elsevier N.V. Uitgeversmaatschappij (publishing)
Gist-Brocades N.V. (pharmaceuticals and biochemical products)
Grinten N.V. (graphics materials and equipment)
Heineken N.V. (brewery)
Hollandsche Beton Groep N.V. (construction and engineering)
IHC Holland N.V. (dredging and offshore drilling)
Internatio-Müller N.V. (wholesale and international trading department stores)
Koninklijke Bijenkorf Beheer N.V. (department stores)
Koninklijke Nederlandsche Papierfabriek N.V. (paper)
Koninklijke Scholten-Honig N.V. (starch and starch products)
Nederlandsche Scheepvaart Unie N.V. (shipping, land and air transportation)
Phs van Ommeren N.V. (tankers and coastal shipping)
Pakhoed Holding (tank storage and pipelines)
Rijn-Schelde-Verolme N.V. (shipbuilding and repair)
Verenigde Machinefabrieken N.V. (engineering)
Verenigde Nederlandsche Uitgeversbedrijven (printing and publishing)

Bank Members of the Amsterdam Stock Exchange

Algemene Bank Nederland N.V. / Vijzelstraat 32 / Amsterdam
(New York and Boston Securities Affiliate: *ABD Securities Corporation* / 84 William Street / New York, New York 10038 / and 53 State Street / Boston, Massachusetts 02109)
Amsterdam-Rotterdam Bank N.V. / Herengracht 595 / Amsterdam
Amsterdamsche Effecten en Commissiebank N.V. / Keizersgracht 701 / Amsterdam

Amsterdamse Crediet-en Handelsbank N.V. / Herengracht 553 / Amsterdam
Bank der Bondsspaarbanken N.V. / Singel 236 / Amsterdam
Bank Mees & Hope N.V. / Herengracht 548 / Amsterdam
Bank Mendes Gans N.V. / Herengracht 619 / Amsterdam
Bank Van Vloten en De Gijselaar N.V. / Tesselschadestraat 12 / Amsterdam
Banque de Paris et des Pays-Bas N.V. / Herengracht 539-541 / Amsterdam
Hollandsche Bank-Unie N.V. / Herengracht 434-440 / Amsterdam
Hollandsche Koopmansbank Lippmann Rosenthal N.V. / Nieuwe Spiegelstraat 6-8 / Amsterdam
Mahlers Bank N.V. / Keizersgracht 452 / Amsterdam
Nederlandse Credietbank N.V. / Keizersgracht 507-517 / Amsterdam
Nederlandsche Middenstandsbank N.V. / Herengracht 580 / Amsterdam
Pierson, Heldring & Pierson / Herengracht 206-214 / Amsterdam
(New York Securities Affiliate: *New Court Securities Corporation* / 1 Rockefeller Plaza / New York, New York 10020)

Banks on the Rotterdam Stock Exchange
Not Members of the Amsterdam Stock Exchange

Cooperatieve Centrale Raiffeisen-Bank / Blaak 35 / Rotterdam
Europese en Overzeese Handelsbank N.V. / Parklaan 32-34 / Rotterdam
Slavenburg's Bank N.V. / Coolsingel 63 / Rotterdam

Leading Dutch Investment Funds

ABN-Beleggingspool / managed by *Algemene Bank Nederland N.V.* / Keizersgracht 706 / Amsterdam
Amro-Pierson Fund / jointly managed by *Amsterdam-Rotterdam Bank N.V.* / Herengracht 595 / Amsterdam and *Pierson, Heldring & Pierson* / Herengracht 206-214 / Amsterdam
Robeco / *Rolinco* / *Utilico* / P.O. Box 973 / Rotterdam

Dutch Investment Information Services

Gids bij de Prijscourant van de Vereeniging voor den Effectenhandel te Amsterdam / Uitgeverij *J.H. de Bussy N.V.* / Herengracht 172 / Amsterdam
Tabel van Laagste en Hoogste Koersen / Het Financieele Dagblad / Weesperstraat 85 / Amsterdam
Van Oss' Effectenboek / *Uitgeverij J.H. de Bussy N.V.* / *Herengracht* 172 / Amsterdam
Wegwijzer voor Nederlandse Effecten / Keesing Systemen / Ruysdaelstraat 71-75 / Amsterdam

Specialized Financial Papers and Periodicals

Banken Effectenbedrijf / Herengracht 136 / Amsterdam
Beleggers Belangen / Prinsengracht 770 / Amsterdam

Beursberichten / Lange Houtstraat 4-8 / Den Haag
Beurs Express / Huddestraat 7 / Amsterdam
Elseviers Weekblad, Editie voor de Zakenman / Postbus 152 / Amsterdam
Feiten en Cijfers / Postbus 23 / Deventer
FEM / N.Z. Voorburgwal 94 / Amsterdam
Het Financieele Dagblad / Postbus 216 / Amsterdam
Financiele Berichten / N. Doelenstraat 12-14 / Amsterdam
De Financiele Koerier / Postbus 3906 / Amsterdam
Handelsbelangen / Helmholtzstraat 61 / Amsterdam
Wall Street / D.W. Brand N.V. / Keizersgracht 215 / Amsterdam
Zakenwereld / Postbus 7898 / Amsterdam

General Interest Publications with Financial Coverage

Accent / Postbus 3038 / Utrecht
Elseviers Weekblad / Postbus 152 / Amsterdam
H.P. Magazine / Singel 136 / Amsterdam

Daily Newspapers with Extensive Financial Coverage

Algemeen Dagblad / Postbus 241 / Rotterdam
Haagsche Courant / Postbus 1050 / Den Haag
NRC-Handelsblad / Westblaak 180 / Rotterdam
Het Parool / Postbus 433 / Amsterdam
De Telegraaf / N.Z. Voorburgwal 225 / Amsterdam
De Tijd / Postbus 348 / Amsterdam
Trouw / De Rotterdammer / Postbus 859 / Amsterdam
De Volkskrant / Postbus 1002 / Amsterdam

15

BELGIUM AND LUXEMBOURG
THE OPEN DOOR

The Belgians claim to have originated the use of the word "bourse" for stock "exchange" in the 14th century when traders in Bruges, then one of the leading cities of the Hanseatic League, conducted their business in front of the house of the Chevalier van der Buerse (who had three purses in his arms). Going to the *buerse* began to mean going to the exchange, and from Bruges the name spread to other trading cities of the Hanseatic League, becoming *bourse* in French, *beurs* in Dutch, *börse* in German, *bolsa* in Italian, and *börs* in Swedish.

Be that as it may, the historical name did not inspire the activities of the modern Brussels Stock Exchange (the main exchange of the country; there are smaller exchanges in Antwerp, Ghent, and Liège). For many years, Brussels was one of the most inactive of the European stock exchanges. It came to life somewhat in 1971 and 1972, primarily as the result of British buying, but total annual trading volume in 1972 of somewhat over $1 billion is still very small compared with most other European exchanges, and as few as 25 of the 700 listed stocks account for about half of the volume. Individual Belgian investors have largely ignored their own stock market. Most of them invest through Luxembourg and Swiss banks because of the bank secrecy in these countries, and their portfolios tend to be international. There are also tax advantages for Belgian residents to invest via Luxembourg.

On October 3, 1973 the Belgian franc (BFr.) was valued at U.S. 2.71¢ and the Luxembourg franc (LFr.) was valued at the same rate.

Foreigners Welcome

It may not be too early, however, to keep an eye on the Brussels Stock Exchange. Its future may be bright. The Belgian government and financial institutions are making major efforts to develop the Brussels exchange into a more effective place to trade stock and raise money. As the headquarters city for the European Economic Community, Brussels has ambitions to become the "Capital of Europe." Belgium, among all European countries, is the most hospitable to international organizations as well as to foreign companies wanting to invest in the country and to establish operations there, and to the many foreigners working for these organizations and companies. In fact, Brussels today seems to be the most popular of the international headquarters cities, not only for Americans who represent their companies in Europe but even for many "internationalized" Europeans who work outside their own countries. In that respect, Brussels has decidedly won out over the two other cities frequently chosen for international operations—Geneva and Paris. The Swiss have made it increasingly difficult for foreigners to live in their country, even temporarily, and Paris is now generally considered too expensive and hostile.

Brussels, on the other hand, encourages foreigners to settle. Among the attractions it offers are an ample choice of modern accommodations, tax breaks to individuals representing foreign companies, easy commuting, good international schools, and good restaurants. Unlike many French, Belgians do not treat foreigners who do not speak their language like imbeciles, and they make every effort to be helpful.

Most importantly, there are no foreign exchange restrictions in Belgium. Money can freely be taken into and out of the country; residents can freely buy and sell foreign securities and gold; and nonresidents can buy Belgian securities. Dividends, interest, and other income earned in Belgium can freely be taken out of the country.

Economy Stimulated

Belgium also freed itself recently from two bad economic heritages —early industrialization and a colonial empire. Early industrialization based on coal mining and steel created bad scars on the Belgian countryside, on the business traditions, and labor relations. It also left

Belgium after World War II with antiquated production facilities. With the help of substantial foreign investments, Belgian industry in the 1960s has made great strides towards modernization, and more modernization is under way.

The colonial empire of the Belgian Congo, huge in relation to the mother country, came to an abrupt end in 1960. This sent heavy shock waves through the population and its business establishment. Yet, in retrospect, this traumatic end to an era may have been a blessing in disguise. It accelerated the complete reorientation of Belgian business and the purposeful internationalization of its economy.

Belgium today exports almost 50% of its production. Of the more than $3 billion in capital investment in the 1960s, about 70% came from abroad—more than half of this from the United States alone. With Britain's entry into the European Economic Community on January 1, 1973, additional capital has flowed into Belgium. Many Belgian firms have been taken over by foreign companies. Brussels has become an important international banking center, and a large amount of international bond issues, including Eurobonds, is being placed there. Much of the money invested through banks and investment funds in Luxembourg is managed in Brussels.

On the negative side is the fact that Belgium is a house divided against itself because of the rift between the Flemish-speaking population and the French-speaking Walloons. Both are very sensitive about the equal use of their own language and about equal representation in all government, social, and educational organizations. The political scene is greatly fragmented because each of the four political parties has a Walloon and a Flemish wing, and in addition there are Walloon and Flemish parties, each concerned only with its own narrow ethnic interests. All factions want ministerial representation, and Belgium, with a population of somewhat less than 10 million, has about three dozen ministers—per capita by far more than any other country in the world. This makes for inefficiencies and delays in many governmental matters.

Another factor that may be considered negative from an investor's point of view is Belgium's heavy dependence on foreign trade, which makes many of its industries vulnerable to the economic trends of its main customers—primarily its Common Market partners.

On balance, however, Belgium's industrial and financial establishments are thriving, and the stock market has reflected this. The index of the averages rose by 52% between April 1968 and April 1973—more than those of other leading European exchanges.

Holding Companies

If an investor wanted to make an overall investment in the Belgian economy he could theoretically do this by buying just one stock—that of one of the larger holding companies. More than half of Belgium's national output is in the hands of holding companies, and there is a vast network of interlocking ownership in finance and industry. The largest holding company, *Société Générale de Belgique,* controls an estimated 30% to 40% of the Belgian economy. It owns 20% of the largest Belgian bank, *Société Générale de Banque,* and it has a substantial stake in about 70 other companies, including financial institutions, insurance concerns, shipping lines, utilities, and industrial companies. It also has a 50% interest in three other holding companies, which in turn have a part-ownership in a total of 20 companies.

In addition to the *Société Générale de Belgique,* there are some 40 other holding companies listed on the Brussels exchange, Some, like the *Société Générale,* are widely diversified including the second largest, *Compagnie Bruxelles-Lambert,* the result of a recent merger of four holding companies. Several have substantial foreign holdings among their assets and others are specialized in one industry.

Stock market performance of the holding companies varies greatly, with some of the smaller or specialized ones often doing better than the very large, diversified ones.

Many Belgian companies traded on the Brussels exchange are partly owned by holding companies, and often they are not independent in their management. Others are partly owned by American or other foreign concerns. This does not necessarily recommend them as an investment since some of the Belgian companies that were for sale were the ones that were in trouble.

The Giants

The two largest Belgian companies are independent, however. And their stocks are among the most actively traded issues. They are *Petrofina,* the largest Belgian petroleum company, with an annual sales volume of about $2 billion, and *Solvay & Cie S.A.,* a large chemical concern, with an annual sales volume of about $1 billion. Business activities of both companies are world-wide. *Petrofina*'s stock price increased from about BFr. 2000 ($54.00) in 1968 to about BFr. 8450 ($226) in mid-1973. *Solvay*'s stock price, on the other hand, remained relatively unchanged during the same time.

Other actively traded stocks include *Gevaert Photo-Producten N.V.,* which, in a joint venture with the German *AGFA* (a division of *Bayer A.G.*), has become the second largest photographic supplier of the world after *Kodak,* and the two largest Belgian department stores, *G B Enterprises* and *Innovation-Bon Marché S.A.*

Utilities are publicly owned in Belgium rather than nationalized as in most other European countries. They are popular investments because of generous, steadily increasing dividends, and a slow but steady appreciation of the stock price.

New Issues

An important event for the Brussels Stock Exchange was the public sale and listing, in November 1972, of the large new issue of common shares of *Bekaert S.A.*, accompanied by an issue of convertible bonds. *Bekaert,* with an annual sales volume of about BFr. 11 billion ($285 million), is a leading international wire manufacturer and supplier of steel wire for the steel-belted radial automobile tire which is used on almost all European cars and which is now increasingly being adopted by the American automobile industry. Before the public offering, *Bekaert* was a closely-held company with no public market for its stock. The offering price was BFr. 2100 ($56.50) and by mid-1973 it had risen to about BFr. 2500 ($67.00). (Most Belgian companies pay dividends only once a year—usually mid-year after publication of the annual report.) The *Bekaert* convertible issue, paying 6¼% on the issuing price of BFr. 2400 ($65.00) rose in half a year to about BFr. 2600 ($70.00).

The *Bekaert* issue was a boost to the Brussels Stock Exchange because its successful placement proved that the Belgian market is now capable of absorbing a large common equity issue and of developing a good trading volume for it. This is expected to encourage other companies to raise money through the sale of common stock rather than through bonds or bank loans.

There are not many large Belgian companies left that are not yet publicly held, but Belgian investors are casting their eyes hopefully at two large family concerns that might one day decide to let the public participate in their operations. One is *Eternit*, a large building materials producer, and the other is *Artois*, the largest Belgian brewery and one of the largest in Europe. The Belgians have the second largest per capita consumption of beer in the world—133 litres per year—following Germany with 144 litres per year.

Fixed-Income Securities

Traditionally, Belgian investors have been inclined towards fixed-income securities, both Belgian and foreign. Yields for Belgian state bonds in mid-1973 were about $7\frac{1}{2}\%$, and for safe corporate bonds about 8%. For non-residents, there is a 20% withholding tax on the interest payments. However, there are a number of Belgian state bonds, as well as bonds of financial institutions, including convertible bonds, that are tax free for non-residents. Also exempt from the withholding tax payable by non-residents are a number of international bond issues sold in Belgium, such as the bonds of the *International Bank for Reconstruction and Development.*

A somewhat unique institution among all fixed-income markets of the world is the Belgian *Fonds des Rentes,* an independent public institution that has been created to maintain a steady market in government bonds as well as in the bonds of public institutions, such as railroads, telephone and telegraph companies, national and regional finance institutions, and municipalities. By buying and selling bonds on the open market, the *Fonds des Rentes* influences the market price of the bonds, and thereby the yield. It also intervenes in the short-term money market. In 1973, the portfolio of the *Fonds des Rentes* represented about 25% of the about 250 listed and unredeemed Belgian bond issues, with an approximate market price of BFr. 700 billion. ($1.9 billion). Yearly transactions of the *Fonds des Rentes* are valued at about BFr. 60 billion ($162 million).

Corporate bonds convertible into common stock have become popular with Belgian investors because they offer a fixed income plus the possibility of an increase in the price of the convertible in line with the movement of the common stock. Yield of convertible issues in mid-1973 averaged slightly above 6%. About a dozen convertible bond issues are quoted on the Brussels Stock Exchange.

During the two rounds of the devaluation of the dollar, the Belgian franc has remained the fourth-strongest European currency, following the German mark, the Swiss franc, and the Dutch guilder. Thus, in retrospect, Belgian fixed-income securities look like a good hedge against currency devaluation even if interest rates are not quite as high as in some other countries.

Investment Trusts

Belgium has a number of well managed investment funds—some legally based in the country, others legally based in Luxembourg but managed in Belgium. For the non-resident, only the Luxembourg-based funds are of interest, since there is a withholding tax of 20% on the dividends paid out by the Belgium-based funds that a non-resident cannot recover in Belgium. The portfolios of the Luxembourg funds are largely international; thus they generally do not offer a pure means of investing in the Belgian economy.

Luxembourg—Investment Haven

The Grand-Duchy of Luxembourg, a country that came into independent existence as recently as 1863, and with a population today of about 340,000, has only a handful of domestic stocks to offer investors, leading among them are *ARBED*, a steel company with a sales volume of about $1.7 billion, and *Brasserie de Diekirch*, a brewery making good beer. However, Luxembourg has become an important international investment center and stock exchange. Almost 400 international bond issues are listed and traded on the Luxembourg Stock Exchange, plus nearly 100 international investment funds and some 50 foreign common stock issues.

Foreign banks and brokers handle a substantial business for Belgian and other foreign investors. Luxembourg offers bank secrecy, as Switzerland does, but it has none of the restrictions against foreign bank deposits and investments in domestic securities that Switzerland has instituted as a result of the dollar crisis. The Luxembourg franc is linked to the Belgian franc, and money, gold, and securities can be moved in and out of the country as freely as they can in Belgium. There are also some tax advantages when investing through a bank or broker established in Luxembourg. There is no withholding tax on dividends and interests earned from foreign investments, and foreign securities traded in Luxembourg are exempt from stamp duty and transfer tax. (On the other hand, a non-resident investing in Belgian securities through a bank or broker located in Belgium pays 20% withholding tax on practically all interest and dividends received.)

Where to Buy Belgian Stocks

Because of this special relationship between Belgium and Luxembourg, a foreign investor wanting to invest in Belgian stocks will be advised by most Belgian banks to open an account at their Luxembourg office. In practice, investment accounts handled by a bank or brokerage house established in Luxembourg will usually consist of international rather than purely Belgian portfolios. In addition to Luxembourg and Belgian banks, many foreign financial institutions are established in Luxembourg. (A representative list is given at the end of this chapter.)

Belgian banks accept both discretionary accounts (all investment decisions are left to their discretion) and consulting accounts (a customer is consulted before a stock is bought or sold). The banks charge a relatively modest management fee.

Belgian brokers also handle individual investment accounts. They are the only ones who can execute orders on the floor of the Brussels Stock Exchange. In this capacity, they fill the same function as the specialist on the floor of the American stock exchanges. Banks must place all their stock orders for less than BFr. 10 million through a broker. Only for larger orders can they try to make the trade outside the exchange. This means that the individual investor, when he buys a Belgian security through a Belgian bank, pays two commissions, one for the bank and the other for the broker. Belgian brokers will accept business from non-resident customers, but this is not very practical because of the withholding tax applicable in Belgium and the communications problems. No Belgian broker has an office in the United States, and only one is represented in Luxembourg.

If an individual investor wants to place a single order for Belgian securities from the United States and without opening an account in Belgium or Luxembourg, he must go to one of the American brokerage houses accepting orders for foreign stocks. The Belgian banks represented in the United States will not handle orders from individual investors, but most will accept institutional business for Belgian stocks.

Information

The standard information book on Belgian stocks is *Memento des Valeurs*, published yearly and distributed by most of the Belgian brokerage houses with their name imprinted on the cover. It provides basic information and financial figures for all actively traded Belgian companies, as well as the stock price ranges over a period of years. However, it does not recommend specific stocks or make projections for the earnings prospects of individual companies.

A much more detailed multi-volume work on Belgian stocks is *Recueil Financier,* published annually by *Etbs. Emile Bruylant,* 65 rue de la Régence, Brussels. This is primarily for professional use.

The Investment Research Group of *European Banks International*

(*EBIC*) publishes a monthly European stock guide that includes a section on the most popular Belgian stocks. *Société Générale de Banque* is the Belgian member of this group and makes the book available to investors in Belgium.

In addition, the Belgian banks and brokers listed at the end of this chapter provide regular information on the Belgian stock market, the Belgian economic scene, and individual Belgian stocks.

Partial List of Major Belgian Banks
Handling Investment Business

Banque du Benelux / 19 place Sainte-Gudule / Brussels
Banque de Bruxelles S.A. / rue de la Régence / Brussels
(New York and Boston Securities Affiliate: *ABD Securities Corporation* /
    84 William Street / New York, New York 10038 / and 53 State
    Street / Boston, Massachusetts 02109)
Banque Degroof S.C.S. / 44 rue de l'Industrie / Brussels
Banque Lambert S.C.S. / 24 avenue Marnix / Brussels
(New York Securities Affiliate: *New Court Securities Corporation* /
    1 Rockefeller Plaza / New York, New York 10020)
Banque de Paris et des Pays-Bas Belgique / 3 rue des Colonies / Brussels
Kredietbank N.V. / 7 Arenbergstraat / Brussels
Société Générale de Banque S.A. / 3 rue Montagne-du-Parc / Brussels
(New York Securities Affiliate: *Sogen International Corporation* / 595
    Madison Avenue / New York, New York 10022)

Partial List of Belgian Brokerage Houses
Accepting Business from Foreign Investors

Dewaay, Sebille, Van Campenhout & Cie / 1 boulevard Anspach / Brussels
Eliot, Pringiers, Valentyn & Cie / 34 rue de la Montagne / Brussels
Peterbroeck, Van Campenhout & Cie / 52 rue des Colonies / Brussels
Puissant Baeyens, Poswick & Cie / 36 rue Ravenstein 36 / Brussels
Remy Frères & Fils, S.N.C. / 138 rue Royale / Brussels
Van Moer-Santerre, S.N.C. / 49 rue de Ligne / Brussels
Marcel Vermeulen & Fils, S.N.C. / 59 boulevard Anspach / Brussels

Partial List of Actively Traded Belgian Stocks

Banque de Bruxelles (banking)
Bekaert S.A. (steel wire)
Cockerill (steel)
Compagnie Bruxelles-Lambert (holding company)
Delhaize Frères & Cie (department store)
EBES (public utility)
Electrobel (electric utilities holding company)
G B Enterprises (department store)
Gevaert Photo-Producten N.V. (photographic materials)
Innovation-Bon Marché (department store)
Intercom (public utility)
Kredietbank (banking)
Petrofina (integrated oil company)
Société Générale de Banque (banking)
Société Générale de Belgique (largest holding company)
Société de Traction et Electricité (utility holding company)
Solvay & Cie S.A. (chemicals)
Union Minière (non-ferrous metals)
Vieille-Montagne (zinc)
Wagon-Lits (sleeping and dining-car operation)

Belgian Investment Funds

Depot Americain / 7 rue d'Arenberg / Brussels
Depot Belge / 7 rue d'Arenberg / Brussels
Depot Intercontinental / 7 rue d'Arenberg / Brussels
Depot d'Obligations International / 7 rue d'Arenberg / Brussels
Fonds Fiducem International / 2 rue de la Régence / Brussels
Fonds de Prevoyance et de Retraite / 24 avenue Marnix / Brussels
Foreign and National Investment Fund / 52 rue des Colonies / Brussels
Institutional Investors Fund / 7 rue d'Arenberg / Brussels
North American Fund, Series A-Income and *Series B-Growth* / 3 rue Montagne-du-Parc / Brussels

Belgian Sources of Information

Memento des Valeurs, available from most Belgian bankers and brokers
Recueil Financier, published by *Etbs. Emile Bruylant* / 65 rue de la Régence / Brussels

Belgian Financial and Business Press

Agence Economique et Financière / 5-7 quai au Bois-à-Brûler / Brussels
La Bourse de Bruxelles / 24 rue Frère Orban / Brussels
Bourse et Industrie / 10 rue des Colonies / Brussels
Le Courrier de la Bourse et de la Banque / 23 rue du Boulet / Brussels
L'Echo de la Bourse / 47 rue du Houblon / Brussels
Financieel Economische Tijd / Tavernierkaai 43 / Antwerp
L'Information Economique et Financier / 223 rue Royale / Brussels
Journal de l'Epargne / 52 boulevard Emile Jacqmain / Brussels
Mercure / 135 boulevard M. Lemonnier / Brussels
Moniteur des Finances / 74 quai au Briques / Brussels
Spécial / 31 rue des Drapiers / Brussels

Belgian Daily Newspapers with Good Business Coverage

La Dernier Heure / 52 rue du Pont Neuf / Brussels
Le Libre Belgique / 12 Montagne aux Herbes Portagères / Brussels
Le Soir / 21 place de Louvain / Brussels
Volkgazet / Antwerp

Stockbrokers of the Luxembourg Stock Exchange— International Investment Accounts

Bank of America S.A. / 8 boulevard Royal / Luxembourg City
Banque de Benelux-La Luxembourgeoise / 10 rue Aldringen / Luxembourg City
Banque Commerciale S.A. / 33 boulevard Royal / Luxembourg City
Banque Générale du Luxembourg S.A. / 14 rue Aldringen / Luxembourg City

Banque Internationale à Luxembourg S.A. / 2 boulevard Royal / Luxembourg City

Banque Lambert-Luxembourg S.A. / 59 boulevard Royal / Luxembourg City

Banque Mathieu Frères / 80 place de la Gare / Luxembourg City

Banque de Paris et des Pays-Bas pour le Grand-Duche de Luxembourg S.A. / 10a boulevard Royal / Luxembourg City

Banque Troillet à Luxembourg / 28 boulevard Joseph II / Luxembourg City

Caisse d'Epargne de l'Etat / 1 place de Metz / Luxembourg City

Compagnie Financière de la Deutsche Bank A.G. / 68 avenue de la Liberté / Luxembourg City

Compagnie Luxembourgeoise de Banque / 34a rue Philippe II / Luxembourg City

Crédit Européen / 21 rue Glesener / Luxembourg City

Crédit Industriel d'Alsace et de Lorraine / 103 Grand-rue / Luxembourg City

Crédit Lyonnais / 26a boulevard Royal / Luxembourg City

Deposit and Finance Bank S.A. / 48 avenue de la Gare / Luxembourg City

Dewaay Luxembourg S.A. / 11 avenue de la Porte-Neuve / Luxembourg City

First National City Bank (Luxembourg) / 16 avenue Marie-Thérèse / Luxembourg City

Investors Bank Luxembourg / 16a avenue de la Liberté / Luxembourg City

James Capel International S.A. / 103 Grand-rue / Luxembourg City

Kredietbank S.A. Luxembourgeoise / 37 rue Notre-Dame / Luxembourg City

Société Générale Alsacienne de Banque / 15 avenue de l'Arsenal / Luxembourg City

Union de Banques Privées (Unibanque) / 17 avenue de l'Arsenal / Luxembourg City

Investment Companies and Mutual Funds Quoted on the Luxembourg Stock Exchange

Luxembourg-Based

Alexander Fund S.A.
Atlantic Alliance Trust S.A.
Austral Trust S.A.
BtF Trust S.A.
Bucklersbury Fund S.A.
Capital International Fund S.A.
Capital Italia S.A.
Centenary Fund S.A.
Convertfund International S.A.
Crosby Fund S.A.
Delta Investment Fund S.A.
Delta Multifund S.A.

Europe Obligations
Finance-Union
First Investor American Trust S.A.
First Investor International Mining & Petroleum Fund S.A.
Fleming Japan Fund S.A.
Fonditalia
Fonds Deltec p. l'Amérique Latine S.A.
Fund of Nations
Hill Samuel Overseas Fund S.A.
Hispano Fund
Hope Street Fund S.A.
Icofund S.A. (International Common Share Fund)
I.I.T.
Intercontinental Technology & Natural Resources S.A.
Interfund S.A.
Interitalia
Intermarket Fund 1 S.A.
International Securities Fund S.A.
Interspar
Intertec
Investissements Atlantique S.A.
Italamerica S.A.
Italfortune International Fund S.A.
Italunion S.A.
Japan Growth Fund S.A.
Japan Pacific Fund S.A.
Kleinwort Benson (Japan) Fund S.A.
Luxam Trust S.A.
Luxfund S.A.
Monterey Trust S.A.
Multi-Trust Fund S.A.
Murray Fund S.A.
117 Group Fund S.A.
117 International Growth Fund S.A.
Pan-Holding S.A.
Panwit Trust S.A.
Rominvest International Fund
Rose Park Trust S.A.
Selected Risk Investments S.A.
Sepro S.A. (Security & Prosperity Fund)
Shareholders Excalibur Investment Corp. S.A.
Standard & Poor's International Fund S.A.
Tokyo Valor S.A.
Trafalgar Fund S.A.
Transpacific Fund S.A.
United States Trust Investment Fund S.A.

Based Outside Luxembourg

Concentra
The Convertible Bond Fund N.V.
Diversified Growth Stock Fund Inc.

Diversified Investment Fund Inc.
The Dreyfus Intercontinental Investment Fund N.V.
Dreyfus Offshore Trust N.V.
Energy International N.V.
EPR Europrogram International
E.U.P.I.C. (European Property Investment Company N.V.)
First Security Capital and Income Fund N.V.
Five Arrows Fund NV.
Fonds Exécutif du Canada Ltée
Fundamental Investors Inc.
General Overseas Fund
The Gresham Street Dollar Fund N.V.
Investment Properties International Ltd.
Massachusetts Investment Growth Stock Fund
Nefo N.V. (De Nederlandsche Fondsen Mij)
Pegasus International S.A.
Robeco N.V.
Rolinco N.V.
Société Générale International Fund Inc.
Suez International Venture Inc.
Tokyo Trust S.A.
USIF Real Estate (United States Investment Fund)
Utilico N.V.
Western Canada Resources Fund Ltd.
Worldwide Securities Ltd.

16

SPAIN AND PORTUGAL
IBERIAN PHOENIX

During the eclipse of Wall Street from 1969 to 1973, Spain was one of the most unexpected bright new stars to appear on the international investment sky—unexpected because the country had been in economic obscurity for almost two centuries.

Like an impoverished noblewoman too proud to display her penury to the prying eyes of a money-minded mercantile world, Spain, after the loss of most of her world-wide empire during the Napoleonic Wars, went into virtual economic seclusion throughout the 19th century when other Western European countries developed, flaunted, and abused their industrial wealth. She collapsed into a paroxysm of self-destruction during the Civil War of 1936-1939. For the next 20 years she lived a pariah existence because of her "neutral" sympathy toward the Axis powers during World War II and her own protective shell against outside influences and opinions often found in governments that have no freely elected opposition.

Coming Out of Seclusion

It was not until 1959 that she decided to join the rest of Europe—at least economically—by devaluating the peseta from 60 to 70 to the dollar and removing most barriers to foreign trade and investments.

On October 3, 1973 the Spanish peseta was valued at U.S. 1.80¢ and the Portuguese escudo was valued at U.S. 4.32¢.

The decision took a while—at least until 1964—to show results, but then it was as if sluice gates had been opened between higher and lower levels of water—between higher and low labor and living costs and between a surplus of labor, and a dearth of it. Tourists and foreign businessmen and their money began to pour into Spain, and Spanish workers and maids swarmed into the factories, farms, and households of other European countries and sent their money back home.

It was not exactly her own bootstraps by which Spain pulled herself up, but by the inflow of foreign exchange from tourism, workers remittances, plant investments by foreign companies, United States military expenditures, and other unilateral remittances. These began to exceed $2 billion in 1970 and reached about $2.5 billion in 1972. They allowed Spain to run a considerable surplus of imports over exports to bring in capital equipment and raise the living standards of its people. Yet, in 1972 the import surplus was only $1.2 billion, leaving about $1.3 billion to add to the foreign currency reserves. These reserves reached $5.2 billion at the end of 1972 and are expected to exceed $6 billion by the end of 1973, putting Spain into the top league of all countries in terms of such reserves.

Industrial Build-Up

United States direct investment in Spanish plant facilities is estimated at about $1 billion, and some 350 American companies now have operations in Spain. Other industrial countries have also made substantial investments. Not only has this raised consumption of manufactured products inside Spain, but it has also made Spain a significant exporter of industrial products, notably automobiles, chemicals, electrical equipment, steel, and ships. Industrial exports are now far ahead of the once dominant exports of agricultural products and minerals.

Paradise Lost

The most dramatic rise in service "exports" has been in tourism, which doubled between 1964 and 1972 from about 14 million to 29 million foreign visitors. In 1973, 32 million were expected—or almost as many as the entire Spanish population of 35 million. This has been a mixed blessing. While it brought in by far the largest income of foreign currency from Spanish industry and gave a great boost to the construction industry, tourism has also impaired the natural beauty of some of the most attractive coast lines in Spain, such as the Costa Brava, Costa Blanca, and Costa del Sol. As everywhere else where tourism is rampant, the local flavor and pristine nature that were the original attractions have been replaced by the sterility of neon-lighted, shoddy-modern tourist facilities, and the thousands of busloads of "packaged" tourists for whom they were built. Real estate prices have shot up, and living costs are following. This development has removed some of the attraction that Spain offered in the past as one of the best bargains in climatically and scenically pleasant retirement havens, especially on its Mediterranean coast and islands. (Much of the interior of Spain has a rather forbidding landscape and climate with extreme heat and bone-rattling cold.)

Gross National Product Growing

Nevertheless, all this has added up to an economic growth that is among the strongest in the world. During the second half of the 1960s, the Spanish gross national product grew at an average rate of 8% in real terms, and this rate continued in the early 1970s and even seemed to accelerate in 1973. The peseta, linked to gold, became a strong currency. It remained linked to the old price of gold of $35 a troy ounce during the two dollar devaluations and has appreciated from 70 to about 58 pesetas per U.S. $1. The peseta exchange rate to the dollar is set every morning by the central bank and may range within a band of plus or minus 5%. At times, it was 56 pesetas to $1.

Even though Spain is not part of the European Economic Community, it has nevertheless negotiated special tariff rates with the EEC, and trade is brisk in both directions.

The only serious economic problem, as in so many other countries of the world, is inflation, with money supply expanding almost three times as fast as the production of goods and services. Some attempts to curb inflation were made or planned in 1973, but the Spanish government, like almost every other government under the spell of Keynesian economic theory, apparently dares not try to see whether economic expansion would not work just as well with sound money and no inflation.

Another uncertain factor from an investor's point of view is the question of whether the transition from the government of the now 80-year-old Franco to another government of perhaps more democratic make-up will occur smoothly and without serious repercussions to the economy.

Stock Market Takes Off

The Spanish stock market index reflected the economic revival. It grew about fivefold between 1960 and 1973. In 1972 it rose 42% above the previous year's average, and by mid-1973 it had again risen by 8% from 1972. Initially it benefitted from other developments besides the economic revival. It was opened in 1960 to foreign investors who began to buy selectively. Then Spanish investment funds were set up which added to the buying throughout the 1960s. Spanish savings banks were required to put 45% of their assets into public or government-guaranteed securities; and finally Spanish resident investors no longer had to pay capital gains tax for securities held over one year.

Up to 1970, the stock market was only a minor source of new capital for corporations and public agencies. Through government incentive, however, new issues since 1971 have become an important factor in financing Spain's economic growth. In 1972, about $1.4 billion of new issues were sold, and they accounted for about 22% of all new financing. New issues of listed stocks are usually offered to existing stockholders at par value, providing them with handsome profits. As a result, trading volume has picked up considerably, and there were signs of speculative excesses in 1973 that may call for a correction.

In spite of this pick-up, the Spanish markets must still be considered very narrow by Wall Street standards. Only about 30 to 40 issues develop sufficient trading volume to allow execution of orders with relative ease. For less actively traded stocks it may often take a few days to execute even a relatively modest-sized order.

Three Exchanges

There are three Spanish stock exchanges—Madrid, Barcelona, and Bilbao. Madrid is the largest, accounting for about 60% of all transactions, and apparently gaining on the other two exchanges, with Barcelona perhaps accounting for 22% of the trades, and Bilbao for the rest. All transactions are executed by brokers who are appointed, in a personal capacity rather than as firms, by the Ministry of Finance. All banks, mutual funds, and portfolio management firms handling investment business must deal through a broker. Transfer of stock is a rather formal business and must be attested either by a broker who is a member of one of the three stock exchanges, a notary public, or a *corredor de comercio,* who is somewhat of a broker's representative in cities that have no stock exchanges. In addition to a stock certificate, a Spanish investor also receives a so-called *póliza de operaciones al contado,* serving as evidence of his ownership of the stock certificates. He may keep this *póliza* when he deposits his stock certificates with a bank, and this may be useful if the certificate gets lost or misplaced. Spanish stock certificates can be either bearer certificates, without the name of the owner, or certificates registered in the name of the owner. In the case of bearer certificates the owner must detach a coupon to collect his dividend. Registration of certificates do not ensure automatic dividend payments, as in most other countries. The owner must present the certificate at a bank to collect the dividend, and the certificate is stamped as evidence of payment.

Foreign Investors Encouraged

Foreigners are fairly unrestricted in the purchase of Spanish securities as long as these are paid for in pesetas derived from the conversion of a foreign currency. Total foreign portfolio investments in a single Spanish company may not exceed 50%. Shares of some companies, notably those involved in national defense and public information, may not be bought by foreign investors. Foreign investments in some other industries are limited to varying degrees. These include mining, motion picture production, hydrocarbon prospecting and processing, banking, shipping, and insurance. Proceeds from the sale of foreign securities originally bought with converted pesetas, as well as dividends and interest income, can be freely taken out of the country.

There is no withholding tax on dividends received by foreign owners of Spanish shares, and foreign investors pay no capital gains tax irrespective of the length of time the securities were held. There is a 24% withholding tax on fixed-income securities, which cannot be recovered, but can be set off against taxable income on the IRS income tax return. There are no Spanish shares, or American Depositary Receipts of Spanish shares, actively traded in the United States. Thus, in most cases, American investors in Spanish securities must pay the Interest Equalization Tax due on the purchase price of most foreign securities.

Unless he can sell the securities to another American investor with the tax included, he will not be able to recover the tax when selling the shares on the Spanish market. Thus, only stocks with substantial growth potential should be of interest to the American investor—

until the Interest Equalization Tax is allowed to expire—and Spanish fixed-income securities are of no interest to him before that time.

Where to Buy Spanish Securities

About 70% of the portfolio investment business in Spain is handled by the commercial banks; and the balance by special portfolio management companies. From a practical point of view, the American investor should contact the United States representative office of a Spanish bank for information (listed at the end of this chapter). The banks cannot transact investment business in the United States, but they will arrange for the investor to open a dollar investment account at their head office in Spain and forward the investor's instructions. They will also provide the investor with investment information available from Spain. The office in Spain acts as a custodian for the stock certificates and attends to all the necessary details of stock transfer, dividend collection, rights offering, etc. When the American investor sells his Spanish stocks, his dollar account will be credited with the proceeds. If he wants to close out his account, the dollars can be taken out of Spain without problems.

Spanish Common Stocks

For an investor wanting to participate in the growth of the Spanish economy, shares of one of the leading banks offer the simplest and probably the safest way. The five or six leading commercial banks reportedly control between them almost 50% of Spanish manufacturing. A new government regulation in 1971 lifting some credit restrictions and offering tax rebates on new industrial investment further strengthened the position of the banks, since much of the new money is raised by the commercial banks. An effort by the government to separate the commercial and investment banking activities of the banks resulted in the formation of subsidiaries in one or the other type of banking so that the overall scope of the business of the controlling bank remained unchanged.

The largest commercial banks roughly in the order of the size of their deposits, are *Banco Español de Crédito, Banco Hispano-Americano, Banco Central, Banco de Bilbao, Banco de Vizcaya,* and *Banco de Santander.* All of them have had excellent stock market records during the years 1960 to 1973, with most of their prices rising tenfold or better.

Electric utilities are also publicly owned in Spain, and their operations are somewhat more in public view than those of manufacturing companies. Their stock market performance has not been as spectacular as that of the banks, but some have shown a good growth record, including *Fuerzas Eléctricas de Cataluña S.A. (FECSA), Iberduero S.A., Hidroeléctrica Española S.A., Union Eléctrica S.A.,* and *Cia. Sevillana de Eléctricidad.*

Construction and real estate operations have been growth industries, but with more risk and cyclical factors. Actively traded stocks include *Dragados y Construcciones S.A., Portland Valderrivas, Vallehermosa,* and *Imobiliaria Urbis.*

The steel industry has greatly benefitted from the boom. The largest integrated steel company, 25% owned by *U.S. Steel,* is *Altos Hornos de Vizcaya S.A.*

Spain's leading automobile manufacturer is *SEAT (Sociedad Española de Automotive de Turismo S.A.),* whose new miniature model reportedly helped boost Spain's automobile exports by more than 50%. Total *SEAT* production of cars and trucks in 1972 was 700,000, and new plant construction planned could bring this figure to 1.3 million by 1976. Performance of the *SEAT* stock was rather undistinguished during the years 1970 to 1972.

Investment Funds

Spanish investment funds are of recent origin. Initially, through a decree in 1958, closed-end investment funds received the green light to operate. Through a second decree in 1964, open-end funds were created, and at the same time foreign investment in these funds was stimulated by guaranteeing foreign investors repatriation of their money on redemption of the fund shares including tax-free dividends and capital gains. Since February 1973, Spanish investment trusts can invest up to 10% of their assets in foreign securities listed on a recognized stock exchange. Nevertheless, with 90% in Spanish securities, a Spanish investment trust represents a good vehicle for a smaller investor to invest in the Spanish economy on a diversified basis.

Information

Spanish companies are very uncommunicative by American standards, and this is no doubt a deterrent to the foreign investor. With a few exceptions, answering mail does not seem to occupy top priority with Spanish corporations and financial institutions. Even though the Madrid and Barcelona Stock Exchanges and most of the leading banks publish investment information, with reports on individual stocks, it takes time to get them if one is not on the spot. The American investor is largely confined to what he can get from the American offices of Spanish banks represented in the United States.

Portugal

Part of the Iberian Peninsula, and with a colonial history as glorious and far-flung as that of Spain, Portugal is nevertheless very different in character from Spain. There is practically no country in the world about which there is such unanimity of praise from visitors. The country's charm lies in its people, landscape, climate, and communities rather than in its historical treasures, although even these are attractive.

Portugal is beginning to follow Spain in the development of an industrial economy and it encourages foreign direct investments in production facilities. However, in 1973 it was not yet a country for foreign portfolio investment. All investments must be approved by the government, and in 1973 such approval was practically impossible to get unless it was requested in order to buy an interest in an operating company with the objective of instilling additional foreign capital and know-how. The small Lisbon Stock Exchange went into wild excesses in 1972 and 1973, with price/earnings ratios of stocks going up to 200 and 300.

There were also restrictions on the purchase by non-residents of income-producing property in Portugal, and mortgages for vacation homes bought by non-residents were difficult or impossible to get.

Given some time, however, to grow and mature, the Portuguese stock markets may eventually also open up to foreign investors, especially when the authorities recognize that a stock market can become a good source of new capital only if it develops active and regular trading volume, including that from "speculators."

Partial List of Spanish Banks Doing Portfolio Investment Business

Banco de Bilbao / Alcalá 16 / Madrid
(New York Office: 767 Fifth Avenue / New York, New York 10022)
Banco Central / Alcalá 49 / Madrid
Banco de Santander / Alcalá 37 / Madrid
(New York Office: 375 Park Avenue / New York, New York 10022)
Banco de Vizcaya / Alcalá 45 / Madrid
(New York Office: 250 Park Avenue / New York, New York 10017)
Banco Español de Crédito / Castellana 7 / Madrid
(New York Office: 375 Park Avenue / New York, New York 10022)
Banco Exterior de España / Carrera de San Jeronimo 36 / Madrid
Banco Hispano-Americano / Serrano 47 / Madrid

Sources of Information

All banks listed above provide investment information.
Also, the Madrid and Barcelona stock exchanges have information on
listed companies on file.
Bolsa de Madrid / Plaza de la Lealtad 1 / Madrid
Bolsa de Barcelona / calle Consulado 2 / Barcelona

Partial List of Actively Traded Spanish Stocks

Banks

Banco de Bilbao
Banco Central
Banco Español de Crédito
Banco Hispano-Americano
Banco de Santander
Banco de Vizcaya

Utilities
Fuerzas Eléctricas de Cataluña S.A. (FECSA)
Iberduero S.A.
Hidroeléctrica Española S.A.
Cia Sevillana Eléctricidad
Unión Eléctrica S.A.

Construction, Real Estate
Cros S.A.
Dragados y Construcciones S.A.
Imobiliaria Urbis
Portland Valderrivas
Vallehermosa

Chemicals, Oil
Cia Española de Petróleos S.A.
Energia e Industria Aragonesas
Insular de Nitrógeno

Petroliber
Unión Explosivos Rio-Tinto S.A.

Automobiles

Citroën Hispania
F A S A-Renault
S E A T

Retail

Galerías Preciados S.A.

Steel Processing

Altos Hornos de Vizcaya S.A.
Nueva Montana Quijano S.A.
Ponferrada

Telephone Utility

Cia Telefónica Nacional de España S.A.

Partial List of Spanish Investment Funds

Ahorrofondo / Alcalá 27 / Madrid
Bonserfond / Alcalá 37 / Madrid
Crecino / General Perón 27 / Madrid
Eurovalor / Cedaceros 11 / Madrid
Financiera Bansander S.A. (Fibansa) / Paseo de Pereda 9-10 / Santander
Gesta / Lagasca 95 / Madrid
Gramco Iberia / General Sanjurjo 57 / Madrid
Inespa / Marqués de Valdeiglesias 6 / Madrid
Inrenta / Marqués de Valdeiglesias 6 / Madrid

List of Spanish Daily Newspapers
With Good Financial Coverage

ABC / Serrano 61 / Madrid
La Gaceta del Norte / Bilbao
Informaciónes / San Roque 9 / Madrid
La Vanguardia / Barcelona

Financial and Business Periodicals

Actualidad Económica (bi-weekly) / Padre Damian 19 / Madrid
Desarrollo (weekly) / Velázquez 61 / Madrid
El Economista (weekly) / Conde Aranda 8 / Madrid
Información Comercial Española (monthly) / Goya 73 / Madrid

17

ITALY
TO LIVE IN PEACE

Italy for many years has been plagued by a flight of capital. This means that many Italians who want to build up a nest egg take their money across the border to Switzerland and have it invested on their behalf in foreign securities or other values. The Swiss border town of Chiasso and the nearby resort town of Lugano have thereby become two important international investment centers.

Thus, there is little reason for a foreign investor to do in Rome what most Romans don't do and invest his money in Italy—except perhaps for the man who wants to retire there (and Italy more than any other country lures its citizens back after they sought their fortunes abroad). But even retirees don't always seem to do that. If they have worked in a country with a relatively stable currency, they can leave their savings there and have the income transmitted, as needed; or they can stop in Switzerland on their way home and leave them there. (They can no longer deposit money in Swiss francs or buy Swiss securities as easily as in the past—as explained in the chapter on Switzerland—but they can have it invested by a professional portfolio manager in safe international securities.)

Poor Investment Climate

There are a number of reasons why Italy in 1973 offered an uncertain picture to a foreign investor.

The Milan Stock Exchange, where 80% of Italian securities trading is carried on, was in an almost steady decline from 1962 to 1972.

On October 3, 1973 the Italian lira was valued at U.S. 0.177¢.

(Other exchanges are in Rome, Turin, Naples, Palermo, Venice, Genoa, Florence, Bologna, and Trieste.) There was a surprisingly sharp upturn during the first part of 1973, but it was difficult to see whether this would be a lasting development. The underlying factors that make the Italian market weak remain. Trading volume, compared to other European countries, is very low. Most of the trading is carried on outside the exchange among the banks, and this trading volume and the prices at which the transactions are made remain unknown to the public. Only 145 Italian companies have listed their stock on the Milan exchange—compared to more than 500 in Germany and about 800 in France, the two other large industrial countries of Continental Europe with relatively poorly developed stock market practices. Information published by Italian companies is even scantier than that published by reticent companies in other European countries. Reportedly, many publicly owned Italian companies keep four sets of books —one for themselves, one for their bankers, one for the tax authorities, and one for their stockholders. Moreover, even with all these books, or because of them, many Italian companies have not been able to show an attractive earnings record over the past few years. There is no clear indication that matters will improve in the future. Several of them are in such bad shape that they would probably welcome nationalization. Labor relations remain a serious problem in Italy. The government seems to remain in a permanent state of stalemate, unable to form any consistent economic policy or pass much needed legislation, including proposed legislation affecting the financial and investment community. Stock registration with the government has been compulsory since 1962 in an effort to collect taxes on dividends and interest, but this has driven Italians even further away from the stock market than they had been before, and their attitude toward their own stock market remains one of great detachment and even contempt. Finally, the Italian currency has remained one of the weakest in Europe, holding the line roughly with the dollar; and thus, it has been anything but a currency hedge. To stop some of the outflow of money, the Italian government, in July 1973, passed a regulation that made it prohibitive for an Italian investor to invest in foreign securities through legitimate channels in Italy.

Cosa Nostra Tradition

It is, of course, easy to be contemptuous or condescending about the Italian economic and financial muddle, but anyone who has watched with some attempt at objectivity the economic and political scene in the United States in the late 1960s and early 1970s is likely to recognize that the difference is only one of degree—and the underlying motivation in Italy may be more human than in the United States.

To understand Italy, one must understand the history of the Italian *cosa nostra*—the closely knit family, tribal, and friendship associations that exist not only in the well publicized Mafia but actually pervade every social strata in Italy. These associations were formed as a protection against foreign invaders and other exploiters of the hardworking peasants and artisans. In one way or another, Italy, throughout its history, until Garibaldi helped unite it as an independent nation in 1860–1870, has been ruled or exploited by foreigners. Sicily has the oldest tradition of defense against foreign occupation. Several hundred years before Christ it was first occupied by the "colonizing" Greeks, then by the Phoenician merchants, and later by the Roman militarists, who, with the sweat of slaves, made Sicily supply most of the grain they needed to give away to the "welfare" population of the City of Rome. The Romans, who started their military career by first conquering the neighboring Etruscans, became, strictly speaking, alien rulers of the rest of Italy. When Rome fell in the 5th century, the Teutonic tribes ransacked the country. In 800 A.D. Charlemagne had himself crowned Emperor of the "Holy" Roman Empire of the German Nation, starting many hundreds of years of German robber baron expeditions into Italy, interrupted occasionally by French and Spanish forays. The dukes and *condottieris* of the Italian city states during the Renaissance were not exactly socialists when they carried on their intercity wars on the backs of the working population that had to pay for these ventures in blood, toil, and money. Nor were some of the more worldly popes, such as the Borgias, amateurs when it came to financial extortion of the faithful. In more recent history, Napoleon had a fling at Italy, and the Austrians ruled Venice and other areas until they were expelled in 1866.

Thus, it is not surprising that the Italians, for sheer self-preservation, have developed a system of mutual self-protection against the authorities, and of evading taxation and other extortions by governing bodies. Because of its more than 2000-year tradition, this system is not easily abandoned, and considering that neither Mussolini nor the democratic politicians of the post-World War II era can be regarded as paragons of virtue, there has so far been little inducement to abandon this system.

To Live in Peace

In fact, it is the family system that makes the Italian economy function in spite of all government ineptitude. Anyone trying to do business in Italy will find himself stymied at every turn unless he links up with a "business family," and as soon as he does, he will be surprised to find how easily he can meet the right bankers, politicians, industrialists, newspapermen, lawyers, and others who can help his cause.

It is the same on the human and social level. The most wonderful examples of mutual assistance for survival were provided by the many Italians who during World War II, often at great risk to themselves, helped prisoners of war, irrespective of uniform or affiliation, to survive and escape to their home countries to "live in peace." (*Vivere in Pace* was the title of a classic film that paid tribute to this eminently human side of the Italians.)

The system does much to lure so many Italians who have emigrated back to their home country and, combined with Italy's scenery, climate, and art treasures, the Italian way of life continues to enrapture foreigners who visit or settle there. But the system is not well suited for an investment market that depends on relatively honest public disclosure. Nevertheless, here, for the record, is some information on the investment scene.

Italian Securities

Among the ten largest Italian companies by capitalization only one—*Lepetit*—shows an attractive earnings record and a correspondingly attractive increase in its stock price. It is a pharmaceutical company, of which the majority is owned by *Dow Chemical Company*.

The largest Italian company is *Fiat*, which produces very popular automobiles but relatively unimpressive earnings.

It is followed by *SIP* (*Società Italiana per l'Esercizio Telefonico par Azionario*), a telephone company with "flat" earnings, that is, about the same earnings every year.

Third is an insurance company, *Assicurazioni Generali di Trieste e Venezia*, which had a modest general upward trend in earnings and a reasonably firm stock price.

The worst performer from 1960 to 1972 was *Montedison*, number four, the large chemical concern, which had declining earnings through most of these years, ending up in whopping losses in 1970 and 1971. A recovery was in sight in 1972.

The largest Italian bank, *Banca Commerciale Italiana*, is number nine, with an indifferent earnings record, as had also *Banco di Roma* and *Credito Italiano*, two other large publicly owned banks.

Olivetti, next to *Fiat* probably the best known Italian company outside Italy, and not among the top ten, showed an erratic earnings picture and a steadily declining stock price throughout the 1960s. The company nearly killed itself when it acquired bankrupt *Underwood* in the early 1960s, and only survived with help from *Fiat*.

Pirelli, the large Italian tire manufacturer, which joined forces in a 50/50 partnership with the British *Dunlop*, in early 1973 was a disaster case and next to insolvency.

Even retail business seems in trouble, judging by the declining earnings of *La Rinascente*, Italy's largest department store and supermarket chain.

There are more than 500 bonds listed on the Milan Stock Exchange, but because of the weakness of the Italian currency they would be of limited interest to a foreign investor.

In 1972, there was a wave of 15 new listings of bond issues convertible into common stocks, which found surprisingly good acceptance by Italian investors. Receiving between 5% and 7% yield, investors apparently found the fixed income plus a possible appreciation of the price, in line with improved prices for common stocks, attractive. For hope springs eternal, and it was said in 1972 that the Milan Stock Exchange was so low that it couldn't possibly go lower, and indeed in 1973 there was a temporary upturn.

Italian Mutual Funds

Italian mutual funds offer a partial opportunity for investing in the Italian economy. All mutual funds that are permitted to be sold in Italy must have at least 50% of their assets invested in Italian securities. There are 17 Italian mutual funds, all of them, because of legal snares, registered in Luxembourg. Performance has been mediocre because of the 50% commitment to the Italian economy, but of course that may improve if the Italian market recovers.

Where to Buy Italian Stocks

Even though trading on the stock exchanges is the exclusive right of government-appointed brokers, and these brokers can theoretically do business with customers, in practice most of the investment business is handled by the banks. The banks have a national network of branch offices, all of which handle investment business, and it is difficult for brokers to compete on this scale. Some of the Italian banks are represented in New York, but they are generally not equipped to do business with individuals.

The five largest banks in Italy with branch office networks are *Banca Nazionale del Lavoro, Banca Commerciale Italiana, Banco di Roma, Credito Italiano,* and *Banco di Napoli.* In general, they will not accept discretionary accounts, which means that each transaction must be authorized by the customer—not a practical procedure unless one lives in the country. A number of private banks will accept discretionary management of larger portfolios, leading among them *Banca Stainhauslin,* Florence, and *Monte dei Paschi di Siena,* Siena. So will a relatively new, but substantial, mutual fund and portfolio management company, *SAFI,* Turin, with offices in Milan, which is half owned by *The Group Agnelli (Fiat)* and half by *SAI, Società Assicurazioni Industriali,* a large insurance company.

A number of regulations govern the purchase of Italian securities by non-residents, notably the one that requires that they be paid for with freely convertible foreign currency or from a foreign lira account. Stock certificates owned by non-residents must be deposited with an authorized Italian bank, or if they are to be taken out, registered with a special number and endorsed *circolante all'estero.* The latter is a time consuming and not very practical way; thus it is advisable to leave Italian securities in the custody of an Italian bank.

Dividends and interest due can be transmitted to a non-resident up to a maximum of 8% per year of the invested capital. There is a withholding tax of 5% for United States residents.

Most trades on the Milan Stock Exchange are for "forward" settlement. Settlement day is a fixed date once a month—so that a trader can have up to 30 days before he settles a transaction. This encourages speculation and in-and-out trades.

Sources of Information

Information available on Italian stocks is limited and not very revealing, although there is a trend towards improvement.

Pioneering work in this area is done by *Edizioni Sasip,* Milan, which publishes stock and bond guides on about 200 companies and is working on the development of security analysis methods for Italian companies. The two partners of the company were instrumental in the organization of an Italian security analysts society in 1972. *Sasip* has also started a joint venture with *DAFSA*, the French securities research firm, which is trying to develop unified security analysis methods throughout Europe.

Among the banks, *Banca Commerciale Italiana* and *Credito Italiano* publish the most comprehensive information on Italian securities and the Italian market, including some material in English.

A few brokers publish information on Italian stocks. One of the leading ones, *Alberto Milla,* has published a guide on Italian convertible securities.

The leading financial newspaper is *Il Sole-24 Ore*, published in Milan.

Partial List of Italian Banks Handling Investment Business

Bergamo: *Banca Provinciale Lombarda* / Via Monte de Pietà 8
Florence: *Banca Steinhauslin* / Via dei Sassetti 4
Milan: *Banca Commerciale Italiana* / Piazza della Scala 6
Milan: *Banca Morgan Vonwiller, S.p.A.* / Via Armorari 14
Milan: *Banca Popolare di Milano* / Piazza Meda 4
Milan: *Banco Ambrosiano* / Via Clerici 2
(New York Securities Affiliate: *Ultrafin International Corporation* / 63
    Wall Street / New York, New York 10005)
Milan: *Credito Commerciale, S.p.A.* / Via Armorari 4
Milan: *Credito Italiano* / Piazza Cordusio 2
Naples: *Banco di Napoli* / Via Roma 177
Palermo: *Banco di Sicilia* / Via Mariano Stabile 182
Rome: *Banca Nazionale dell'Agricoltura* / Via Lovanio 16
Rome: *Banca Nazionale del Lavoro* / Via Vittorio Veneto 119
Rome: *Banco di Roma* / Via del Corso 307
(New York Securities Affiliate: *EuroPartners Securities Corporation* /
    1 World Trade Center / New York, New York 10048)
Siena: *Monte dei Paschi di Siena* / 53100 Sienna
Turin: *Cassa di Risparmio Torino* / Via XX Settembre 31
Turin: *Instituto Bancario San Paolo di Torino* / Piazza San Carlo 156

Leading Credit Institution

Instituto Mobiliare Italiano / Via delle Quattro Fontane 121 / Rome
    (owns *Fonditalia*, largest Italian mutual fund based in Luxembourg)

Portfolio Management Company

Safi Management / Via Manzoni 9 / Milan

Partial List of Milanese Brokers

Agente di Cambio Milla / Via Morone 8
Agente di Cambio Tagi / Piazza S. Maria Beltrade 1
Agenti di Cambio Foglia Albertini / Via della Posta 3
Ettore Fumagalli / Via Meravigli 16
Leonida Gaudenzi / Via delle Orsole 4B
Pietro San Martino / Via della Posta 7

A Representative List of Italian Stocks as Published by Banca Commerciale Italiana

Banking

Banca Commerciale Italiana
Banco di Roma
Credito Italiano
Mediobanca

Finance

Bastogi
Breda
Finsider
GIM
IFI
Invest
La Centrale
Pirelli & C.
Pirelli S.p.A.
SME
STET
Sviluppo

Insurance

Alleanza Assicurazioni
Assicurazioni Generali
Compagnia Assicurazioni Milano
Fondiaria Incendio
Fondiaria Vita
L'Abeille
L'Assicuratrice Italiana
RAS
SAI
Toro-Compagnia Assicurazioni Torino

Real Estate

Aedes
Beni Immobili Italia
Beni Stabili
Generale Immobiliare (Roma)

Industrial

ANIC (chemicals)
Burgo (paper)
Cantoni C. (textiles)
Cementir (cement)
Condotte Acqua (construction)
Cucirini C.C. (textiles)
Dalmine (steel tubes)
Erba C. (pharmaceuticals)
Eridania (sugar)
Eternit (building materials)
Falck (iron and steel)
FIAT (automotive)
Italcementi (cement)
Italgas (gas)
Italsider (iron and steel)
Lepetit (pharmaceuticals)
Magneti M. (electrical equipment)
Magona d'Italia (steel sheets)

Marelli E. (electrical engineering)
Metallurgica Italiana (metals)
Mira Lanza (detergents, soaps)
Mondadori (publishing)
Monte Amiata (mercury)
Montedison (chemicals)
Montefibre (synthetic fibers)
Motta (candies)
Olivetti & C. (office machines)
Pertusola (lead and zinc)
Pierrel (pharmaceuticals)
Richard Ginori (chinaware and building materials)
Rumianca (chemicals)
SAFFA (matches, paper, chemicals)
Siele (mercury)
Snia Viscosa (synthetic fibers)
Terni (steel)

Miscellaneous

Alitalia (airline)
CIGA (hotels)
La Rinascente (retailing)
SIP (telecommunications)

Italian Investment Funds

Only funds with at least 50% of their portfolio in Italian securities can be sold in Italy. For legal reasons, Italian funds are registered in Luxembourg, but they are sold in Italy through banks and sales organizations.

Amitalia Fund S.A. / 10 boulevard Royal / Luxembourg City, Luxembourg

Capital Italia S.A. / 37 rue Notre-Dame / Luxembourg City, Luxembourg

Fonditalia International / 1 place de Metz / Luxembourg City, Luxembourg

Interfund S.A. / 1 place de Metz / Luxembourg City, Luxembourg

International Securities Fund / 14 rue Aldringer / Luxembourg City, Luxembourg

Intertrust International Fund S.A. / 103 Grand-rue / Luxembourg City, Luxembourg

Italamerica S.A. / 23 avenue de la Porte-Neuve / Luxembourg City, Luxembourg

Italfortune International Fund S.A. / 11 boulevard Grande-Duchesse Charlotte / Luxembourg City, Luxembourg

Italunion / 11 boulevard Grand-Duchesse Charlotte / Luxembourg City, Luxembourg

Mediolanum Selective Fund / 37 rue Notre-Dame / Luxembourg City, Luxembourg

Rominvest International Fund / 2 boulevard Royal / Luxembourg City, Luxembourg

Independent Investment Research

Sasip / Via S. Vittore al Teatro 1 / Milan

Leading National Newspapers with Financial Coverage

Corriere della Sera / Via Solferino 28 / Milan
Daily American (English-language) / Due Macelli 23 / Rome
Il Messagero / Via del Tritone 152 / Rome
La Stampa & Stampa Sera / Via Roma 80 and Galleria S. Federico 16 /
   Turin

Italian Financial Press

Espanzione / Via San Martina 14 / Milan
L'Espresso / Via Cervo / Milan
Il Fiorini / Via Parigi 11 / Rome
Il Globo / Plaza Indipendenza 11 / Rome
Mondo Economico / Via Mercanti 2 / Milan
Ore 12 / Piazza S. Lorenzo in Lucina / Rome
Panoramo / Via Beatrice di Savoia 20 / Milan
Il Sole-24 Ore / Via Monvisco 26 / Milan
Successo / Via Manzoni 44 / Milan

18

AUSTRIA
SOUND AND SYLVAN

Austria today is the minuscule left-over of what was one of the largest and most powerful empires in the world. At the height of its glory, when the Hapsburg dynasty also ruled over Spain and its possessions, "the sun never set" over this empire. But even in its sunset days before World War I—the days of Viennese waltzes, Kaiser Franz Joseph, Mayerling, and *Der Rosenkavalier*—the empire was still the largest in Europe excluding Russia.

This came to a sudden halt at the end of World War I, when Austria was reduced to its present size. From 1938 to 1945 it was briefly incorporated into Hitler's Third Reich, but emerged afterward as a neutral nation in its 1918 shape. All that remains of the past glory is an oversized capital (where about 23% of the total population of about 7 million lives) and an oversized bureaucracy.

Nevertheless, Austria today represents a sound economy. Its currency is among the strongest in the world, having been revalued *vis-à-vis* the dollar almost as much as the Swiss Franc and the German mark. Tourists who flock in from all parts of the world, including the Iron Curtain countries, are one of its main sources of foreign currency income. Traditions and memories of the old empire are what attracts them—the gigantic palace of Schönbrunn; the Opera and

---

On October 3, 1973 the Austrian schilling was valued at U.S. 5.65¢.

Johann Strauss; the Ringstrasse, ringed by what must be the largest assembly of neo-something-or-other architecture anywhere in the world; the Heurigen, the potent new wine served by the vintners in the villages on the slopes of the Vienna woods; the Prater, the amusement park with its giant wheel; and the coffeehouses, where for the price of a cup of coffee a guest can sit for hours to read a dozen newspapers. And many tourists also enjoy the lovely scenery of the rest of Austria, ideal for both summer and winter vacations.

Fixed Income for Retirement

Austria's beauty also makes it an attractive country to retire to. It is less crowded than Switzerland, and south of the Alps it offers a particularly pleasant climate—dry, warm summers and crisp winters, ideal for skiing. It is for people with retirement in mind that Austria is of primary investment interest. The firm currency provides a safety feature against currency losses. The most advantageous investment vehicles are fixed-interest securities, which in 1973 paid a yield of between 7% and 8%. What is most important, however, is that Austrian residents under certain conditions can buy fixed-income securities with tax benefits, including income-tax-free interest. The regulations are somewhat complicated, and the counsel of an investment advisor of an Austrian bank is recommended.

A non-resident can also buy Austrian fixed-income securities with foreign currency, and there is no withholding tax. He would, of course, have to declare the income from Austrian fixed-income securities in the country where he pays his income tax. About 450 fixed-income securities are traded on the Vienna Stock Exchange.

Limited Investment Opportunities

Otherwise, Austria offers only limited opportunities to the investor. Because of the great attraction of fixed-income securities, very little financing is done through common stock. About 70 Austrian stocks are listed on the Vienna Stock Exchange. Trading volume in most of them is slight. In many companies, a large percentage of the stock is in the hands of the Austrian government or the banks. This limits the number of shares available for trading. The largest Austrian bank, *Creditanstalt-Bankverein*, is 60% government owned, and the bank in turn has major holdings in many Austrian corporations. This close control of many companies has in the past given rise to the accusation that the Vienna stock market is "rigged." In fact, it may have been merely the very thin market that created wide fluctuations in stock prices—and this is still liable to happen today.

Such erratic movement of the market occurred in 1961 and 1962 when prices rose to giddy heights, only to collapse again at the end of 1962. The disillusioned Austrian investors turned to foreign stocks, but by the end of the 1960s they were even more disillusioned by the collapse of the United States market and the IOS fund of Bernard Cornfeld, whose sales force had been very active in Austria (see footnote on page 229). In the meantime, the Austrian stock market remained in the doldrums, and by the end of the 1960s many Austrian stocks looked greatly undervalued by international standards.

To stimulate interest, some Austrian companies split their stocks, while maintaining the dividend rate, which means that the effective dividend income was doubled. Foreign buyers came into the market, notably from Switzerland, Germany, England, and the Netherlands, and in the second half of 1972 the Austrian market again took a sharp upward turn. This rising trend carried on well into 1973, in contrast to several other stock exchanges, including New York, which declined early in 1973.

Among the stocks bought by foreign investors were *Creditanstalt-Bankverein*; *Semperit A.G.*, a tire and rubber manufacturer; *Veitscher Magnesitwerke-A.G.*, one of the world's largest manufacturers of refractory bricks, used in steel making; *Felten & Guilleaume*, a copper and steel wire manufacturer; and brewery stocks, such as *Gösser Brauerei-A.G.* and *Österreichische Brau-A.G.*

There is no restriction on the purchase and ownership of Austrian shares by non-residents provided the shares are paid for in freely convertible foreign currency. There is a withholding tax of 20% on dividends due to non-residents.

Like several other European countries, Austria has a central depository and clearing agency for securities where change of ownership can be registered by simple bookkeeping entry. Most Austrian shares are bearer certificates—which means they are not registered in the owner's name—and dividends must be collected by detaching a coupon. For practical reasons, a non-resident is well advised to leave his Austrian shares with a custodian bank.

Investment Trusts

Because of the limited opportunities of investing in Austrian common stock, most Austrian investment trusts include foreign securities, or they are composed entirely of foreign securities. Five funds of the leading Austrian investment trust management company, *Österreichische Investment-Gesellschaft m.b.H.*, are traded on the Vienna Stock Exchange, as well as the shares of seven foreign investment trusts, including the internationally traded Dutch funds, *Roboco, Rolinco,* and *Utilico.* The shares of four Austrian funds not traded on the Vienna exchange—*Atlasfond, Combirent, Sparinvest,* and *Intertrend* —are nevertheless quoted in the official stock exchange bulletin— *Amtliches Kursblatt der Wiener Börse*—at their net asset value at which they can be bought through Austrian banks.

Where to Buy Austrian Securities

Because of the limited trading volume of Austrian shares, an investor might find it difficult to buy Austrian shares anywhere but in Austria or through Swiss, Dutch, and British banks or brokers.

In Austria, an investor can buy securities from any office of a financial institution whether it is a member of the Vienna Stock Exchange or not. Non-members place their security orders through members and split the commission. The role of the government-appointed brokers (*Sensale*) and free brokers are comparable to those of specialists and floor brokers. They do not normally deal with individual investors.

The three leading banks with well developed investment services are *Creditanstalt-Bankverein, Österreichische Länderbank A.G.,* and *Girozentrale.* The leading private bank providing investment services and portfolio management is *Schoeller & Co.* The banks charge commission plus fees for complete portfolio management and custodial services, but commissions only if stock certificates are delivered to the investor.

Sources of Information

Sources of information on stocks are scanty in Austria. Austrian companies themselves are not very communicative by American standards. There is no security analysts society in Austria, and what might be described as security analysts are usually also portfolio managers.

The leading banks providing investment services publish a certain amount of stock market information, including reports on individual companies, but the viewpoint is global rather than strictly Austrian.

The *Creditanstalt-Bankverein* and *Österreichische Länderbank A.G.* provide a certain amount of information in English.

Some international investment information services include reports on a few Austrian companies, notably *Capital International S.A.*, in Geneva (15 rue du Cendrier).

In relation to the size of the country, Austria has an unusually large number of newspapers and periodicals, including almost 20 specialized business and financial publications. The leading stock market publications are *Börsen Rundschau* and *Trend*.

Leading Bank Members of the Vienna Stock Exchange

Allgemeine Sparkasse in Linz / Promenade 11-13 / Linz-Donau
Bank Gebrüder Gutmann Nfg., Aktiengesellschaft / Schwarzenberg-
  platz 16 / Vienna
Berger & Companie, Bankhaus / Rathausplatz 4 / Salzburg
Creditanstalt-Bankverein / Schottengasse 6-8 / Vienna
*Girozentrale und Bank der österreichischen Sparkassen Aktiengesell-
  schaft* / Schubertring 5 / Vienna
Österreichische Länderbank Aktiengesellschaft / Am Hof 2 / Vienna
*Raiffeisen-Zentralkasse Niederösterreich - Wien registrierte Genossen-
  schaft mit beschränkter Haftung* / Seilergasse 6 / Vienna
Schoeller & Co. / Renngasse 3 / Vienna
Spängler Carl & Co., Bankhaus / Schwarzstrasse 1 / Salzburg

Some Actively Traded Austrian Stocks

Banks and Insurance

Creditanstalt-Bankverein
Internationale Unfall- und Schadensversicherungs-A.G.
Österreichische Länderbank A.G.

Construction

Perlmooser Zementwerke A.G.
"Universale" Hoch- und Tiefbau A.G.

Magnesite

Veitscher Magnesitwerke-A.G.

Chemicals and Rubber

Semperit A.G.
Stölzle Glasindustrie A.G.
Treibacher Chemische Werke A.G.

Electrical

*Felten & Guilleaume, Fabrik elektrischer Kabel, Stahl- und Kupferwerke
  A.G.*

Breweries

Österreichische Brau-A.G.
Brüder Reininghaus Brauerei-A.G.
Gösser Brauerei-A.G.
Brauerei Schwechat A.G.

Foods

Leipnick-Lundenburger Zuckerfabriken A.G.

Machine Tool and Metallurgy

Hutter & Schrantz A.G.
Jenbacher Werke A.G.
Steyr-Daimler-Puch A.G.
Waagner-Biró A.G.

Paper

Leykam-Josefsthal A.G.

Textiles

A.G. der Vöslauer Kammgarn-Fabrik

Austrian Investment Management Companies

Österreichische Investment-Gesellschaft m.b.H. / Schottengasse 6 / Vienna
  (Funds: *Allinvest, Allrent, Securta, Selecta*)
Sparinvest-Kapitalanlage-Gesellschaft m.b.H. / Schubertring 5 / Vienna
  (Funds: *Atlasfond, Combirent, Intertrend, Sparinvest*)

Austrian Business and Financial Press

Bank und Börse / Strozzigasse 26 / Vienna
Börsen Rundschau / Annagasse 8 / Vienna
Finanznachrichten / Bankgasse 1 / Vienna
Trend / Marc-Aurel-Strasse 10-12 / Vienna
Wiener Börsen-Kurier / Biberstrasse 2 / Vienna

Vienna Daily Newspapers with Financial Coverage

Arbeiter Zeitung / Rechte Wienzeile 97 / Vienna
Die Presse / Muthgasse 2 / Vienna
Kronenzeitung / Muthgasse 2 / Vienna
Kurier / Lindengasse 52 / Vienna
Nö Volksblatt / Löwelstrasse / Vienna
Volksstimme / Höchstädtplatz 3 / Vienna
Wiener Zeitung / Rennweg 12a / Vienna

19

SCANDINAVIA AND FINLAND
THE COOL NORTH

The relationship of the four Nordic countries to the rest of Europe
is to some extent reflected in their geography. Only Denmark has
direct land connections with Western Europe. Denmark is also the
only Nordic country to join the European Economic Community
(EEC). Norway, Sweden, and Finland are separated from Western
Europe by the sea and Russia. Norwegians, surprisingly to many of
themselves and to other Europeans, voted down membership in the
EEC in 1972. Sweden decided that membership in the EEC would
not be compatible with its neutrality, which it has maintained since
1814. And Finland, as a result of its hapless wars with Russia
(1939-1945), must maintain its own kind of neutrality under the
giant wings of its neighbor.

From the viewpoint of a foreign investor, this situation is also
reflected in the investment opportunities in the four Nordic countries.
Only Denmark, since its entry into the EEC on January 1, 1973, has
made it possible for foreign investors to buy stock of its publicly
owned companies without restrictions. In anticipation of this event,
the Copenhagen stock index doubled during 1972. Both Norway
and Sweden make it difficult for foreign investors to buy their se-

On October 3, 1973 the Danish krone (DKr.) was valued at U.S. 17.58¢; the
Finnish mark (FM) was valued at U.S. 27.3¢; the Norwegian Krone (NKr.)
was valued at U.S. 18.19¢; and the Swedish krone (SKr.) was valued at U.S.
23.82¢.

curities, and foreign ownership in publicly held companies is limited
to varying degrees. Finland limits foreign ownership of Finnish companies to 20%. Its stock market is the least active of the four.

Free Enterprise "Socialism"

To some armchair conservatives, the Nordic countries, and especially Sweden, are suspect because of their "rampant socialism,"
as it is often referred to, a socialism in the opinion of some that puts
the Swedes into the category of state-controlled Marxist economies
or near-communism. For anyone patient enough to look at the facts,
however, economic enterprise in the four Nordic countries will appear
as private and free as in most other countries of the non-communist
world, and more private and freer than in some of them, although
the programs of the socialist parties envision government control of
merchant banks, insurance companies, and other industries. What is
loosely described as "socialism" is only social services provided from
tax income by democratically elected governments which ran on the
platform of providing such social services. What is often overlooked
is the fact that under their economic systems, whatever one may want
to call them, the Nordic countries have reached the highest ranks in
per-capita income among all countries of the world. In 1971 Sweden
was second in its gross national product per capita, closely behind
the United States and ahead of Canada. Denmark was sixth, Norway
seventh, and Finland fourteenth, about equal with England. Since
the latest dollar devaluation in February 1973, Sweden claims the
first spot, ahead of the United States.

A Limit to Taxation?

What might give concern to free-enterprise proponents and potential investors in these countries is the fact that the cost of these
social services has made the Nordic countries undisputed leaders in
the world in raising taxes. Sweden, in 1971, led all countries of the
world with tax receipts that were 49% of the gross national product.
Norway, with 48%, was second as a tax raiser, Finland, with 38%,
was sixth, and Denmark, with 37½%, was seventh, slightly behind
England and West Germany. (The United States was sixteenth with
30%.)

With such high taxes, the question arises: What are the limits to
which taxes can be raised without creating mass resistance or evasion

by the taxpayers, and without seriously impairing personal endeavor and, thereby, economic growth?

The first rumblings of a tax revolt occurred in Denmark where a non-partisan candidate for political office named Mogens Glistrup proposed to abolish all income taxes and all social services. The government apparatus for administering the social services had become so expensive, he argued, that the individual taxpayer would be financially better off if he paid no income taxes at all and took care of his own social services. The small government apparatus needed to provide other government functions could easily be financed through the sales tax, the candidate said. In their election in November 1973, the Danes elected Mr. Glistrup and a number of his followers to seats in the Folketing.

World Trade Dependence

Another significant factor in the investment climate of the Scandinavian countries, excluding Finland, is their great dependence on world trade, making their economies subject to the business trends of their main trading partners—Western Europe and the United States. In exports of goods and services as a percentage of gross national product, Norway, in 1971, with about 40%, was third among all countries of the world, closely behind the Netherlands and Belgium. Shipping services are Norway's main "export," with Norway having by far more ships per capita on the Seven Seas than any other country in the world. Denmark was fifth, with about 29% of its gross national product going into export, the largest export item being agricultural products. Sweden was seventh, with about 25%; the largest exports, about 25% of the total, were machinery and automobiles. Sweden must earn an increasingly larger amount in foreign exchange to pay for the rapidly increasing tourist expenditures abroad of its citizens in search of sun and fun.

In view of the great dependence on foreign trade of the Scandinavian countries, it is surprising to find these countries somewhat isolated when it comes to an interchange of portfolio investments with foreign countries. (There are just as many restrictions on Scandinavian investors in foreign securities as there are on foreign investors wanting to invest in Scandinavian securities.) This seems to be partly the relic of strict foreign exchange controls imposed during the Depression and World War II, and partly an effort to prevent control of local industry by far larger and financially stronger nations.

Denmark Opens the Door

Denmark was obliged to drop most of its restrictions with its entry into the EEC. Foreign investors can now buy Danish common stocks. Because of the very high yields on bonds—up to 13%—some restrictions still remain on the purchase of Danish bonds by foreign investors, but these are expected to disappear in a two-year transitional period during which, it is hoped, yields on Danish bonds will be more in line with the yields from bonds of other EEC member countries. More than 80% of Danish bonds are private bonds issued by mortgage credit associations, but these are guaranteed by the state. The balance includes state and local government bonds, shipping bonds, and general corporate bonds. Trading volume in bonds on the Copenhagen Stock Exchange is about 50 times larger than that of common stock (DKr. 5 billion [$870 million] versus about DKr. 100 million [$17.5 million]).

Only a few more than 100 stocks are listed on the Copenhagen Stock Exchange, and trading volume in most of them is negligible. The stock that is most likely to strike a familiar chord among investors outside Denmark—at least the beer drinkers among them—is that of the brewery that brews Carlsberg and Tuborg beer, *Førenede Bryggerier*. Apart from benefitting from a spectacular sales and earnings rise, the company's stock received a strong boost from the general upswing in the Danish market in 1972, with the price almost tripling.

Also benefitting from the general upswing in stock prices in 1972 were the three leading Danish banks—*Den Danske Landmandsbank, Kjøbenhavns Handelsbank A/S,* and *Privatbanken i Kjøbenhavn A/S.* A fourth bank, *Finansbanken A/S.,* according to a *Wall Street Journal* story, tried to boost both its business and the demand for its stock by offering a higher interest rate on deposits to those customers who at the same time bought about $400-worth of the bank's common stock.

Old Asia hands will be familiar with the *Danish East Asiatic Co.* (*Østasiatiske Kompagni A/S*), a commodity trading company operating its own shipping line, which for many years has been Thailand's main trading partner. One of its major products is the teak wood that distinguishes modern Scandinavian furniture exported to the United States. With a fairly steady increase in sales and earnings, the company's stock price more than doubled in 1972.

Shipbuilding is a highly cyclical business, as reflected in the erratic sales and earnings picture of the leading Danish shipbuilder, *Burmeister & Wain Skibsbyggeri*. Recently, the company has benefitted from the offshore oil exploration boom in the North Sea, with the stock price recovering from an all-time low.

The most attractive feature of the Danish stock market is probably the building that houses it. Finished in about 1624, it is the oldest stock exchange building in the world in continuous use. With red brick walls and a green, oxidized copper roof, it is an outstanding example of the Nordic brick architecture that stretches from the Flemish Coast to the upper reaches of the Baltic. Classified as "Dutch Renaissance," the Copenhagen Stock Exchange building is topped off by four dragons whose tails are turned skyward to form the spire.

Only officially recognized brokers can deal on the floor of the stock exchange. They also deal directly with the public, as do the banks. Banks can trade among each other or through brokers, but they cannot operate on the floor of the exchange.

Danish shares are registered in the buyer's name, but a simple endorsement makes them negotiable for anyone who holds them. Coupons must be detached to collect dividends. For practical reasons, a foreign investor should leave his shares in the custody of a bank or broker.

Information on Danish stocks is scanty. Many companies don't even disclose their sales volume. Legislation is in preparation, however, that would require companies to conform to disclosure practices recommended for all member countries of the European Economic Community.

The *Danish National Bank* publishes an annual report in English with a section on the securities market. Limited information on Danish stocks and investment funds is found in *Green's Danske Fonds og Aktier* published by *Børsen's Forlag*. The two leading financial publications are the daily *Børsen* and the weekly *Finanstidende*.

Sweden Keeps Door Half Shut

In 1970, economists and other soothsayers predicted a five-year average annual growth rate of 3.7% in real terms for the Swedish economy. For the first two years there was practically no growth, and the five-year prediction for 1971-1975 was reduced to 3.1%. Unemployment also rose unexpectedly. The only positive item was the fact that the balance of trade, for the first time in many years, was favorable in 1971 and 1972. In spite of this somewhat disappointing development, the stock market index crept upwards in 1971 and 1972.

Sweden has a number of industrial companies of world-wide renown, among them the two automobile manufacturers *Volvo A.B.* and *SAAB-Scania*; the electrical appliances and electronics manufacturer of vacuum cleaner fame, *Electrolux A.B.*; the world-wide roller bearing manufacturer *SKF (Svenska Kullagerfabriken A.B.)*; and the *L.M. Ericsson Telefon A.B.* With such internationally known companies it is surprising that, with the exception of *Ericsson* and a few others traded on foreign markets, Swedish stocks are not easily available outside Sweden.

Ericsson is the only Swedish stock that can be bought in the United States in the form of American Depositary Receipts, which are traded over-the-counter. The company is a major supplier of telephone and other telecommunications equipment for the international market. It operates more than 120 subsidiaries and affiliates in about 100 countries. Its annual report in English is an outstanding example of good disclosure practices. Earnings and stock price trends since 1968, however, have been undistinguished.

Purchases of other Swedish securities by a non-resident are extremely difficult. Unless the stock is already owned by a non-resident, such purchases must be approved by the *Riksbank* (the Swedish central bank). Approval is not automatically given and depends to some extent on the industry involved. Shares of Swedish banks, insurance companies, and defense products manufacturers are completely taboo to foreigners. Permission to buy shares of Swedish shipping companies, mining enterprises, other natural resources companies, and real estate operations is rarely given to foreign investors. Foreign ownership in most Swedish companies is usually limited to 20% of the voting shares or to 40% of the total share capital. This ownership limitation is accomplished through the issuance of four types of different shares—Class A "bound" and "free" and Class B "bound" and "free." Foreign investors can buy only "free" shares. Class A shares have one vote per share; Class B shares may have 1/100th vote per share or 1/1000th vote per share in older companies but not less than 1/10th vote in companies founded after 1944. Usually 80% or more of the Class A shares issued are bound. For all practical purposes Swedish bonds are also barred to foreign investors.

Many Swedish securities can be bought in Sweden by foreign investors without special permit from the *Riksbank* if so-called "switch currency" is used—these are the proceeds of a sale of Swedish securities by a foreign investor. Switch currency can be obtained at a premium above the regular rate of exchange. The premium is on deposit while the shares are held and can be recovered when the shares are sold. There is a 30% withholding tax on dividends paid to non-residents.

On the other side of the coin, the Swedes themselves are restricted in their investments in foreign securities. Foreign mutual funds are banned in Sweden. Thus, the Swedes are more or less confined to their own stock market and to Swedish mutual funds (several of which have foreign securities in their portfolios).

Investment interest among Swedes is quite high—with about 6% of the population being active shareholders (not much lower than in the United States). In 1972, Swedish investors became particularly active, boosting Stockholm's stock trading volume to about SKr. 1.6 billion ($375 million), about double the volume in each of the two preceding years. It is estimated that about the same volume is transacted directly among the banks off the floor of the exchange by telephone.

One oversized potential investor in common stocks was standing in the wings in 1973—the *Swedish National Pension Fund*. Since the fund was established in 1960, its assets have grown to SKr. 60 billion ($14.4 billion); that is as large as the deposits of all the Swedish commercial banks combined. The fund is growing at the rate of SKr. 10 billion ($2.4 billion) a year. In recent years, it has been buying between 80% and 90% of all industrial bonds issued. In 1973, the fund was permitted to invest in Swedish common stock through a specially set up investment fund with an initial capital of SKr. 500 million ($120 million). The effect of this step on stock prices is hard to predict for it will depend on whether the fund will act as a bona fide investor or as an arm of the government to buy control of private industry.

Both banks and brokers sell securities to the public, and both banks and brokers can be members of the Stockholm Stock Exchange. The five largest banks accounting for about 80% of the total assets of the 14 Swedish commercial banks also dominate the securities business to about the same extent. However, the banks cannot hold securities for their own account.

In 1971, Sweden instituted a new system of stock transfer under which a central depository was established. Transfer of ownership can be registered there, without physical transfer of stock certificates.

Owners also receive dividends automatically if their names are registered with the central depository, and there is no longer a need, as there was in the past, to send in a coupon to claim a dividend. An owner can appoint a nominee to be on the registry of the depository or he can have the shares registered in his own name in an "open deposit of a bank." The latter would be the most practical approach for a foreign investor.

Disclosure practices in Sweden are generally good. Several larger Swedish companies publish their annual reports, or a summary thereof, in English. *Svenska Aktiebolag* publishes data on most Swedish stocks in Swedish, as well as an abridged English version titled *Some Prominent Swedish Companies.* Banks and brokers also publish information about Swedish securities. A daily stock market index is prepared by the brokerage firm of *Jacobsen & Ponsbach.* The two leading financial publications are *Veckans Affärer* (which also publishes an annual volume, *Sweden's 200 Biggest Companies,* which contains tables and summaries in English) and *Affärsvärlden-Finanstidningen.*

Norway Restricted

Even though Norway has encouraged direct foreign investments in its economy, foreign portfolio investments in Norwegian securities is severely restricted, and thus of very limited interest to the foreign investor. All investments in Norwegian securities must be approved by the *Norges Bank* (the Norwegian central bank), and in many cases approval of the company involved must also be obtained. Foreign ownership in banks is limited to 10% of the outstanding shares, in industrial and oil companies to 20%, and in shipping companies to 40%. Some other companies have their own limitations to foreign share ownership. Moreover, there is a 25% withholding tax on dividends payable to non-residents.

The one Norwegian company that has encouraged foreign investments is *Norsk Hydro,* a 57% state-owned public utility that is also a large chemical and fertilizer manufacturer. The company is also involved in North Sea oil exploration, an activity that was partly responsible for a spectacular rise in the company's stock from a low of about NKr. 70 ($12.60) in 1970 to well above NKr. 700 ($126) in 1973. The stock is actively traded on the Paris and London stock exchanges, and permission to own these shares is automatically granted by the *Bank of Norway (Norges Bank).*

North Sea oil exploration activities have kept the Oslo stock market in a general upward trend. (There are also smaller exchanges in Bergen and Trondheim). Individual stocks of some of the larger companies have not always reflected this trend. The stock of *Kvaerner Industrier A/S,* a leading shipbuilding company, and those of the leading banks, *Bergens Privatbank, Christiania Bank og Kreditkasse,* and *Den Norske Creditbank,* have remained more or less on the same level for several years. The stock of *Kosmos A/S,* a leading shipping line, also remained relatively unchanged over a period of years, but showed an upswing in 1973.

Some 150 stock issues and about 250 bonds are listed on the Oslo Stock Exchange.

Both banks and brokerage houses are members of the Oslo Stock Exchange, and both can deal with the public.

A widely used reference book on Norwegian stocks is the *Håndbok over Norske Obligasjoner og Aksjer,* published by a leading brokerage firm, *Carl Kierulf & Co. A/S.* Another broker, *Gunnar Bøhn & Co. A/S,* publishes a stock guide entitled *Aksjer Oslo Børs.*

The only business news in English is published once a week in the daily commercial and shipping paper, *Norges Handels og Sjøfarts Tidende.*

Finland Very Limited

For all practical purposes, Finland offers extremely limited investment opportunities to the foreign investor in spite of healthy economic growth and a hard-working, intelligent population.

Foreign investments in Finnish companies are in most cases limited to 20% of the outstanding shares. Less than 50 stock issues are listed on the Helsinki Stock Exchange. Some of them are quite inactive. Total annual trading volume on the exchange is hardly more than FMk. 100 million ($27 million). The state has a direct ownership in many industries because after World War II few companies could finance themselves through private channels. Even today, financing is rather by debt than through the sale of common stock. Large share ownership by the *National Bank of Finland* and the *National Pension Institute* also limits the number of shares available for public trading.

Britain's and Denmark's entry into the EEC has curtailed Finland's trade with two of its major trading partners, and in mid-1973 there was some concern in Finland whether the economy could be kept on an even keel. Finland has negotiated a free-trade agreement with the

Common Market Countries that provides for a graduated mutual tariff reduction over a period of 11 years. Trade with the nine members of the EEC accounted for about 45% of Finland's foreign trade in 1972.

In the other direction, Finland is walking a tightrope in its trade relations with Soviet Russia and the Eastern bloc nations, regulated through the Comecon pact. About 15% of Finland's foreign trade is with Comecon nations and 12% with the Soviet Union, and this trade is not always governed strictly by the free play of supply and demand and market price. According to a *Wall Street Journal* article, it involved, among other things, a yearly hunting party of Finland's president, Urho Kekkonen, with Soviet Communist Party leader Leonid Brezhnev.

There is apparently no information in English on Finnish stocks. Whatever investment information is available is published in Finnish, by the Finnish banks and brokerage houses. Both banks and brokers can be members of the Helsinki Stock Exchange and deal in securities with the public.

Leading Danish Banks and Brokerage Houses
Doing Investment Business

Andelsbanken AMBA / Vesterbrogade 25 / Copenhagen
Den Danske Provinsbank A/S / Kannikegade 4-6 / Aarhus
Den Danske Landmandsbank / Holmens Kanal 12 / Copenhagen
R. Henriques & Son Jr. / Hejbroplads 9 / Copenhagen
Privatbanken i Kjøbenhavn A/S / Borsgade 4 / Copenhagen

Partial List of Actively Traded Danish Stocks

Aarhus Oliefabrik A/S (foods)
Burmeister & Wain Skibsbyggeri (shipbuilding)
Den Danske Landmandsbank (banking)
Danske Sukkerfabrikker A/S (foods)
Førenede Bryggerier (Carlsberg and Tuborg beers)
Kjøbenhavns Handelsbank A/S (banking)
Nordiske Kabel-og Traadfabriker A/S (wire and cable)
Østasiatiske Kompagni A/S (trading and shipping)
Privatbanken i Kjøbenhavn (banking)
Superfos A/S (chemicals)

Danish Mutual Funds

Bankforeningernes / *Investeringsforening* / Bredgade 32 / Copenhagen
Dansk Sparinvest / H.C. Anderson Boulevard 37 / Copenhagen
Investor / Ny Vestergade 17 / Copenhagen

Principal Sources of Information

Green's Danske Fonds og Aktier (Directory of Funds and Shares) published by *Børsen's Forlag* / P.O. Box 2103 / Copenhagen

Danish Business and Financial Publications

Børsen / Montegarden, Vognmagergade 2 / P.O. Box 2103 / Copenhagen
Danmarks Handels og Sofartstidende / Valbygaardsvej 62 / Copenhagen-Valby
Finanstidende / St. Kannikestraede 16 / Copenhagen
Fund Guide International / Kompagnistraede 34 / Copenhagen
Tidsskrift for Industri / H.C. Anderson Boulevard 18 / Copenhagen

Danish Newspapers With Good Business Coverage

Berlingske Tidende / Pilestraede / Copenhagen
Politiken / Politikens Hus, Raadhusplads / Copenhagen
Jyllands-Posten / Vilby / Jutland

Members of the Stockholm Stock Exchange

Banks

Göteborgs Bank / Box 40106 / 103 43 Stockholm 40
Östergötlands Enskilda Bank / Box 7079 / 103 82 Stockholm 7
Skandinaviska Banken / Box 40085 / 103 42 Stockholm 40
Skaraborgs Enskilda Bank / Box 16311 / 102 61 Stockholm 16
Skånska Banken / Box 7035 / 103 81 Stockholm 7
Sparbankernas Bank Aktiebolag / Box 4049 / 102 61 Stockholm 4
Stockholms Enskilda Bank / Box 16067 / 103 22 Stockholm 16
Sundsvallsbanken / Box 16279 / 103 25 Stockholm 16
Svenska Handelsbanken / Box 16341 / 103 26 Stockholm 16
Sveriges Kreditbank / Box 7042 / 103 81 Stockholm 7
Uplandsbanken / Box 16165 / 103 24 Stockholm 16
Wermlands Enskilda Bank / Box 16140 / 103 23 Stockholm 16

Brokers

Aktiebolaget Bankirfirman Langenskiöld / Hovslagargatan 5B / 111 48
Stockholm C
Aktiebolaget Fondkommission / Skeppsbron 8 / 111 30 Stockholm C
Bankirfirman E. Öhman J:or Aktiebolag & Co., Kommanditbolag / Box
7061 / 103 82 Stockholm 7
Fondkommissionärsfirman Berg Kommanditbolag / Box 16200 / 103 24
Stockholm 16
Fondkommissionärsfirman Hägglöf Kommanditbolag / Box 16162 / 103
24 Stockholm 16
Jacobson & Ponsbach / V. Trädgårdsgatan 11 B / 111 53 Stockholm C

Partial List of Actively Traded Swedish Stocks

ASEA-Allmänna Svenska Elektriska A.B. (electrical equipment—owns
23% of *Electrolux,* 32% of *Svenska Fläktfabriken,* and 49% of
Skandinaviska Elverk)
Atlas Copco A.B. (pneumatic machinery)
Boliden A.B. (zinc, lead, copper)
Electrolux A.B. (electrified appliances, radio, TV—23% owned by *ASEA*)
L.M. Ericsson Telefon A.B. * (telephone equipment)
SAAB-Scania (automobiles, aerospace)
Sandvikens Jernverks A.B. (steel)
Skandinaviska Elverk (electric utility—49% owned by *ASEA*)
Svenska Cellulosa A.B. (forest products)
Svenska Fläktfabriken A.B. (machinery—32% owned by *ASEA*)
Svenska Kullagerfabriken A.B. (roller bearings, steel products)
Svenska Tändsticks A.B. (matches—owns 32% of *British Match*)
Ångfartygs A.B. Tirfing (shipping)
Uddeholms A.B. (forest products, steel)
Volvo A.B. (automobiles)

* ADRs traded on the United States over-the-counter market.

Partial List of Swedish Mutual Funds

Interfond/Interfond Stiftelsen / Nybrogatan 7 / Stockholm
Skandifond/Skandinaviska Banken / Sergels Torg 2 / Stockholm
Skandinavinvest/Skandinaviska Banken / Sergels Torg 2 / Stockholm
Sparinvest/Stiftelsen Sparinvest / Peter Myndes Backe 12-14, Box 4049 /
Stockholm

Sources of Information

Svenska Aktiebolag (an abridged English-language edition is available
under the title *Some Prominent Swedish Companies*) published by
Kungl. Boktryckeriet P.A. Norstedt & Söner / Box 2030 / S103 12
Stockholm.
Stockholm Stock Exchange index and reports are published by *Jacobson
& Ponsbach* / V. Trädgårdsgatan 11B / Stockholm

Swedish Business and Financial Publications

Affärsvärlden-Finanstidningen / Box 1760 / 111 87 Stockholm
Industri Förbundets Tidskrift / Storgatan 19, P.O. Box 5501 / Stockholm
Veckans Affärer (also publisher of *Sweden's 200 Biggest Companies*) /
Box 3188 / 10 363 Stockholm 3

Swedish Newspapers With Good Business Coverage

Dagens Nyheter / Rålambsvägen 17 / Stockholm
Göteborgs Handels - och Sjöfartstidning / Kopmansgatan 10 / Göteborg
Svenska Dagbladet / Rålambsvägen 7 / Stockholm
Sydsvenska Dagbladet / Krusegatan 19, Box 145 / Malmö

Leading Norwegian Banks and Brokers Doing Investment Business

Andresens Bank A/S / Kirkegaten 6 / Oslo
Bergens Privatbank / Torvalmennig 2 / Bergen
Gunnar Bøhn & Co. A / S / Universitetsgate 22 / Oslo
Christiania Bank og Kreditkasse / Stortorvet 7 / Oslo
Den Norske Creditbank / Kongensgate 24 / Oslo
Fondsfinans A/S / Haakon VII's gate 6 / Oslo
Carl Kierulf & Co. A/S / Øvre Slottsgate 17 / Oslo
Smith & Smith A/S / Prinsens gate 6 / Oslo
Tennants Fonds- og Aktiemeglerforretning A/S / Tollbugaten 27 / Oslo

Partial List of Actively Traded Norwegian Stocks

Hafslund A/S (utility)
Kosmos A/S (shipping)
Kvaerner Industrier A/S (shipbuilding)
Norsk Hydro (utility, chemicals, fertilizer, oil exploration—57% state
owned)
Union A/S (forest products)

Norwegian Sources of Information

Aksjer Oslo Børs published by *Gunnar Bøhn & Co. A / S /* Universitetsgate 22 / Oslo
Håndbok over Norske Obligasjoner og Askjer published by *Carl Kierulf & Co. A / S/* Øvre Slottsgate 17 / Oslo

Norwegian Financial and Business Publications

Farmand (weekly)/ R. Amundsensgate 1 / Oslo
Kapital (weekly) / Box 18 / 1345 Østerås
Naeringsrevyen (weekly) / Drammensvn. 30 / Oslo
Norges Handels og Sjøfarts Tidende (daily) / Sjøfartsbugningen / Oslo

Leading Norwegian Daily Newspaper

Aftenposten/ Akersgate 51 / Oslo

Member Firms of the Helsinki Stock Exchange Dealing in Securities

Bensow Oy-Ab / E. Esplanadikatu 22 / Helsinki
Pankkiiriliike Ane Gyllenberg Oy / P. Esplanadikatu 33 / Helsinki
Helsingin Osakepankki / Aleksanterinkatu 17 / Helsinki
Pankkiiriliike L. Hiisi Ky / Temppelikatu 21 C 64 / Helsinki
Kansallis-Osake-Pankki / Aleksanterinkatu 42 / Helsinki
Lamy Oy / Dagmarinkatu 8 / Helsinki
Pankkiiriliike S.A. Lundelin Ky / Mannerheimintie 124 A 12 / Helsinki
Osuuspankkien Keskuspankki Oy / Arkadiankatu 23 / Helsinki
Pohjoismaiden Yhdyspankki Oy / Aleksanterinkatu 30 / Helsinki
Pankkiiriliike Erik Selin Ky / E. Esplanadikatu 22 / Helsinki
Oy Suomen Pankkiirilaitos / E. Esplanadikatu 22 / Helsinki
Säätöpankkien Keskus-Osake-Pankki / Aleksanterinkatu 46 / Helsinki

Finnish Economic Publication

Talouselämä / Fredrikinkatu 34 / Helsinki

Finnish Newspapers With Financial Coverage

Helsingin Sanomat / Ludviginkatu 2-10 / Helsinki
Kauppalehti / Yrjökatu 13 / Helsinki

20

TAX HAVEN SPECIALS
EUROBONDS AND OFFSHORE FUNDS

Two important international investment vehicles of limited appeal to the United States resident investor are Eurobonds and offshore funds. Both are subject to the Interest Equalization Tax and, unless registered with the Securities and Exchange Commission, neither a new Eurobond issue nor a new closed-end offshore fund issue can initially be offered in the United States—and they are rarely registered with the SEC. A share of an open-end offshore fund can never be legally offered in the United States since the fund continues to offer new shares, and thus technically remains a "new issue" all the time. However, both are of great interest to many investors outside the United States, especially those who can take advantage of tax havens. Therefore, the two types of securities are discussed here briefly for the record.

Eurobonds

The heavy loss of dollars to foreign creditors, which was discussed earlier, and the Interest Equalization Tax have created a huge market in Eurodollar bonds and loans in what can best be described as a financial no-man's-land outside the jurisdiction of any national fiscal authority. Eurodollars are American dollars owned by a non-resident of the United States—and that can include corporations, banks, and other organizations. Eurodollars can be held by a resident of any country of the world, except the United States, and not necessarily in Europe, but also in Japan, Australia, Hong Kong, Singapore, etc. In the Far East, they are sometimes called Asia dollars, but it's the same animal by a different name.

The development of the Eurodollar bond business meant quite a substantial loss of long-range foreign currency earnings for the United States. Until 1963, the United States had been the most important capital market for foreign governments and other foreign agencies and institutions wanting to raise money. These foreign borrowings were a major long-range source of income for this country. A foreign organization borrowing $100 million at 5% for ten years would pay back $150 million within these ten years—$100 million in capital and $50 million in interest.

On a short-term basis such a loan did, of course, mean an outflow of capital from the United States. Taking the short-sighted, short-term view in 1963, the United States government imposed the Interest Equalization Tax in an effort to reduce the outflow of dollars. The tax was intended to "equalize" the difference between the lower interest rates prevailing in the United States and the higher rates prevailing in Europe. In practice, the tax stopped almost completely all placements of foreign bond issues in the United States.

However, the tax did not stop the outflow of dollars, which continued at an increasingly faster rate until by 1973 there were an estimated $100 billion owned by non-residents of the United States. One can say this money is in no-man's-land because it is outside the control of any government bank or other government fiscal authority. It can flow freely from one country to another, greatly adding to local inflation wherever it appears.

The foreign borrowers—national governments and government agencies, municipalities, and international agencies—which formerly came to the United States to borrow money, in the early 1960s began to tap these Eurodollars as a source of capital. London became the primary marketplace for these bond issues.

In 1965, American corporations began to join the flock of foreign borrowers of Eurodollars. At the time, the United States government began to restrict American corporations in the amount of money they could transfer abroad to finance their overseas expansion. These corporations also turned to the Eurodollar pool and raised money outside the United States by selling both straight debt as well as bonds convertible into the common stock of the American parent company.

Some other currencies held outside their homelands joined the Eurodollar market so that a new term was coined to describe this homeless money—Eurocurrency. Deutsches mark issues have been the most popular, but there have also been issues in French francs, Dutch guilders, and even Luxembourg francs. Some issues in British pounds Sterling Australian dollars, and Danish kroner give the investor the option of demanding repayment in Deutsche marks in case of devaluation of the original currency.

Issues in European currency units (ECU) and European units of account (EUA) afford even greater protection against devaluation by giving the investor the choice of repayment in a number of different currencies.

In all, a total of $32.4 billion in Eurobond issues (including the equivalents of other currencies) was sold from 1963 to 1972, according to figures published by *Morgan Guaranty Trust Company*. United States corporations accounted for $9.2 billion of the total. During the first eight months of 1973, a total amount of $2.477 billion was sold.

Eurocurrency bond issues are attractive to institutional investors as well as to many individuals in many parts of the world, except the United States, because of their generally attractive yields and the fact that no tax is withheld on interest payments.

Eurobonds are usually listed on a recognized stock exchange to make them eligible for purchase by institutions and other investors that by law or established policy can invest only in listed securities. The most frequently used exchanges are those in Luxembourg and London. A few issues are listed on the New York Stock Exchange (after registration with the SEC). This makes these bonds eligible collateral for margin accounts—a feature of interest to a foreign investor who maintains a brokerage account in the United States.

Even though most Eurobond issues are listed on an exchange, most of the trading is done over-the-counter among the leading dealers in these securities (see the listing at the end of this chapter). Transfer of ownership of Eurobonds is usually accomplished via a clearing house service by bookkeeping entry. Two leading Eurobond clearing house services have been set up—*Cedel,* by a group of banks in Luxembourg, and *Euro-clear,* by *Morgan Guaranty Trust Company*.

The two dollar devaluations temporarily dampened the market in Eurodollar issues. Investors who held such dollar bonds since before August 1971, have lost about 30% of their investments in terms of many other currencies.

Borrowers in countries whose currencies have been revalued upwards in relation to the dollar have gained if they repay the loan in their own currency.

Offshore Funds

The 1960s saw the rapid spawning of mutual funds in all parts of the world. Many of them went "offshore," which in everyday language means outside the reach of harsh tax authorities and regulatory bodies. Offshore funds are legally registered in a country that is lenient as far as taxes and regulations are concerned, while the actual management is often in another country, and fund shares are sold wherever possible.

Many offshore funds are managed by reputable banks, brokers, and investment management firms in England, the United States, Switzerland, and other countries. But there have also been a number of offshore funds with management and sales promotion practices that are far removed from those approved by the Securities and Exchange Commission in the United States.

Offshore funds are particularly attractive to investors who sit in tax havens or are otherwise unencumbered by taxes. Offshore funds usually pay little or no tax in the place of their registration, and there is no withholding tax on the dividends they pay to their shareholders.

A United States citizen or resident who buys shares of an offshore fund at his own initiative must pay the Interest Equalization Tax of 11.25% of the purchase price.

The most popular locations for offshore funds are the Bahamas, Cayman Islands, Channel Islands, Liechtenstein, Netherlands Antilles, and Panama. Luxembourg, even though enforcing strict regulation for the management of mutual funds, has also attracted a number of offshore funds because of the tax advantages it offers. All Italian mutual funds are registered in Luxembourg because the Italian government became bogged down in its effort to pass legislation that would make it possible for mutual funds to be headquartered in Italy.

Since their heyday in the 1960s, the number of offshore funds has shrunk, and it is not easy to keep track of all of them. The most complete directory for funds in all parts of the world, including offshore funds, is the *Investment Companies International Yearbook* published by *Scheinman Ciaramella International,* 505 Park Avenue, New York, New York 10022.

Dealers in Eurodollar Bonds *

H. Albert de Bary / Amsterdam
Algemene Bank Nederland N.V. / Amsterdam
Amsterdam-Rotterdam Bank N.V. / Amsterdam
Bank of America Ltd. / London
Bank Mees & Hope N.V. / Amsterdam
Bank of London and South America / London
Bankers Trust International / London
Banque Troillet / Geneva
Bondpartners / Lausanne
Bondtrade / Brussels
Brown Harriman International Ltd. / London
Deltec Trading Company Ltd. / London and Lausanne
Dewaay Luxembourg S.A. / Luxembourg City
Dominion Securities Corporation Ltd. / London
First Boston Europe Ltd. / London
First Chicago Ltd. / London
Hambros Bank Ltd. / London
Hill, Samuel & Co., Ltd. / London
Kidder Peabody Securities Ltd. / London
Lloyds & Bolsa International Bank Ltd. / London
Merrill Lynch, Pierce, Fenner & Smith / Geneva and London
Samuel Montagu & Co., Ltd. / London
Nederlandsche Middenstandsbank N.V. / Amsterdam
Nesbitt Thomson Ltd. / London
Oyens & Van Eeghen / Amsterdam
Pierson, Heldring & Pierson / Amsterdam
Privatbanken i Kjøbenhavn / Copenhagen
Scandinavian Bank Ltd. / London
Strauss, Turnbull & Co. / London
C.G. Trinkaus & Burkhardt / Düsseldorf
Western American Eurodeal Ltd. / London and Zurich
White, Weld & Co., Ltd. / London
Wood Gundy Securities Ltd. / London

* Source: CCH Editions Ltd. / 5 Charterhouse Building / London

Eurobond Issues by Currency*

	1968	1969	1970	1971	1972
		(U.S. $ million equivalent)			
U.S. dollars	2,361.5	1,630.5	1,733.0	2,188.0	3,288.0
Deutsche marks	662.5	1,053.6	542.2	807.4	1,149.6
French francs	20.3	—	—	46.8	465.3
Dutch guilders	—	33.1	390.8	290.0	392.9
Luxembourg francs	—	—	—	16.0	142.8
£/DM	28.8	—	—	36.0	99.0
Australian $/DM	—	—	—	—	35.7
DKr/DM	—	—	—	—	32.2
European Currency Units	—	—	50.0	85.0	30.0
Sterling	—	—	—	—	26.1
European Units of Account	57.0	60.0	54.0	166.5	—
Totals	3,130.1	2,777.2	2,770.0	3,635.7	5,661.6

* Source: White, Weld & Co., Ltd.

Internationally Syndicated Debt Issues*

(U.S. $ million equivalent)

	Straight Debt		Convertible Debt		Total Issues	
	First 8 months 1972	First 8 months 1973	First 8 months 1972	First 8 months 1973	First 8 months 1972	First 8 months 1973
U.S.$	1,230.0	875.0	677.0	350.0	1,907.0	1,225.0
DM	705.9	730.7	—	—	705.9	730.7
Dfls	288.1	191.9	—	—	288.1	191.9
EUA	—	36.0	—	—	—	36.0
ECU	30.0	—	—	—	30.0	—
FFr	337.3	151.1	19.5	—	356.8	151.1
LuxFr.	89.3	91.8	—	—	89.3	91.8
£	26.1	—	—	—	26.1	—
£/DM	46.9	32.6	52.1	—	99.0	32.6
A$/DM	35.7	—	—	—	35.7	—
DKr/DM	32.2	—	—	—	32.2	—
Leb. £	—	18.1	—	—	—	18.1
	2,821.5	2,127.2	748.6	350.0	3,570.1	2,477.2

* Source: White, Weld & Co., Ltd.

GLOSSARY

This glossary covers primarily those technical investment terms used in this book, plus a few other commonly used terms. More complete glossaries can be found in New York Stock Exchange literature and various stock market and investment handbooks.

American Depositary Receipt (ADR): Certificates issued in the United States in lieu of original foreign securities deposited with a bank abroad. ADRs are actively traded in the United States in the same way as common stock.

arbitrage: The simultaneous buying and selling of a security on two different stock exchanges to take advantage of the price differential; or the buying of one security convertible into another, and the selling of the other, to take advantage of the price differential.

arbitrager, arbitrageur: A security trader making arbitrage deals.

Asiadollars: The same as Eurodollars—dollars owned by non-residents of the United States. If the dollars are in the hands of residents or banks in the Far East they are often called Asia dollars.

asset value (of an investment trust or fund): The market value on any given day of all the securities held by an investment trust or mutual fund, plus cash on hand, usually expressed on a per-share basis.

bargain: A transaction on The Stock Exchange, London.

bearer certificate: A certificate for a stock or bond not registered in the owner's name. Anyone holding the certificate can collect the dividends or interest due (usually by detaching a coupon) and can sell it without having endorsed it. In other words, a bearer certificate is comparable to cash.

beneficial owner: The ultimate owner of a stock certificate who receives the "benefits," such as dividends, associated with stock ownership. The term is often used when the apparent owner is a custodian who holds the stock certificate in trust for the "beneficial" owner.

blue chip: Stock of a well known large company, implying maximum safety of investment.

blue sky laws: Laws passed by individual states of the United States to protect the investor from fraud.

bond: A certificate of long-term, interest-paying debt issued by a corporation, government, or other organization to raise money.

broker: An individual or firm who buys and sells securities on behalf of an investor on a commission basis.

call (*call option*): A contract to buy a certain number of shares at a specific price within a specific period of time.

call of bonds: A redemption of bonds by the issuer before maturity, usually at a previously specified price that is higher than the redemption price at full maturity.

capital gain (*loss*): Profit or loss from the sale of a security or other capital asset.

central bank: A government or quasi-government bank usually responsible for the money supply, foreign exchange reserves, and financial dealings of a country.

clearing bank: A British commercial bank which "clears" checks but also conducts almost every other conceivable banking business.

clearing house: A firm or agency that facilitates the receipt and delivery of stock certificates via bookkeeping entries to reduce the physical movement of stock certificates.

closed-end investment trust or fund: An investment trust with a limited number of shares which are traded in the same manner as other securities and often listed on stock exchanges. The price of the shares is determined by supply and demand and often varies from the per share net asset values of the trust.

common stock: A share ownership in a publicly owned company, usually entitling the owner to a vote during shareholder meetings and to the receipt of a dividend if the company pays a dividend (which is not necessarily the case even if a company earns money).

convertible bond: A bond that a holder, under specified conditions, may exchange into common stock.

coupon: A small piece of paper attached to "bearer" bonds or shares that must be detached and presented to a paying agent to collect a dividend or interest payment due.

custodian: A bank, broker, or trust agency that holds an investor's securities for safekeeping and will usually attend to any action necessary in connection with the ownership, such as collecting dividends and interest due, exercising rights, or voting at shareholders meetings (if so instructed by the owner).

debenture: A long-term debt certificate, paying interest, and secured by the general credit of the issuer rather than a specific property.

demand deposit: A bank deposit that a depositor can withdraw at any time without notice.

dilution: An increase in the number of outstanding shares, thereby reducing the value of each share held by existing shareholders.

discount: (1) The amount under face value for which a bond is selling; (2) the amount under asset value for which the shares of a closed-end investment fund are selling; (3) the amount under conversion value for which a convertible bond is selling.

discretionary account: The broker has the authority to buy and sell securities on behalf of the customer without consulting him.

dividend: That part of the earnings of a company that is distributed to shareholders on a per-share basis. Dividend distribution is usually not automatic even if a company makes money. Each dividend is "declared" by the board of directors, usually on a quarterly basis in the United States; on a semi-annual or annual basis in most other countries.

equity: (1) The ownership interest of a common or preferred stockholder in a company, i.e. the number of shares he holds. If a company sells "equity" this usually means that it raises money through the sale of common stock or bonds convertible into common stocks; (2) the excess value of securities over the debit cash balance that a customer has in a margin account with his broker.

Eurodollars: Dollars owned by non-residents of the United States.

Eurocurrency: Any European currency owned by a non-resident of the country issuing the currency.

ex-dividend: A stock trading without giving the buyer the right to collect a recently declared dividend (which the previous owner collects).

ex-rights: A stock that trades without recently issued rights to buy additional shares of the company. The rights may either have been exercised by the previous owner or sold separately.

fixed-interest security: A bond or debenture on which a fixed rate of interest is paid.

flat earnings: Earnings that remain more or less unchanged.

front-end load: A sales commission charged by a mutual fund at the initial sale of shares to the investor.

gilt edged: A British expression for securities of greatest safety, usually government or government guaranteed bonds.

holding company: A company that controls several others without itself conducting any business.

index: A statistical average of the prices of a certain number of stocks traded on a stock exchange used to measure the average price action on the exchange.

institutional investor: An organization, such as a bank, insurance company, investment trust, pension fund, etc., making substantial investments, often on behalf of others.

investment banker: A firm that raises money for corporations by selling new public issues of securities or placing private debt commitments with lenders.

investment company or trust: A firm that invests money of participating shareholders in a diversified portfolio of securities.

jobber: A dealer on The Stock Exchange, London, who makes a market in a certain number of securities, dealing with brokers or other jobbers, but not with the public.

Kaffirs: South African gold stocks.

leverage: This usually refers to borrowings of a company that are heavy in relation to the number of outstanding shares. Such a company is often called "highly leveraged." The per-share prices of the stocks of highly leveraged companies tend to rise more quickly in profitable years than the shares of less highly leveraged companies, and they also decline much faster in poor years.

linked bonds or debentures: A security whose price is linked to the cost-of-living index or a fixed exchange rate for a foreign currency or gold.

listed securities: Corporate stocks or bonds admitted to a stock exchange for trading.

liquidity: Active trading on a stock exchange, making it easy to buy and sell securities within a narrow price range.

margin, margin account: A margin account permits an investor to buy a security by paying only a limited percentage of the purchase price (the margin) and borrowing the balance from his broker.

market maker: A security dealer ready to buy or sell securities of a certain company, usually not listed on a stock exchange.

marking: The recording of a transaction on The Stock Exchange, London.

maturity: The date on which a bond or other long-term fixed-income security comes due and is redeemed.

merchant bank: A British banking house engaged in corporate financing, investment banking, portfolio management, and other banking activities, except checking and savings accounts.

mutual fund: An open-end investment fund (q.v.).

NASD: The National Association of Securities Dealers Inc., an American organization of over-the-counter securities brokers and dealers.

NASDAQ: A computerized information network that provides brokerage offices throughout the United States with price quotations of most securities traded over-the-counter.

new issue: Shares offered to the public for the first time either of a company that has never offered shares to the public before or that is offering additional shares to those that have been issued before.

no load (fund): An investment fund that charges no sales commission for the sale of its shares (usually closed-end, q.v.), but if traded on an exchange or over-the-counter, the usual brokerage commission is paid by the investor.

odd lot: A stock transaction for fewer shares than the normal trading unit (usually 100 shares).

open-end investment trust or fund: An investment fund that continually issues new shares as it receives new capital or redeems shares of owners who want to sell them. Shares are usually sold at net-asset value, minus sales commission, which can be quite high.

offerings: Public sale of a parcel of securities at a fixed price, usually by a group of underwriters (q.v.).

option: The right, purchased at a certain price, to buy or sell a specific number of securities at a specific price on a specific day.

over-the-counter (OTC): An open market for securities not listed on a regular stock exchange.

par value: The nominal or face value of a stock, usually far below market price.

pink sheets: Sheets published daily in the United States and printed on pink paper listing all the brokerage houses that make markets in over-the-counter stocks, including American Depositary shares for foreign stocks. Pink sheets are available at practically every American brokerage office.

portfolio: The different securities held by an individual investor, or an institution, such as an investment fund.

preferred stock: Stock taking precedence over common stock of the same corporation in the case of dividends and liquidation payments.

price/earnings ratio: The market price of a stock divided by its reported or anticipated earnings per share.

puts and calls: Options that give the right to buy or sell a fixed number of securities at a specified price within a specified period of time.

registered certificates: Stock certificates registered in the owner's name.

rights: A claim given to existing stockholders to buy additional shares of the company at a specific price within a specific time. Rights not exercised can usually be sold on the open market before expiration.

Securities and Exchange Commission (SEC): A United States government agency that regulates and polices security trading and information disclosure of publicly owned companies.

security: In investment language, a certificate that gives the owner a share in a publicly owned company or that certifies a loan to the lender. The term usually applies to common and preferred stock, bonds—interest bearing as well as bonds convertible into common stock—and warrants and rights for the future purchase of a security.

security analyst: An investment professional who collects information on companies and industries to "analyze" the value of particular securities for investment purposes.

shares: Used interchangeably with common stock to denote a part ownership in a publicly held company, issued to raise capital for the company, and traded on stock exchanges and other security markets.

specialist: A member of a stock exchange who makes a market for a number of stocks by buying all shares offered and selling all shares wanted. He is usually expected, in the United States, to buy and sell within a narrow price range to "maintain an orderly market."

stock dividend: The payment of stock in lieu of a cash dividend. A 5% stock dividend means that a holder of 100 shares receives 5 additional shares. If no cash dividend at all is paid by the company, the shareholder gets really no value. All that has happened is that the same sized pie—the net worth of a company—is split into 105 slices rather than 100, and earnings per share are correspondingly diluted (q.v.). A stock "dividend" of 20% or more is really in the nature of a stock "split." (q.v.)

stock split: The issuance of one additional share for each share held by a shareholder without making him pay for it, as is the case when rights (q.v.) to buy additional shares are offered to shareholders.

Sometimes splits are made by a different formula—3 new shares for 1 held, or 3 for 2, etc. Sometimes such stock "splits" are called stock "dividends" (q.v.). Stock splits are usually made to increase the number of outstanding shares and keep the price within the range that is most popular with investors. If the cash dividend remains unchanged for both old and new shares, a stock split or dividend represents an increase in the cash dividend. For instance, a 3 for 2 stock "split" or a 50% stock "dividend" is then an effective increase of 50% in the cash dividend.

stop order: An order to buy at a price above the current market price of a stock or sell below the current market price.

street name: Registration of shares in the name of the broker, without the owner taking physical delivery of the shares.

time deposit: A bank deposit that a depositor can withdraw only after a specified period of time.

transfer agent: A bank or other institution which transfers shares from one owner to another on behalf of the company that has issued the shares.

troy ounce: A weight used for gold and silver = 1.09714 regular ounces.

underwriter: A securities firm which commits itself, usually together with a group of other firms, to buy a new issue of securities for resale to the public.

unit trust: The name for open-end mutual funds in England and some other countries.

warrant: A certificate authorizing the holder to buy a specified number of shares of a company at a specified price within a specified period of time. The time limit is much longer, often by several years, than that for "rights" to buy shares.

yield: The annual income in dividends or interest which an investment returns, expressed in percentage of the market price of the security.

CHARTS

1 January 1970 = 100

CAPITAL INTERNATIONAL INDEX   THE WORLD INDEX

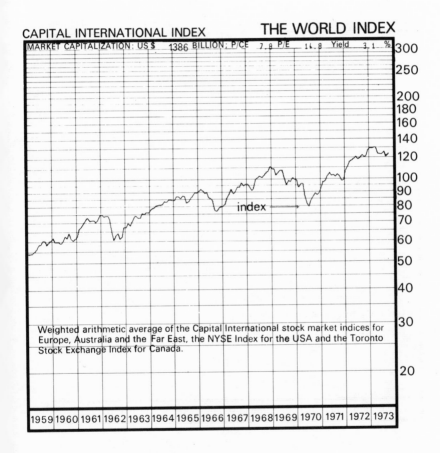

MARKET CAPITALIZATION: US $ 1386 BILLION; P/CE 7.8 P/E 11.8 Yield 3.1 %

index ⟶

Weighted arithmetic average of the Capital International stock market indices for Europe, Australia and the Far East, the NYSE Index for the USA and the Toronto Stock Exchange Index for Canada.

1959 1960 1961 1962 1963 1964 1965 1966 1967 1968 1969 1970 1971 1972 1973

1 January 1970 = 100

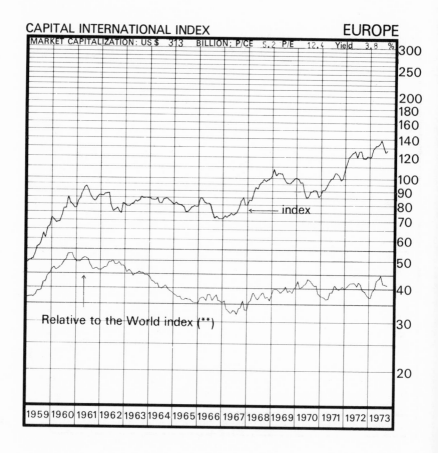

CAPITAL INTERNATIONAL INDEX   EUROPE

MARKET CAPITALIZATION: US $ 313   BILLION; P/CE   5.2   P/E   12.4   Yield   3.8   %

300
250
200
180
160
140
120
100
90
80
70
60
50
40
30
20

index

Relative to the World index (**)

|1959|1960|1961|1962|1963|1964|1965|1966|1967|1968|1969|1970|1971|1972|1973|

1 January 1970 = 100

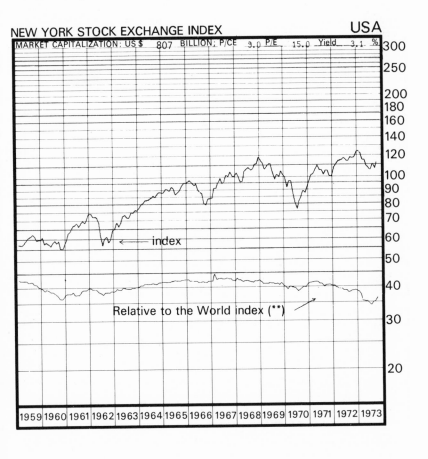

NEW YORK STOCK EXCHANGE INDEX   USA

MARKET CAPITALIZATION: US $ 807   BILLION; P/CE   9.0 P/E   15.0   Yield   3.1 %

← index

Relative to the World index (**)

1 January 1970 = 100

CAPITAL INTERNATIONAL INDEX   UNITED KINGDOM

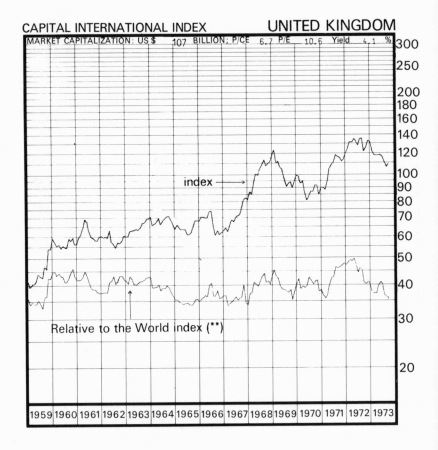

MARKET CAPITALIZATION: US $ 107 BILLION; P/CE 6.7 P/E 10.6 Yield 4.1 %

index →

Relative to the World index (**)

1959 1960 1961 1962 1963 1964 1965 1966 1967 1968 1969 1970 1971 1972 1973

1 January 1970 = 100

TORONTO STOCK EXCHANGE INDEX   **CANADA**

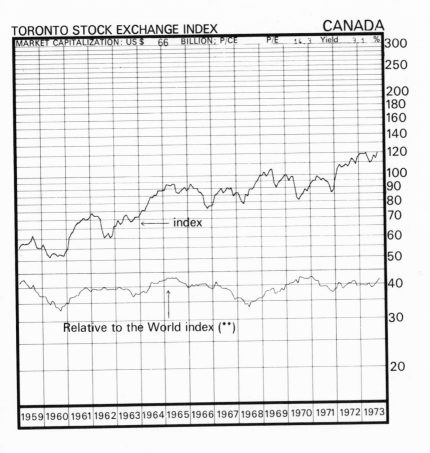

MARKET CAPITALIZATION: US $ 66 BILLION; P/CE   P/E 14.3 Yield 3.1 %

index

Relative to the World index (**)

1959 1960 1961 1962 1963 1964 1965 1966 1967 1968 1969 1970 1971 1972 1973

1 January 1970 = 100

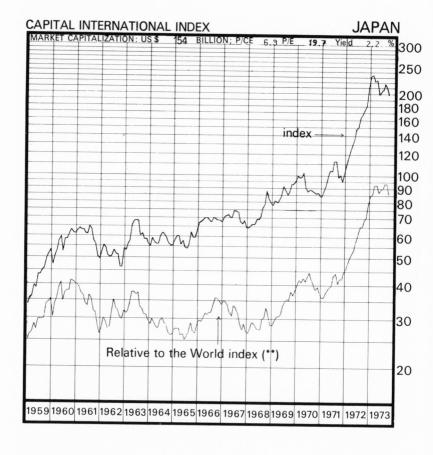

CAPITAL INTERNATIONAL INDEX   JAPAN

MARKET CAPITALIZATION: US $ 154   BILLION; P/CE   6.9   P/E   **19.7**   Yield   2.2   %

index ⟶

Relative to the World index (**)

| 1959 | 1960 | 1961 | 1962 | 1963 | 1964 | 1965 | 1966 | 1967 | 1968 | 1969 | 1970 | 1971 | 1972 | 1973 |

1 January 1970 = 100

CAPITAL INTERNATIONAL INDEX **GERMANY**

MARKET CAPITALIZATION: US $ 52 BILLION; P/CE 3.7 P/E 11.3 Yield 4.2 %

index ⟶

Relative to the World index (**)

1959 1960 1961 1962 1963 1964 1965 1966 1967 1968 1969 1970 1971 1972 1973

1 January 1970 = 100

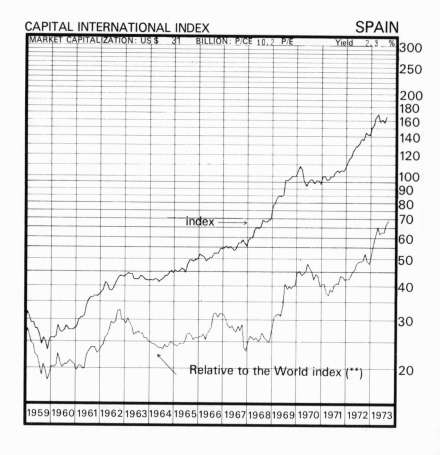

CAPITAL INTERNATIONAL INDEX   **SPAIN**

MARKET CAPITALIZATION: US $ 31   BILLION: P/CE 10.2 P/E   Yield   2.3 % 300

1 January 1970 = 100

CAPITAL INTERNATIONAL INDEX   SWITZERLAND

MARKET CAPITALIZATION: US $ 20 BILLION; P/CE P/E 3.3 Yield 2.5 %

← index

Relative to the World index (**)

1959 1960 1961 1962 1963 1964 1965 1966 1967 1968 1969 1970 1971 1972 1973

1 January 1970 = 100

CAPITAL INTERNATIONAL INDEX   FRANCE

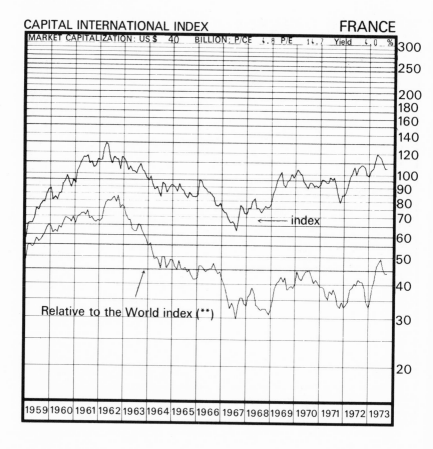

MARKET CAPITALIZATION: US $ 40 BILLION; P/CE 4.8 P/E 14.7 Yield 4.0 %

←—— index

Relative to the World index (**)

1959 1960 1961 1962 1963 1964 1965 1966 1967 1968 1969 1970 1971 1972 1973

1 January 1970 = 100

CAPITAL INTERNATIONAL INDEX
AUSTRALIA

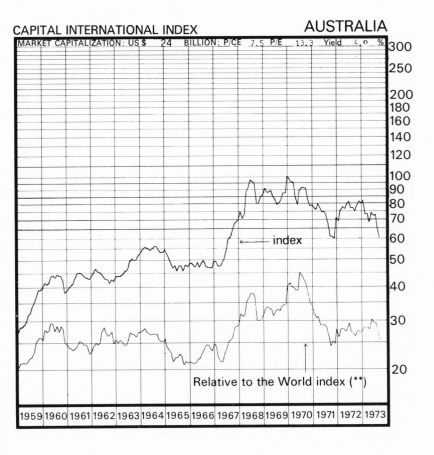

MARKET CAPITALIZATION: US $ 24 BILLION; P/CE 7.5 P/E 13.3 Yield 4.0 %

←— index

Relative to the World index (**)

1959 1960 1961 1962 1963 1964 1965 1966 1967 1968 1969 1970 1971 1972 1973

1 January 1970 = 100

CAPITAL INTERNATIONAL INDEX   **ITALY**

MARKET CAPITALIZATION: US $ 19   BILLION; P/CE   7.7   P/E   Yield   2.1   %

index

Relative to the World index (**)

1959 1960 1961 1962 1963 1964 1965 1966 1967 1968 1969 1970 1971 1972 1973

1 January 1970 = 100

CAPITAL INTERNATIONAL INDEX   NETHERLANDS

MARKET CAPITALIZATION: US $ 17.3   BILLION; P/CE   3.7 P/E   8.1   Yield   5.6   %

index ⟶

Relative to the World index (**)

1959 | 1960 | 1961 | 1962 | 1963 | 1964 | 1965 | 1966 | 1967 | 1968 | 1969 | 1970 | 1971 | 1972 | 1973

1 January 1970 = 100

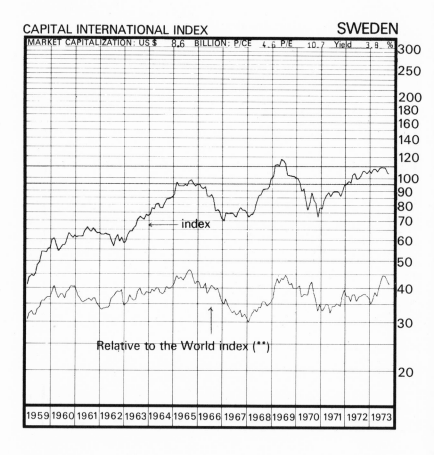

CAPITAL INTERNATIONAL INDEX   **SWEDEN**

MARKET CAPITALIZATION: US $ 8.6   BILLION: P/CE   4.6 P/E   10.7   Yield   3.8   %

1 January 1970 = 100

CAPITAL INTERNATIONAL INDEX   NORWAY

MARKET CAPITALIZATION: US $ 2.4 BILLION; P/CE 12.0 P/E 31.1 Yield 1.6 %

index ⟶

Relative to the World index (**)

1959 1960 1961 1962 1963 1964 1965 1966 1967 1968 1969 1970 1971 1972 1973

1 January 1970 = 100

CAPITAL INTERNATIONAL INDEX   BELGIUM/LUXEMBOURG

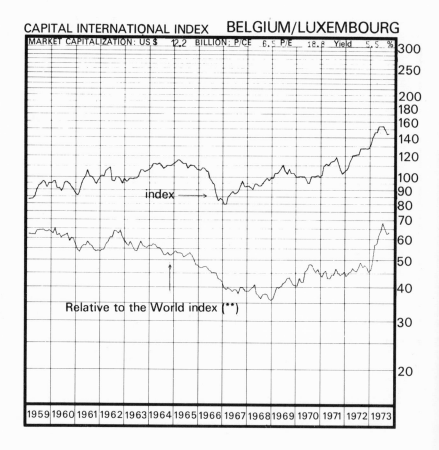

1 January 1970 = 100

CAPITAL INTERNATIONAL INDEX   DENMARK

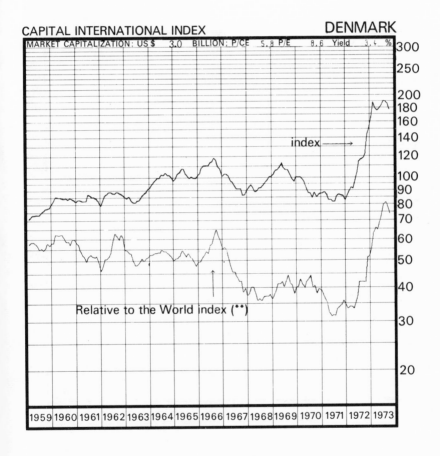

MARKET CAPITALIZATION: US $ 3.0   BILLION: P/CE   5.8 P/E   8.6   Yield   3.4   %

index ⟶

Relative to the World index (**)

1959 1960 1961 1962 1963 1964 1965 1966 1967 1968 1969 1970 1971 1972 1973

1 January 1970 = 100

CAPITAL INTERNATIONAL INDEX   AUSTRIA

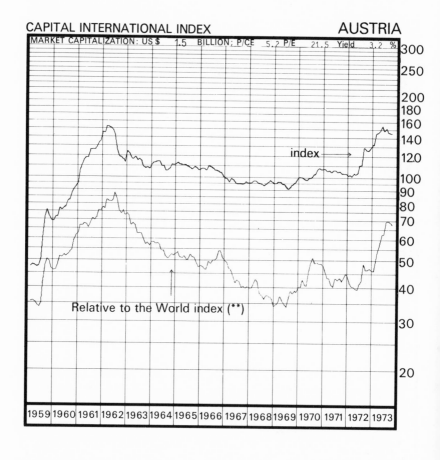

1 January 1970 = 100

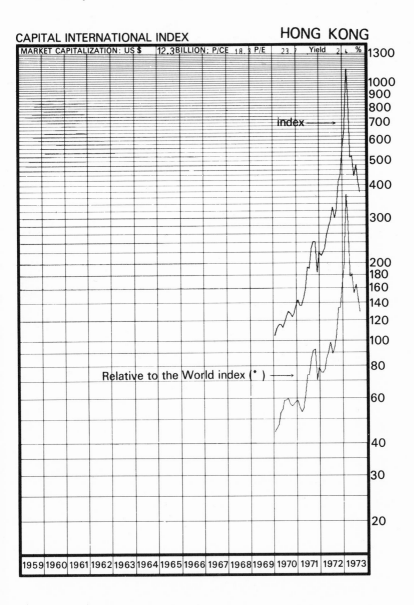

CAPITAL INTERNATIONAL INDEX   HONG KONG

MARKET CAPITALIZATION: US $ 12.3 BILLION; P/CE 18.8 P/E 23.7 Yield 2.4 %

index →

Relative to the World index (*) →

1 January 1970 = 100

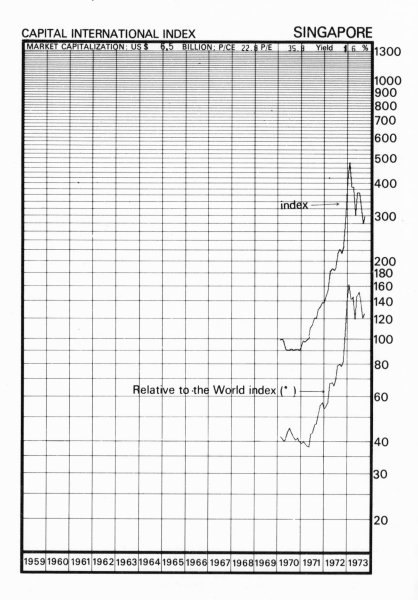

CAPITAL INTERNATIONAL INDEX   **SINGAPORE**

MARKET CAPITALIZATION: US $ 6.5   BILLION; P/CE 22.8 P/E   35.8   Yield   1.6 %

index →

Relative to the World index (*)

1959 1960 1961 1962 1963 1964 1965 1966 1967 1968 1969 1970 1971 1972 1973